AMISH QUILTS

D1611511

Rachel and Kenneth Pellman

Good Books

New York, New York

Acknowledgments

We wish to give special recognition and thanks to Rebecca Haarer who helped collect quilts for photographing and sered as a consultant for this project. We are also pleased with the way Jonathan Charles captured these wonderful masterpieces on film. In conversation with local Amish neighbors, we found both quilts and valuable information. For that we thank those friends. We are grateful to The People's Place for permitting us to borrow "Excerpts from a Grandmother's Diary" for this project. And finally we were warmed by the cooperation of the many folks who generously permitted us to exhibit their treasured quilts on the following pages.

Photograph Credits

All photographs throughout the book were taken by Jonathan Charles except the following: Jerry Irwin, 1, 25 (top), 82; Kenneth Pellman, 8, 11, 20 (bottom), 40 (bottom), 45, 46 (bottom), 62 (left), 63 (top), 68 (bottom), 80 (bottom), 88 (bottom), 100 (bottom), 104, 105, 126; David Lauver, 9, 25 (bottom), 44, 58 (bottom), 92 (bottom); Richard Reinhold, 12 (bottom), 26 (bottom), 100 (bottom), 62 (right), 63 (middle, bottom), 64 (bottom), 72 (bottom), 84 (bottom), 106 (bottom), 110 (bottom), 114 (bottom); Steve Scott, 76 (bottom).

Good Books books may be purchased in bulk at special discounts for sales promotion, corporate gifts, fund-raising, or educational purposes. Special editions can also be created to specifications. For details, contact the Special Sales Department, Good Books, 307 West 36th Street, 11th Floor, New York, NY 10018 or info@skyhorsepublishing.com.

Good Books is an imprint of Skyhorse Publishing, Inc.®, a Delaware corporation.

Visit our website at www.goodbooks.com.

10 9 8 7 6 5 4 3 2 1

Library of Congress Cataloging-in-Publication Data is available on file.

Cover design by Abigail Gehring

Print ISBN: 978-1-68099-064-5
Ebook ISBN: 978-1-68099-107-9

Printed in China

Table of Contents

The World of
Amish Quilts

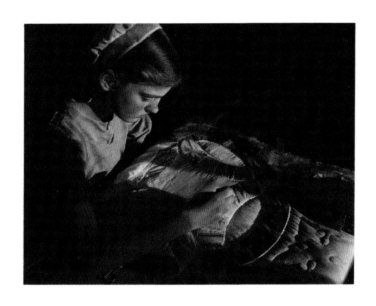

The World of Amish Quilts

How can the splash of color, synonymous with many Amish quilts, well up from a people whose life is so reserved and disciplined? Is it not both a visual and theological irony for the "quiet of the land" to mix such austerity and beauty?

An encounter with antique Amish quilts is incomplete if it does not include some understanding of the people who made them. If one studies Amish quilts without relating the finished textile to the community of its origin, one is left with only a partial look at these wonderful bedcovers.

The Amish are traditionally recognized for their strict lifestyle. Black hats, drab carriages and sad faces are quick labels often used to identify them. But by wearing the right kind of glasses—those that look beyond oversimplification—one will discover that the Amish live in a delightful world of faith, community and beauty.

Beauty and craftsmanship are traditions among the Amish. Meticulously manicured lawns and gardens, correctly shocked stalks of field corn, well groomed houses and barns belong to their way of life. They find joy in the push of a bean through the springtime soil, in filled chairs around the supper table, and Sunday visits. Loaded canning shelves and full hay mows satisfy their bodies and spirits. To do something well and attractively is always more gratifying for them than doing one of those qualities without the other.

Who Are These People?

Who are these people? Where did they come from? Where are they going? Why do they live the way they do?

The Amish are, most basically, a people committed to God. They believe that their lifestyle and practice must embody their faith. They intend to live, in every part of life, consistently with Jesus' teachings in the New Testament.

The Amish believe that Jesus taught his followers to be a community to each other that nurtures its members to greater faithfulness. It is from this unique belief that the Amish receive much of the solidarity they need to continue living with the tensions they feel with the outside world. One cannot be Amish alone. It requires the support and fellowship of others who share the same beliefs. The community becomes the conscience for the individual. And the community discerns together the do's and don'ts for its members.

Community is a Refuge

Most Amish do not see their community as restrictive. Rather, it is a harbor from rampant Western individualism they believe responsible for the demise of the church, home and family. It is against this backdrop that the Amish church continues to grow, having doubled in size in the last twenty years. There is peace, security and joy in living as the Amish do. Though not without its struggles and problems, the Amish community nurtures its members in wonderful and precious ways.

So as a result of trying to follow their faith daily in life the Amish find themselves to be separate from the world. Because they are committed to their faith-life, they are wary of anything that could become a possible route to acculturation into the "world." The Amish believe that becoming involved in the larger society takes one away from family, community and church. Their leaders are constantly concerned with the purity of their fellowship. So they tend to draw lines in black and white areas before the issues become gray to help identify their church's separation from the world.

The Old Order Amish, the strictest of all the Amish groups, have traditionally shunned the use of electricity from local power companies, have not permitted telephones in their homes, have rejected ownership of automobiles and usually discontinue their formal education on the completion of grade eight. Their farming is generally done with horses and mules. Dress regulations are quite severe. Solid colored fabrics are usually the rule for men's and women's clothing. Their primary language within the community is Pennsylvania Dutch (Deutsch) although they are also fluent in English. Yet the Amish are not simply figures cut from the very same form. They are individuals, and as a result, diverse within the structures. It is this blend of diversity and regulation that keeps the Amish culture alive and vital.

The Problem with Technology

For the Amish, advanced technology is not evil or wicked in itself. They do not think that a vehicle with four wheels that travels at high rates of speed is neces-

sarily designed by ungodly forces. But the Amish do believe that the automobile is a major factor in breaking up the family. A car in the driveway increases the temptation to be places other than home, thus making it difficult to spend the majority of evenings each week with one's family.

The same concern is behind the Amish rejection of electricity from local power companies. The Amish are not opposed to the correct alignment of electrons and neutrons that produces electricity. Their caution is that if it is too readily available in the house, members could be tempted to acquire all kinds of appliances and gadgets that may lead to the accumulation of possessions and luxury. They may buy a radio. And if a radio, why not a television? And if one has a television, why not watch movies that are aired? And if one watches movies at home, why not go to the theater and cinema as well? They believe the drift into the world can be subtle. That explains why the Amish are so leery of keeping up with style and technology. Separation from the world, they believe, is a biblical value that also holds them together as a people of God.

Not a Fly-by-Night Group

The Amish find their roots in the Protestant Reformation. They are a Christian group whose origins are with the reformers who believed that the break Martin Luther and Ulrich Zwingli were making from the state church was neither as extensive or severe as it should be. At that time in the 1500s, the word "Amish" was not used.

The leaders of this radical left wing of the Protestant Reformation believed in a separation of the church and state. One could live peaceably within the boundaries of the state but only with the keen understanding that one's first allegiance was to God. If the requests of the state ever conflicted with the group's understanding of Christ and his teachings, the state would have to take a back seat.

This small group also practiced adult baptism. They believed baptism to be a symbol of one's commitment to Jesus and the way of life he demonstrated while living on earth. Biblical study showed these reformers that the way of Jesus and the way of the world had difficulty coexisting. Because of potential physical and emotional persecution from people outside their convictions, this group believed one must thoroughly understand these possible hazards before committing oneself to following the values Jesus taught. They believed only adult minds had the capability of making such a tough decision. That is why they performed voluntary baptism for adults. Because of this practice they were nicknamed by their taunters, "Anabaptists." This title does not mean anti-Baptists, but rather re-baptized.

The Anabaptist movement officially began in Zurich, Switzerland on January 21, 1525 when the first group of adults took turns baptizing each other. The beliefs of this group found ready acceptance from many people throughout Europe. The movement flourished, spreading quickly through Germany, France, and the Netherlands. A prolific writer and articulate man from Friesland became known as a prominent leader of the Anabaptists. His name was Menno Simons. It's from his name that people in his church were eventually nicknamed Mennonites.

Church Concerned with Purity

In 1693, a Mennonite minister, Jacob Amman, had a conviction that the church was getting too lax in the

There is a serenity about the Amish way. Early morning always brings lots of chores to be done around the farm regardless of the season.

enforcement of the discipline that separated them from worldliness. Amman led a difficult and painful split from the Mennonites. The people who followed him were nicknamed Amish.

Because of identical origins and similar faith understandings, the Amish and Mennonites remain much more alike theologically than different. They are like religious cousins. Their differences are primarily evident in their lifestyles and practices rather than their basic beliefs.

What Distinguishes Antique Amish Quilts

The quilts in this book are antique Amish quilts. The dates of their origins range from the mid-19th century to the early 20th century. Amish women do continue making quilts today. But these recent quilts look drastically different from the old ones as a result of modern materials and dyes. These contemporary quilts, though made by Amish, are not included in this collection.

Why have many of these antique quilts gained the attention of art critics in the larger world? Why are they in such demand by collectors? Why are they escalating in value as investment objects? There are many answers. It is nearly impossible to acquire the same fabrics and dyes used in antique Amish quilts. Natural fibers dyed at home with natural pigments produced a warm vibrance, unattainable in modern fabrics. There is also an exceptional artistic quality present in these quilts.

Art, for itself, is frowned on within the Amish community. Amish women never formally study color or line in an attempt to design an aesthetically pleasing quilt. That a quilt functions warmly and well as a bedcover was a quiltmaker's primary concern. Because these quilts were not designed to be art objects, they become most interesting if they are not removed from the context in which they were constructed.

An "Innocent" Creativity

Something about the wholeness of life in the Amish community has produced and permitted the mix of superior craftsmanship and visual quality. Creativity has thrived in Amish quilts. The Amish communities' uneducated approach to color has resulted in daring bursts and subtle blends of color. Within the Amish setting little attention is given to color-coordinating clothing or home decor. One wears the colors allowed by the church and plants the flowers created by God. It seems to be this freedom from color theory and an uninhibited use of bright colors that has produced some wonderful masterpieces. Not all old Amish quilts, however, fall into this delightful category!

Children are an integral part of the Amish community. Their dress and language reflect who they are expected to become.

What Inspired These Patterns?

Trying to decide the origin of any given quilt pattern soon becomes mere speculation. But an understanding of the rural agrarian environment that produced these quiltmakers is helpful. Fences around pastures certainly create straight line imagery, depicted in Bars and Rail Fence patterns. Star quilt patterns and the heavenly bodies seem to have a common motif. Fan quilts and buggy wheels may be related. Windmills that pump water and Pinwheel patterns have a similar design. And the parallels between nature and quilt patterns continue. This type of conjecture is difficult to prove. But finding skyscraper, subway and computer motifs in Amish quilts is even more difficult!

Many Amish quilt patterns have specific names but abstract geometric shapes. Realism in pieced quilt tops is not generally permitted by the Amish church. Images are suggested but not definitely constructed. For example, one can see an interlocking log motif in the Log

Turgid colors and geometric shapes are typical in the quilts of this disciplined people. Stars created from diamond-shaped pieces of fabric are common among Eastern and Midwestern Amish.

Cabin even though there is no door, roof, or windows. And because of the difficulty of attaching two curved pieces of fabric to each other without puckers, most pieced quilt shapes have straight edges. Squares, rectangles, diamonds and triangles make up the basic group of geometric designs used. The majority of Amish quilts are assembled using these four main shapes.

Putting Quilts Together

Quilt tops are constructed in two primary ways—by piecing and by appliquéing. Piecing means that the top layer of fabrics on a quilt are sewn to each other along common edges. The result is a single layer of fabric with seam allowances on the reverse side. This piecing is usually done with a sewing machine.

Appliquéing is the process of sewing by hand, one piece of fabric to the surface of another, making sure raw edges are hidden. Because a quiltmaker does not want a quilt to have a puckered surface when it is finished, this procedure is more tedious and time-consuming than piecing. Appliquéing is usually done when curved pieces of fabric are required in the pattern under construction. The tiny hidden stitches of skillful appliquéing are achieved only by long-time veteran quilters.

While straight-edged geometric shapes usually make up the pieced top, the lavish quilting that nearly smothers a finished quilt is often full of curves and circles. Realism is more acceptable in this intricate stitching. Fruit and flower designs are found occasionally in quilting, alongside the more common feather, plant, waffle, and medallion motifs.

Quilting Stitches are Functional

The elaborate stitchery that envelops these bedcovers is viewed as functional within the Amish world. A quilt is composed of three layers. The quilting is needed to hold those three layers together. The top is the pieced or appliquéd surface. This side of the quilt boasts of the colors and pattern which gives the quilt its name.

Quilts also have backs. The surface rarely has any pieced or appliquéd pattern and is the bottom layer of the quilt. (Frequently the skill of the quilter is more visible on this reversed side because there is no variation of color or pieces to compete with the viewer's attention.) Sandwiched between the top and back is the lining. This middle layer provides warmth, but also serves to enhance the quilting. Because the lining is usually thicker than the top or back, its puffy quality shows off the masterful stitches of Amish quilters.

The word "quilting" is both a noun and a verb. The verb "quilting" is the actual process of hand-stitching the three layers of the quilt together. Great care and attention is given to keeping those small running stitches as tiny and straight as possible. With old fabrics and old linings, a good quilter could line up as many as five stitches on a needle at one time and get two full needles' worth of stitches per inch. The finished stitches are also referred to as "quilting." They anchor the lining between the top and back to keep it from bunching up.

Knotting Comforters

Another method of attaching the layers of a quilt together is by knotting. This process is much less tedious and time-consuming. One stitch with a heavy thread is drawn through all three layers of the quilt, and then the two ends of the thread are knotted together on top. This procedure is done in regular two or three inch intervals. The ends of the thread, which are often a contrasting color, are not clipped closely. Instead the tails are nearly an inch long to be sure the knot does not open. These knotted bedcovers are usually called comforters.

Diversity in Amish Quilts

People often perceive the Amish to be backward and against all change. But is a group who contributes almost nothing to air pollution, for example, really backward? Their home-grown meat and vegetables lack chemical preservatives; crime and divorce are nearly unheard of within their community. But this is not to imply that the Amish are static. They do experience change, but at a less frantic pace than most of their non-Amish neighbors. Their increased use of diesel power, extensive use of pneumatic tools and appliances, and their more frequent riding of bicycles signal change in some of the communities.

Nor has the quilting world of the Amish been exempt from change either. Pattern types and variations, the size of pieces, and color have all evolved. There are marked geographical and chronological differences visible in Amish quilts. The eastern settlements are older than those in the West, so Amish quilts from Pennsylvania can be traced to an earlier period than those from Ohio or Indiana. It also appears fair to suggest that there was greater wealth among the Lancaster County Amish than those in the Midwest. It seems like-

This funeral procession depicts the support of the community for its members even in death. These buggies have just left the funeral service held at the home of the deceased, and are on their way to a family grave plot where the body will be laid to rest.

ly that many Lancaster County women bought fabric for the express purpose of making quilts. Center Diamond patterns, for instance, require larger pieces of fabric than would be left as scraps from making clothing. The Pennsylvania communities were more economically stable than were the newer communities settling in the Midwest. The financial instability that came from moving to new areas was reflected in the more common use of clothing scraps in the quilts made by Midwestern women. Frugality, as well as the limited accessibility of fabric stores, also accounts for the popularity of certain quilt patterns. Along with smaller pieces, Midwestern quilts also boasted more lively colors.

More Borrowing in the Midwest

The distances between Midwestern Amish settlements were greater than in Pennsylvania. So the Amish visited less with each other and had greater interaction with their "English" (the Amish term for people who are not in their church) neighbors. With that increased outside influence, the Midwestern Amish adopted more daring patterns, borrowing some from neighbors and reworking old standard patterns. Consequently there is a broader spread of patterns and colors from these far-flung communities than from the more densely populated eastern settlements. But no matter their geographic origin, antique Amish quilts possess an energy that is rooted in a complex milieu of diversity and conformity, of restriction and freedom.

Center Diamond or Diamond in Square

10. Detail of Plate 12 on facing page.

The suggestion of quilt designs are found all around the farm. Here the standing wheat creates the Diamond in Square; the sheaves the quilting stitches.

The first permanent settlement of Amish in America was in Lancaster County, Pennsylvania. Here, within the strict boundaries of Amish culture, the art of quilting flourished.

One of the oldest and plainest Amish quilt patterns is the Center Diamond, or Diamond in Square, found almost exclusively in Lancaster County quilts. In fact, this design, when discovered in other areas, can often be traced to Lancaster roots.

The pattern is very simple. A large square, made of one central fabric and tipped on its side, forms the diamond. Large triangles fill in the corners to create another square, which is then outlined by one or more borders. Borders may be broken by the addition of corner blocks. The number of colors used may be only two or as many as five.

The fact that such large sections of unbroken fabric are required for this pattern indicates fabrics were likely purchased expressly for use in a particular quilt. By contrast, many other Amish quilt patterns require small patches of fabric and can therefore accommodate scraps left over from other home sewing projects, or salvageable portions of worn-out clothing—a reflection of a frugal lifestyle.

It is difficult to decide what is more outstanding about this quilt—the bold pattern, or the quilting. Center Diamond quilts, with their large open spaces, are usually lavishly quilted with tight, tiny stitches. They are often quilted in dark thread, creating a soft, subtle design on the deep, rich colors of the quilt top surface.

Quilting designs vary, but the central diamond generally has some sort of large, dominant design. Frequently this is a large eight-pointed star inside a feather wreath, or a series of wreaths, the central one filled with small diamonds or cross-hatching. Narrow inner borders, if they are present, may be quilted with rambling grapevines, the pumpkin seed pattern or other narrow designs.

The wide outer borders repeat the generous quilting with elegant curved feathers, ferns, some floral patterns, baskets and other graceful patterns. Corners, especially where blocks are set in, may contain a new and different design rather than continuing the border pattern around the corner.

Although few quilts are signed and dated, careful observation may reveal initials or a date discreetly quilted among the graceful lines of the quilting design.

12. Center Diamond, dated 1914. Wool, 78 x 77.
Lancaster County, Pennsylvania. The People's Place,
Intercourse, Pennsylvania. The date and quilter's initials
are beautifully quilted above and beside the overflowing
fruit basket in one corner.

13. Center Diamond, c. 1900. Wool, 73 x 73. Lancaster County, Pennsylvania. Joy Glick Hess.

14. Diamond in Square, 1935-36. Wool, 77 x 77. Lancaster County, Pennsylvania. Collection of Catherine H. Anthony.

15. Center Diamond. c. 1915-20. Wool, 80 x 80. Lancaster County, Pennsylvania. Rebecca Haarer. This quilt was sent to LaGrange County, Indiana as a relief gift following the Palm Sunday tornados of 1965.

16. Center Diamond, 1910. Wool, 74 x 76. Lancaster County, Pennsylvania. Ron and Marilyn Kowaleski, Grant St. Antiques, Lancaster, Pennsylvania.

17. *Center Diamond, dated 1903. Wool. 77 x 77. Lancaster County, Pennsylvania. William B. Wigton.*

18. *Center Diamond with Sunshine and Shadow, 1920. Cotton, 75 x 75. Lancaster County, Pennsylvania. Ron and Marilyn Kowaleski, Grant St. Antiques, Lancaster, Pennsylvania.*

19. *Center Diamond, c. 1920. Wool (cashmere), 76 x 74. Lancaster County, Pennsylvania. Privately owned. The maker of this quilt filled nearly the entire center diamond with a series of feather wreaths.*

20. Center Diamond, 1910-20. Wool, 72 x 75. Lancaster County, Pennsylvania. The People's Place, Intercourse, Pennsylvania. Note the unusual use of bright orange in this Lancaster quilt.

21. Center Diamond, c. 1920. Cotton, 80 x 80. Lancaster County, Pennsylvania. Jay M. and Susen E. Leary.

22. Center Diamond, 1925. Wool, 75 x 75. Lancaster County, Pennsylvania. Collection of Catherine H. Anthony. This quilt shows some of the more common quilting motifs for the Center Diamond pattern.

23. Sawtooth Diamond, 1911-12. Wool. 87 x 87. Leola, Lancaster County, Pennsylvania. Collection of Catherine H. Anthony. Note the exquisite feather quilting on the inside border and the tiny diamonds in the triangles surrounding the center square.

24. Sawtooth Center Diamond, c. 1915. Wool, 77 x 79. Lancaster County, Pennsylvania. Privately owned. Piecing the tiny triangles and fitting them on the edge of the squares required mathematical precision and planning. This quilter had different solutions for different corners.

25. Sawtooth Center Diamond, c. 1920s. Wool, challis, 82 x 82. Lancaster County, Pennsylvania. Paul and Lorraine Wenrich. Note the careful planning used in execution of the sawtooth pattern. Triangles in opposite corners mirror each other.

26. Sawtooth Diamond, c. 1910-15. Wool, 86 x 86. Lancaster County, Pennsylvania. William B. Wigton.

Sunshine and Shadow

27. Sunshine and Shadow, c. 1925-30. Wool, crepe, rayon, cotton, 82 x 84. Lancaster County, Pennsylvania. William B. Wigton. Effective blending of colors in varying shades in this quilt, which also appears on the cover, adds to its drama. Colors are those often used in Amish clothing. A rose motif quilting design fills the border.

Life is full of sunshine and shadows. Death and life exist side by side in the Amish community where birth and old age are equally respected.

There is a striking, almost shocking quality to the Sunshine and Shadow Quilt. Its association with a people of a quiet and subdued lifestyle seems paradoxical. Yet this quilt pattern embodies the spirit of joy and vibrance in the life of an Amish family.

Sunshine and Shadow gets its name from the light and dark effect created by the harmonizing and juxtaposition of a large variety of bold solid colors. The result may be a subtle blending of light to dark or a dramatic opposition of the two.

The Sunshine and Shadow pattern was done largely in Lancaster County, Pennsylvania, but spread to the Midwest when Amish settlements were established there. Therefore, the earliest Sunshine and Shadow quilts are likely Pennsylvania quilts while later ones may be from any Amish area.

This is a simple pattern, consisting of small squares of fabric sewn together and contained by one or several borders. The squares are arranged by color to form a series of brightly colored expanding diamonds. Sometimes the squares are tipped on their sides to form a pattern of squares.

The Sunshine and Shadow quilt traditionally has a wide outer order. Inner borders may or may not be present. Borders may be plain or contain corner blocks.

Because small squares constitute a large part of this quilt, it fits the principle of frugality practiced among the Amish. Most Amish clothes are handmade, often by the women of the household. The scraps left over from these projects could be cut for use in such a quilt. The small pieces required could also come from the still sturdy portions of worn-out clothing.

Quilting on this pattern is lavished on the borders. Here feathers are one of the most common motifs but other full designs are also used. The center squares are often quilted near the seams or simply cross-hatched in diagonal lines. Occasionally a more elaborate stitching like the clamshell design is used on each tiny square. Inner borders usually have their own quilting designs the same width as the border itself.

The Sunshine and Shadow arrangement of squares worked with printed fabrics rather than plain may be called Trip Around the World and is often done by non-Amish women. It is the solid fabric and wide borders of the Sunshine and Shadow quilt that make it distinctive and traditionally Amish.

29. Sunshine and Shadow, c. 1930. Cotton, wool, 81 x 84.
Lancaster County, Pennsylvania. Jay M. and Susen E.
Leary. A wide range of colors makes this quilt dance.

30. Sunshine and Shadow, dated 1926. Cotton, 72 x 80. Mifflin County, Pennsylvania. William and Connie Hayes. The corners of this quilt are less well planned than the center so that the pattern of concentric diamonds breaks near the outside.

31. Sunshine and Shadow, c. 1930. Wool and cotton, 86 x 86. Lancaster County, Pennsylvania. Collection of Catherine H. Anthony. A well-planned gradation of colors creates a magical light and dark interplay in this quilt.

32. Sunshine and Shadow, early 1940s. Wool challis, crepe, 84 x 82. Lancaster County, Pennsylvania. Paul and Lorraine Wenrich.

33. Sunshine and Shadow, c. 1900. Wool, 84 x 84. Lancaster County, Pennsylvania. Jay M. and Susen E. Leary. The squares in this quilt are tipped on their sides which creates a series of concentric squares rather than diamonds.

34. Sunshine and Shadow, 1940s. Cotton, crepe, 88 x 86. Lancaster County, Pennsylvania. The People's Place, Intercourse, Pennsylvania. A rambling rose pattern is quilted on the outside borders of this later quilt.

35. Sunshine and Shadow, c. 1930. Cotton, wool, crepe, 86 x 86. Lancaster County, Pennsylvania. Jay M. and Susen E. Leary. This quiltmaker combined the Sunshine and Shadow pattern with the Center Diamond to create a different look.

Color Among the Amish

Probably the most distinctive quality about Amish quilts is their color. Other quilters from the past would on occasion use exclusively solid fabrics. But Amish women consistently used only solid colors for their quilts. Most antique quilts are made from fabric scraps, usually left over from other sewing projects. Since much Amish clothing, especially women's dresses, men's shirts, and children's clothing, has traditionally been made at home, it is the fabric left from these handmade dresses and shirts that creates the vivid, deep colors found in Amish quilts.

Amish clothing at a quick glance seems dark and somber because of its heavy use of black. But children's clothing and young women's dresses are gaily colored blues, greens, purples, pinks and dark reds. Although the styles are conservative (children wear miniature models of adult clothing), the colors are bold and bright. The colors, it seems, match the children's energies.

"Naive" Color Combinations

Amish quilts are also generally spoken of as "dark." However, there are few quilts as daring and bold in color as those made by the Amish. How can this seeming paradox be explained? Amish quiltmakers, because of their limited access to color and fashion trends, work in a nearly uninhibited color world. Most children in the larger society begin early in their lives to subconsciously develop a color sense. Their socks match their pants; their pants match their shirts; their sweaters are coordinated. All this takes place in homes where carpets, draperies, and walls are synchronized with accessories and furnishings.

In an Amish setting, one style of clothing is worn, and only part of its color changes from day to day. One never need worry about whether one's pink dress matches one's black stockings and black shoes. Most Amish homes do not contain upholstered furniture, their walls are generally painted a solid blue or green, and carpets, where found, are often hand-woven rag rugs. This lack of color consciousness among the Amish leaves them completely open to any possible combination of fabrics from their scrap bag.

Amish women were not told that color hues vary depending on their reference point. But they could see—and feel—that fact. Numerous quilts were pieced without the maker's knowledge of the science of what she was doing. She saw it and knew inherently that the two colors brought out the best in each other. For example, many antique Amish quilts have touches of black and red, two choices which add spark to nearly any color scheme. Amish women simply recognized it as a

Though simple, Amish houses are warm and friendly. Attention is given to cleanliness and order.

pleasing combination. Their approach to color was new, fresh, and followed gut-level instincts. Perhaps that is why these quilts have such wide appeal. Everyone's creative sense knows when something is correct, but too often the "modern" person knows too much to make these free decisions.

Clothing Colors Used Primarily

Among the Old Order Amish there were and are stipulations about clothing colors. The more conservative groups of eastern Pennsylvania avoid red, red-orange, orange, and yellow. But burgundy hues are permitted. Amish groups in Mifflin County, Pennsylvania, use many bright, gaudy colors, including yellows. Midwestern Amish also tend to allow bright and varied clothing colors.

Occasionally a "stray" color appears in an antique Amish quilt. One Amish woman explained how these color exceptions may have happened: midwestern Amish women often bought fabrics from peddlers who went from home to home with their wares. A good peddler learned to know his territory and how to market his merchandise. He knew what kinds of fabrics appealed to his Amish clients and made bundles of those fabrics, offering them at a bargain rate. But among the desirables he might place some pieces that were slow movers. One Amish woman wanted a bundle of fabrics that contained a piece of bright red cloth. Knowing that this particular color was out of her domain, she explained to the peddler that she would like the bundle but with an exchange for the red. Apparently having had trouble moving the red elsewhere, he refused to swap. So she purchased, along with her needs, a piece that she could use only in a secondary function. This bright red cloth became quilt fabric.

Some Quilt Fabrics Purchased

Not all old quilts are made from scraps. Large sections of fabrics used for backings and borders needed to be purchased. But the principle of frugality is strong among these people. So remnant shopping and bargain hunting for fabrics was likely common and would account for some of the exceptional colors used. Backings were sometimes printed fabrics, even though prints were seldom permitted for clothing.

These old quilts delight and surprise the viewer with their vibrance and lasting beauty. They bridge the gap from a separate people to the modern world. Their beauty, though perhaps understood in different ways by each group, is loved and appreciated by both.

Many Amish are employed at home on the farm. As a result, parents and children spend more time together than in families where one or both parents drive to work.

Bars

39. Bars, c. 1890-1900. Wool, 72 x 87. Lancaster County, Pennsylvania. William B. Wigton.

Harvest is a time for thanksgiving. The Bars quilt pattern is reflected in this evening photo, and the quilting motif is parallel to the rows of stubble.

Bars is a pattern of stark simplicity—straight vertical pieces surrounded by a border. There may be only two colors used alternately or an assortment of colors differing in each vertical bar.

Although it does appear among the midwestern Amish, the Bars pattern is a simple, plain one and was made largely among the Pennsylvania Amish. These quilts usually have wide borders covered with generous quilting, typical of Pennsylvania Amish quilts.

The most basic Bars quilt lacks any ornamentation other than the quilting designs, but variations of the Bars pattern exemplify the spirit of adventure and exploration found among this outwardly austere people.

The Split Bars variation adds interest by splitting the larger bands of color with additional narrow bands. Some quilters added a pieced inner border, while others created patterns within the bars themselves. The Wild Goose Chase pattern, for example, has a series of triangles ascending and descending the bars, giving the illusion of birds in flight. A collection of Nine Patch blocks can be stacked inside the bars to give a more interesting design.

The quilting designs on a Bars quilt more than adequately compensate for what may seem to be cold, stark piecing. The entire inner section of bars is sometimes treated as a whole and quilted in continuous lines of small even diamonds or in some graceful, flowing design. Or each bar may be quilted in continuous lines of small even diamonds or of a graceful, flowing design. Or each bar may be quilted in its own motif, giving a sampling of many different quilting designs. The open borders create a challenge for any avid quilter to use an abundance of feathers, cables, or other delicately stitched patterns.

It is not possible to make definitive statements about the inspiration for such a quilt design. However, it is likely that a people so close to the earth would be inclined to incorporate patterns of the field and the garden into other areas of life. One only needs observe a few of the meticulous gardens and fields of the Old Order Amish to see their pride in strong, straight lines. Plowed furrows in long even stretches, horizontal slats on wooden fences, or tobacco barns with opened vents could have provided the impetus for Amish women to create the Bars quilt.

41. Bars, 1910-20. Wool, 78 x 73. Lancaster County,
Pennsylvania. The People's Place, Intercourse,
Pennsylvania.

42. Bars Variation (Nine Patch), c. 1905. Wool, flannel back, 90 x 68. Elkhart County, Indiana. Rebecca Haarer.

43. Bars, c. 1870-80. Wool, cotton, 84 x 66. Mifflin County, Pennsylvania. William B. Wigton. Unlike most Pennsylvania quilts, this one does not have a border. Note the extravagant quilting designs used throughout the quilt top.

44. Bars, c. 1900. Wool, 79 x 69. Lancaster County, Pennsylvania. Orpha M. Hege. The border quilting design contains baskets filled with fruit. Pears and apples are quilted between baskets.

45. Wild Good Chase in Bars, c. 1880-90. Cotton, 69 x 79. Mifflin County, Pennsylvania. William B. Wigton.

46. Wild Goose Chase, Bars Variation. c. 1915. Wool, 84 x 66. Lancaster County, Pennsylvania. Rebecca Haarer. This quilt traveled from Pennsylvania to Indiana in a relief box to victims of the Palm Sunday tornados in 1965.

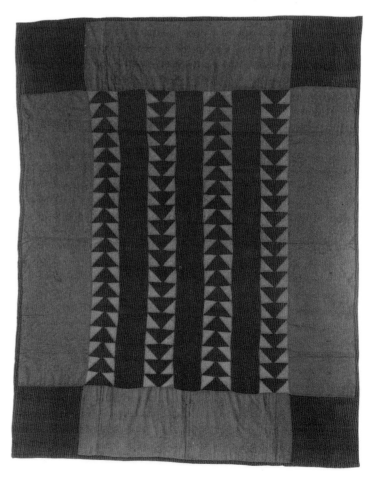

47. *Split Bars, 1933. Cotton, 80 x 80. Lancaster County, Pennsylvania. Collection of Catherine H. Anthony. The rose quilting design used on the borders is also repeated in the bars design.*

49. *Bars Variation, c. 1900-10. Cotton and wool, 73 x 63. Iowa. Judi Boisson Antique American Quilts, New York.*

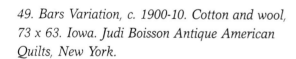

48. *Bars, c. 1930. Cotton, 83 x 85. Lancaster County, Pennsylvania. Jay M. and Susen E. Leary. An inside border with pieced diamonds adds interest to this design. Pineapples are quilted among feathers on the exterior border.*

50-51. Sampler, dated 1926. Cotton, 71 x 82. Mifflin County, Pennsylvania. Judi Boisson Antique American Quilts, New York. This rare quilt is a sampler pattern on one side with bars on the reverse side (see below). Quilting is a simple cross-hatch design throughout.

Multiple Patch Quilts

52. Blockwork, c. 1910. Glazed cotton, 67 x 73. Holmes County, Ohio. Judi Boisson Antique American Quilts, New York. This pattern looks like a collection of miniature center diamond blocks collected and set together into one quilt.

This grouping covers a range of quilts from the simple One Patch pattern to the more complex Double Nine Patch, with variations on all these designs.

The One Patch is just what its name implies—a quilt made up of a series of single patches sewn together in a random or an organized fashion. The Four Patch is a series of blocks consisting of small patches in groups of four. The Double Four Patch uses a set of two four-patch blocks pieced with two solid patches the size of the quartet patch to form a square of four blocks. A series of these "double-four" blocks are sewn together, with sashing setting each square of four blocks apart.

The Nine Patch is the same idea worked in a series of threes. Nine small patches (three horizontal by three vertical patches) are sewn together to make a square. The Double Nine Patch uses five of these nine-square patches pieced together with four solid patches the size of the nine-patch to form the quilt top. Variations include the Four Patch in a Nine Patch, Nine Patch, or Four Patch in a Block Work.

The pattern is a simple one, but the many possibilities allowed within the patches make it intriguing. Seldom are all the patches within a quilt done in the same color scheme. This multitude of color differences makes this a quilt with sparkling potential.

Because of the small pieces and numerous color possibilities, it is an excellent pattern for a "scrap quilt." Any small snippet or scrap can be worked in at some spot.

This pattern was likely a first choice for many girls beginning their piecing skills. The simple straight lines make it easy to piece but the size and number of patches create enough challenge for a novice to tackle it with pride.

It is not only a beginner's quilt, however. The magnificent craftsmanship found in many of these quilts shows they are obviously the work of experienced and skilled hands.

The Amish are not opposed to education, but they are cautious about too much formal training, especially in consolidated schools. The interplay of light and dark blocks in this Amish school is similar to the geometry in Multiple Patch quilts.

54. Double Nine Patch, c. 1930. Cotton, 83 x 82.
Lancaster County, Pennsylvania. Jay M. and Susen E.
Leary. A pieced inner border of bright colors adds interest
to this pattern.

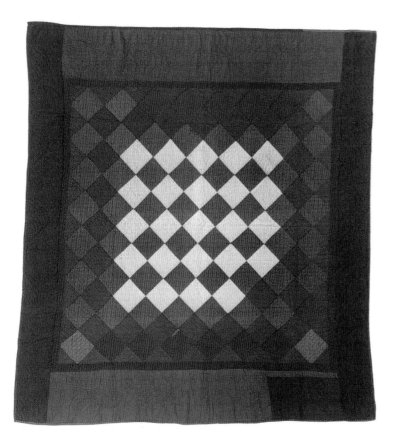

56. Four in Block Work. c. 1930. Cotton, rayon, 73 x 86. Mifflin County, Pennsylvania. William B. Wigton. The framing of the four-patch blocks is reminiscent of the Center Diamond pattern.

55. One Patch, c. 1915. Cotton, worsted wool, 76 x 69. Medford, Wisconsin. Judi Boisson Antique American Quilts, New York. Although this is a very simple pieced pattern, the borders of the quilts are elegantly quilted with fiddlehead ferns.

57. Double Four Patch, dated 1913. Wool, 83 x 71. Elkhart County, Indiana. Joseph M. B. Sarah.

58. Double Four Patch, c. 1920. Cotton sateen, 68 x 78. Mifflin County, Pennsylvania. William B. Wigton. Tiny initials are embroidered on the border of this quilt.

59. Four Patch-Nine Patch, c. 1920. Cotton sateen, 71 x 80. Mifflin County, Pennsylvania. Judi Boisson Antique American Quilts, New York.

60. Four Patch in Nine Patch, c. 1920-25. Cotton sateen, 83 x 77. Mifflin County, Pennsylvania. Reed Hayes. Black and pink squares mark a grid across the quilt top.

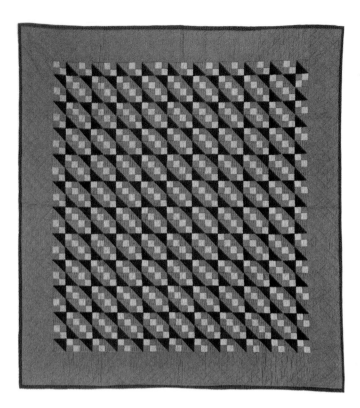

61. *Four Patch and Triangles Combination, c. 1910. Cotton, 78 x 84. Mifflin County, Pennsylvania. William B. Wigton. Four patches with triangles form diagonal lines that shoot across the quilt top. A strong border contains the vibrance of this design.*

62. *Nine Patch, c. 1900. Wool, mohair, 70 x 80. Mifflin County, Pennsylvania. William and Connie Hayes. Careful placement of blue squares creates a rectangle in the center of the quilt. Red squares repeat the pattern in an outer rectangle.*

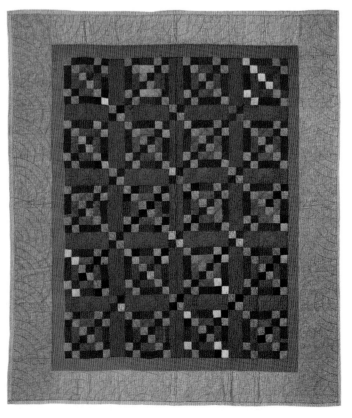

63. *Four in Split Nine Patch, c. 1925. Cotton, 67 x 76. Mifflin County, Pennsylvania. William B. Wigton. Four-patch blocks are matched with rectangular shapes to achieve this interesting block work.*

64. Nine Patch, 1890. Wool, 77 x 84. Belleville, Mifflin County, Pennsylvania. Ron and Marilyn Kowaleski, Grant St. Antiques, Lancaster, Pennsylvania. A saw-tooth inner border frames the nine-patch blocks.

65. Double Nine Patch, c. 1925-1930. Wool, wool-rayon, 74 x 76. Lancaster County, Pennsylvania. William B. Wigton. Triangles form an unusual inner border for this otherwise typical design.

66. Double Nine Patch, c. 1915. Cotton, 46 x 78. Holmes County, Ohio. William B. Wigton. The unusual dimensions of this quilt suggest that it was probably made for a hired man's bed.

67. Nine Patch Variation, c. 1930. Cotton, 64 x 76. Mifflin County, Pennsylvania. William and Connie Hayes.

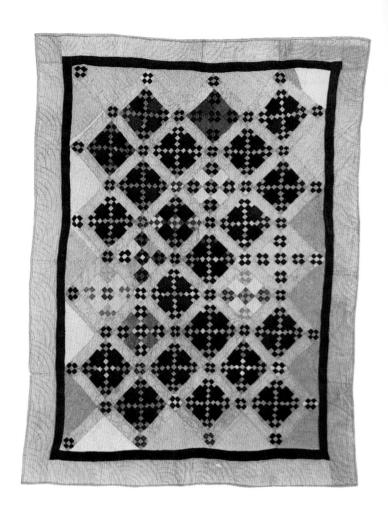

68. *Double Nine Patch, c. 1910. Cotton, 61 x 79. Collected LaGrange County, Indiana. Rebecca Haarer. Triangles surrounding the sashed nine-patch blocks are pieced at several places indicating that the maker was likely using some scraps.*

69. *Double Nine Patch, c. 1910. Cotton, wool, 68 x 74. Collected in LaGrange County, Indiana. Rebecca Haarer. This is truly a scrap quilt! Even the tiny squares in the nine-patch blocks are sometimes pieced.*

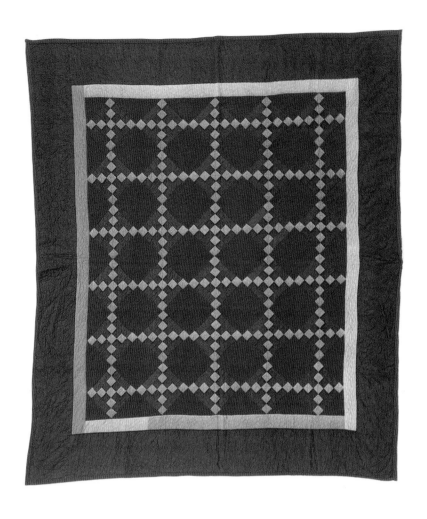

70. *Nine Patch in Block Work, c. 1910. Cotton, 69 x 79. Mifflin County, Pennsylvania. William B. Wigton. Careful placement of pink patches create a chain pattern on the quilt surface. This is very similar to the Single Irish Chain quilt in photo #72.*

71. *Nine Patch in Block Work, c. 1920. Cotton, wool, 74 x 83. Mifflin County, Pennsylvania. William and Connie Hayes. Only one block in this quilt deviates from the norm of using four pink squares in the borders of the nine-patch blocks.*

Irish Chain

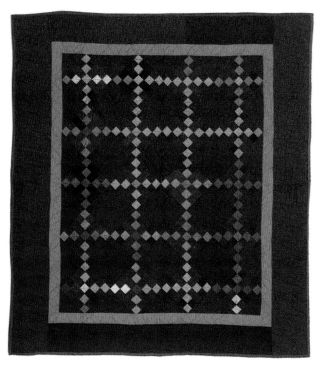

72. *Single Irish Chain, c. 1920. Cotton sateen, 64 x 70.*
Wayne County, Ohio. William B. Wigton.

These three girls are watching a game of baseball played
on a Sunday afternoon in the neighbor's meadow. The
fence pattern reminds one of an Irish Chain quilt.

Here is a quilt with simple elegance—clear, sharp lines with ample space for generous quilting. The Irish Chain pattern can be pieced as a single row of blocks, as a double row, or as a triple row. The category is determined by the number of blocks creating the "chain" that runs diagonally or vertically through the quilt.

The single Irish Chain quilt can be constructed rather simply by making a series of simple Nine-Patch blocks in two colors. These are then tipped on their corners and sewn together alternately with solid squares of the same color to form the single Irish Chain. Other variations of the pattern are much more complicated, requiring very careful placement of color to create the chain effect.

The double and triple chain varieties often combine a bit of appliqué with the piecework. These patterns are sewn together so that a multiple patch is alternated with a solid patch of fabric, the same size as the multiple patch. To achieve a consistent chain effect, small squares must be added to the corners of these solid patches. It is often easiest to appliqué those additional squares on top, rather than trying to piece a right-angled corner.

The solid squares between the chain pattern, as well as the typically wide borders on these quilts, provide ample space for the outstanding quilting skills evident in Amish quilts. Curved, flowing quilting lines provide a contrast for the angles created by the pieced chain.

While the colors and fabrics used in Amish Irish Chain quilts make them distinctive, this is not a pattern unique to Amish quilt makers. Irish Chain quilts were made by quilters in general. At some point, an Amish woman likely borrowed the pattern from a neighbor or friend and from there it probably circulated among Amish quilters.

74. *Triple Irish Chain, c. 1920. Cotton, 72 x 88. Mifflin
County, Pennsylvania. William B. Wigton.*

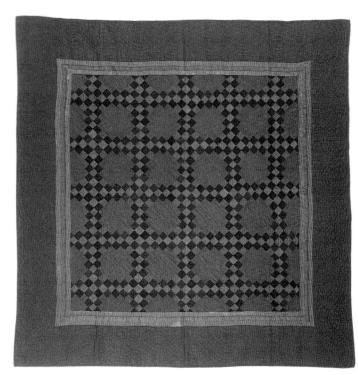

75. Double Irish Chain, dated 1927. Cotton, 73 x 74. LaGrange County, Indiana. Faye and Don Walters.

76. Triple Irish Chain, c. 1915-20. Wool, 76½ x 76½. Lancaster County, Pennsylvania. Joseph M. B. Sarah.

77. Triple Irish Chain, 1864. Cashmere, cotton, 68 x 88. Lancaster County, Pennsylvania. Anna Lois Umble.

78. Double Irish Chain, c. 1920. Wool, 77 x 79. Lancaster County, Pennsylvania. Jay M. and Susen E. Leary.

79. Triple Irish Chain with embroidered Baskets, c. 1930-40. Cotton, 72 x 76. Belleville, Mifflin County, Pennsylvania. Romaine S. Sala.

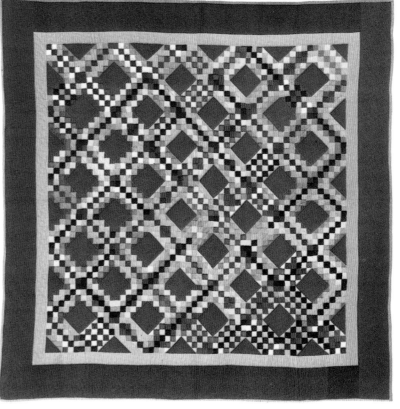

80. Triple Irish Chain Variation, dated 1940. Cotton, 77 x 81. Collected in Holmes County, Ohio. Judi Boisson Antique American Quilts, New York.

81. Triple Irish Chain Variation, dated 1944. Cotton, 78 x 79. Tuscarawas County, Ohio. Judi Boisson Antique American Quilts, New York.

Quilts in the Life Cycle

A people who live from the land know well its seasons and changes. And their own day-to-day lives flow in rhythm with the earth's movement.

The Earth Gives

Spring is the time for planting fields, gardens, and flower beds. Housecleaning gets underway with the women scrubbing the house from top to bottom, airing the mattresses, beating the rugs, wiping walls and ceilings, washing windows to a sparkle, and emptying and cleaning cupboards and drawers. With warmer weather comes vigor for these projects. There is a freshness in the air indoors and out. Lawns are raked free of debris and primped and prepared for the burst of color promised by newly planted flower beds.

Field work begins and ends with the sun. Men and those children no longer in school spend long days standing on the plow behind a team of horses. Their

Children are loved and enjoyed in the Amish community. They grow up eating, drinking, playing, and working "Amishness" and usually join the church as young adults.

reward? The smell and texture of newly turned earth!

Summer and the closing of school bring extra hands to help hoe the corn, top tobacco, and cut and bale hay before the rain comes. It is a rushed time, but rich in the earth's plenty. There are strawberries to pick, peas to pod, beans to shell and corn to be husked. There are new potatoes and tender asparagus to be collected. Cantaloupes, watermelons and fresh fruits offer themselves for snacks and desserts. Not only is there enough to fill summertime tables, but all the fruits have been planted in excess so as to be preserved for the winter months.

Fall comes and with it the children's return to school, the last of the harvest and quieter days on the farm. Fall housecleaning sweeps away the summer clutter. Window screens are replaced with storm windows; hay mows and corn cribs are stacked full; silos burst with food for cattle during cold months. And when the days become shorter and winter's nip is in the air, butchering day arrives. Meats are canned, smoked, or frozen for use throughout the cold months.

The Earth Grows Quiet

Winter is a time for repairs and maintenance around the farm. There are fewer demands from the fields and garden, so the farm family fixes their energies on other projects. It is during these slower times when the earth is frozen and silent that many women turn to quilt making.

It would be misleading to say that all Amish women enjoy quilting. For some it is as natural as housecleaning and gardening. For others it is tedious work and something they simply prefer not to do. But for many women, it is a fulfilling undertaking, learned at the elbows of their mothers and kept alive by tradition and their own enthusiasm.

Growing Up

Discipline is strict in Amish families and is evidenced in the children's ability to sit quietly during the three hour Sunday morning church services. Children are treated firmly but not harshly. They learn early to take responsibility around the farm and are often given specific chores in both house and farm work. One of the skills often taught young children is to hand stitch small patches together for a quilt top. Not only do they learn a specific skill, but these children are at the same time being taught perseverance, patience, and lack of idleness. Young girls eventually learn to embroider and finally to make their own clothing. Along the way, most girls follow the example of the older women in their lives and also learn to quilt.

Families Wrapped in Love—and Quilts

Part of the magic of quilting is that it can be done in groups. Fun and visiting happen around the quilting frame. Young Amish women, like teenagers everywhere, dream about their futures. For most the choices are clear-cut—marriage, family, and carrying on their way of life. It is not unusual for an Amish girl in her early teens to begin making several quilts in anticipation of her marriage and children.

Among the Amish, large families are received with great joy. And in preparation for these gifts from God, expectant mothers and grandmothers turn to making crib quilts. Most women are not employed outside of the home. They view mothering and caring for their homes as honorable and worthwhile positions. The responsibility of raising children in a God-fearing manner is foremost in the minds of these parents.

How do Amish women, with their large families and basic, back-to-earth lifestyle, find time to quilt? Time is a relative concept. Many Amish homesteads operate as extended families with two or three generations living under one roof. Although each family lives separately, there is daily interaction between generations. Consequently, both moral support and physical help flow in all directions. And children, although they are the primary responsibility of their parents, relate closely to grandparents whose lifestyle and values match what they see at home.

Parents work hard at establishing "Amish" values in their offspring. However, as children become teenagers, they are gently freed of parental ties and the choice to leave or stay within the community is one that must be made by each individual. For many young adults marrying and joining the church happen at about the same time. Both are lifetime commitments supported by family and church.

The Amish are, in general, a restrained people. They show little overt emotion or affection. But in place of kisses and embraces, Amish women demonstrate their love through their offerings of quilts and favorite foods, both lovingly prepared and assembled. Many mothers make quilts to present to their sons and daughters at the time of their marriages.

Some quilts seem to have been intended as heirlooms and show quilts, for use on beds only on Sundays and when company was coming. Both the memories of their owners and the condition of their bedcovers bear out this intent. These quilts are in such excellent condition that it seems they were never used. Perhaps the makers knew that the love invested in each tiny quilting stitch would serve as long time testament to that affection.

The Amish care for their own elderly instead of leaving that to Social Security. Additions are built onto the original farmhouse to make room for two or three generations.

Quilting Belongs to All Ages

Growing old is not a tragedy in the Amish world. Age carries the respect of wisdom and the elderly are cared for with dignity. Aging family members are nursed at home unless they require hospitalization. Around the farm there are jobs that can keep men busy even though their strength and health may be failing. There is nearly always a son or grandson for them to assist.

Women stay involved in domestic chores and child care until it becomes physically impossible for them. Here again quilting fits into the life cycle. Old age and new blood work elbow to elbow on a project that symbolizes Amish life. One generation learns from the next with the knowledge that time goes on and with it the cycle of life. Death is seen as a natural part of having lived. When one becomes old, death is the doorway to a new life and a stepping stone for the next generation.

Log Cabin

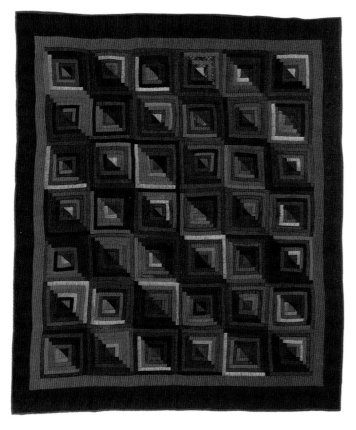

84. *Log Cabin—Diagonal Furrows Variation, c. 1900-10. Wool, 66 x 78. Mifflin County, Pennsylvania. William and Connie Hayes.*

Mutual aid is a way of life for the Amish. Barn raisings are common in Amish settlements, both in the actual construction of barns and in the Log Cabin quilt pattern.

A favorite with quilt makers in general, the Log Cabin also thrived among Amish quilters. Its possibilities are almost infinite. There are Barn Raising, Courthouse Steps, Straight Furrows, and Pineapple or Windmill Blades variations. And each of those can be made with solid borders, pieced borders, or no border at all.

The Log Cabin quilt is often a scrap quilt. Its narrow "log"-shaped pieces in varying lengths could accommodate many scraps that were not large enough for other patterns. Perhaps this is why so many Log Cabin quilts flourish in so many diverse constructions.

Assembly of this quilt is straightforward. It begins with a center square. The block is then rotated one-quarter turn and the next log (the length of the square plus the previous log) is added. This continues with varying numbers of logs to form the basic log cabin patch.

Patches are often arranged with light fabrics on one half of the block and dark fabrics on the other half, which when sewn together produce a larger pattern on the quilt top.

The visual images are apparent. One can see the sun streaming through the rafters of a barn under construction. Straight furrows are sharp and clear and the dark patches conjure up images of rich, dark soil waiting to burst forth with harvest. The tiny steps of the logs create the Courthouse steps, and the Windmill Blades variation seems to spin as easily as the windmill pumping water on an Amish farm.

Log Cabin quilts are one of the exceptions to the general rule of elaborate quilting on Amish quilts. These quilts are sometimes quilted only on the borders, sometimes not at all. In some cases the quilt top, lining, and backing are connected in the piecing process. The blocks are then sewn together, eliminating the functional need for quilting. In other cases, quilts are "tied" or "knotted" (tacked with heavy string at regular intervals) rather than quilted. That may have been done because the narrow width of the logs creates the problem of having to quilt through a seam allowance, thus making quilting less pleasurable and less fine. When Log Cabin patterns are quilted, the stitching is usually minimal in the pieced part of the quilt and more abundant on the borders.

86. Log Cabin, c. 1890-1900. Wool, 82 x 84. Mifflin County, Pennsylvania. William B. Wigton. A strong contrast in colors makes the barn raising design in this quilt very obvious. The pieced borders continue the theme of narrow strips.

87. Log Cabin—Courthouse Steps Variation, c. 1910-20. Cotton, wool, 68 x 76. Collected in LaGrange County, Indiana. Rebecca Haarer. Borders on this quilt contain beautifully quilted feather designs.

88. Log Cabin—Courthouse Steps Variation, c. 1880-90. Wool, 71 x 67. Collected in Indiana. Judi Boisson Antique American Quilts, New York. A pieced border along two sides of the quilt provides extra width and adds interest to the design.

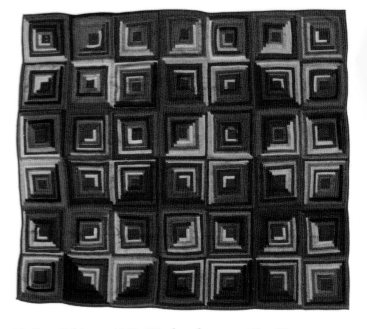

89. Log Cabin, c. 1880. Wool and cotton, 79 x 71. Lancaster County, Pennsylvania. Naomi E. Yoder. Tiny initials of the man for whom this quilt was made are cross-stitched in the center square on the bottom left block.

48

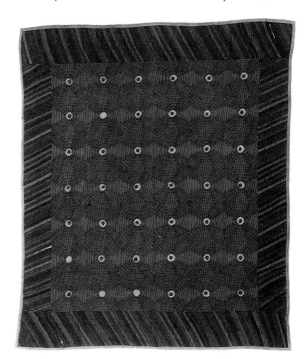

90. Pineapple, c. 1920-30. Cotton, 75 x 82. Ohio.
Judi Boisson Antique American Quilts, New York.
Careful use of fabric creates a double pattern in
this quilt. Fine quilting as well as the addition of
the sawtooth border at top and bottom show this to
be the work of a master.

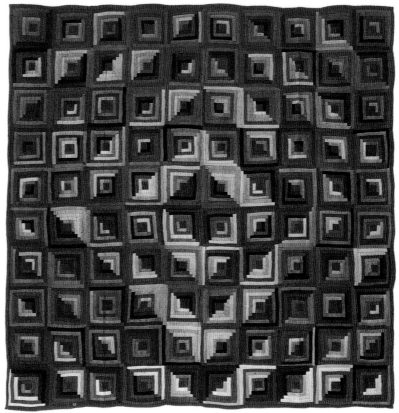

92. Log Cabin—Barnraising Variation, c. 1890. Wool,
80 x 80. Mifflin County, Pennsylvania. The Darwin D.
Bearley Collection. A carefully planned group of log
cabin patches have been tipped on their sides in assembly to create a pattern of concentric squares.

93. Log Cabin—Barn raising Variation, c. 1920.
Cotton, wool, crepe, 78 x 78. Lancaster County,
Pennsylvania. Jay M. and Susen E. Leary.

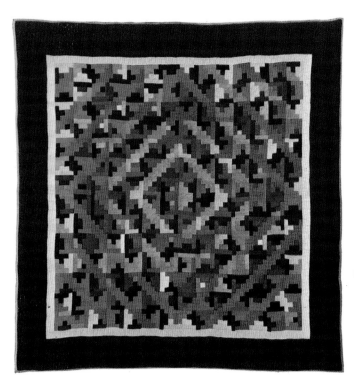

94. *Log Cabin—Barn Raising Variation, 1920. Cotton, wool, 68 x 70. Topeka, LaGrange County, Indiana. Rebecca Haarer. Light and dark patches appear to be mixed in this bedcover but the quilter has successfully achieved an overall barn raising effect. This top was pieced by Sarah Miller for her son Jacob and quilted by Sarah and Jacob's bride.*

95. *Log Cabin—Barn Raising Variation, 1932. Cotton, 86 x 76. Emma, LaGrange County, Indiana. Rebecca Haarer. Bright yellow contrasts with other colors to create the barn raising effect. The entire quilt is covered with tiny quilted diamonds.*

96. *Log Cabin—Barn Raising Variation, dated 1920. Cotton, wool, 68 x 70. Topeka, LaGrange County, Indiana. Rebecca Haarer. The unusual addition of a pieced inner border creates a double framing effect.*

Double T

It is often difficult to document how patterns were developed or named. The Double T, however, looks like what it is called—a T that mirrors itself in two directions. Perhaps this particular pattern began as a Nine Patch (see the center of the Double T patch).

This pattern is seldom found among Amish quilts of Pennsylvania. It is a Midwestern quilt pattern, perhaps learned by an Amish woman from a neighbor. There seems to have been much more borrowing by the Midwestern Amish of patterns from outside their community; at least, these Amish used many more patterns than did the Pennsylvania Amish. Perhaps the same spirit of adventure and necessity that allowed Amish families to move West is reflected in their more experimental attitudes in quiltmaking.

Quilting is an integral part of most Amish quilts. This pattern is no exception. Borders and open blocks between piecework encourage the abundance of stitching that helps make these quilts the masterpieces they are.

97. Double T, c. 1920. Cotton, 80 x 70. Northern Indiana. Nancy Mern. A triple inside border and generous quilting add to the beauty of the quilt.

Detail of above quilt. Note the quilt's subtle color variations in blue.

Stars

99. Broken Star, c. 1920-30. Cotton, 85 x 85. Ohio. Judi Boisson Antique American Quilts, New York. The use of the tiny nine patch blocks bring together the corners of the triple inside border. Fiddlehead ferns are quilted throughout the border.

Numerous quilt patterns deal with the heavenly bodies. Perhaps this fascination with the sky stems from the fact that so much of rural life begins and ends at the bidding of the sun.

The rising and setting sun are particularly important in an Amish home. Without electric lights, sewing is frequently done inside a window where one can reap the full benefit of the sun's light. While gas lamps provide ample light for reading or a game of checkers, the coming of darkness brings rest and time for work to cease.

Probably the most dramatic of the star quilt patterns are the Lone Star and the Broken Star. In these, a large star seems to burst from the center of the quilt, sending light to the ends of its eight points. In the Broken Star, the additional energy of a pieced border surrounding the central star causes the pattern to appear to pulsate.

Successful construction of these quilts requires meticulous accuracy in cutting and piecing the small diamonds. A minute error will be numerously multiplied when trying to match the diamonds' corners in this magnificent quilt.

Quilting adds another striking feature to these already dramatic bed covers. Open corners surrounding the stars and wide outer borders seem always to inspire fresh energy and imagination in quilters. This ornamental stitching adds depth and grace to the quilt.

Star quilts come in an abundance of shapes and sizes. In addition to the large star patterns there are many smaller star designs worked in a series of blocks.

One of the features that make the Amish star quilts so outstanding is their fabrics. Many of these star quilts have backgrounds of very dark colors, making the star itself seem to sparkle like the stars in a clear night sky.

Star patterns, although popular with quilters in general, seem to have been accepted and widely used by the Amish. It suggests a wonderful blending of their respect for God's creation and their love of beauty.

Star motifs are common in Amish quilts and handcrafts. Perhaps this intrigue with heavenly bodies stems from these people's work, beginning and ending at the bidding of the sun.

101. Broken Star, c. 1925-30. Cotton, 72 x 72. Ohio.
William and Connie Hayes.

103. Broken Star, dated 1938. Cotton, 90 x 90, Holmes County, Ohio. Judi Boisson Antique American Quilts, New York.

102. Broken Star, c. 1930-40. Cotton, 89 x 89. Holmes County, Ohio. Judi Boisson Antique American Quilts, New York.

104. Lone Star, 1921. Cotton, 74 x 68. LaGrange County, Indiana. Rebecca Haarer. Effective use of color creates an outline of the star. Red diamonds on the points of the star add spark and vibrance.

105. Lone Star, c. 1930. Cotton, 74 x 74. Ohio. William B. Wigton. The maker of this quilt intentionally or accidentally reversed the placement of a green and yellow diamond at the widest point of this star.

107. *Stars and Blocks, late 1920s. Cotton, 72 x 85. Holmes County, Ohio. Collection of Catherine H. Anthony.*

106. *Series of Stars, c. 1920. Cotton, wool, 78 x 78. Lancaster County, Pennsylvania. Jay M. and Susen E. Leary.*

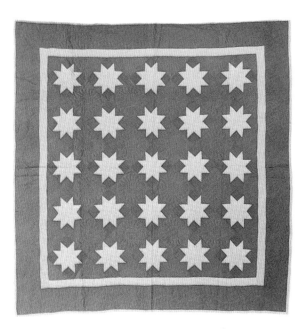

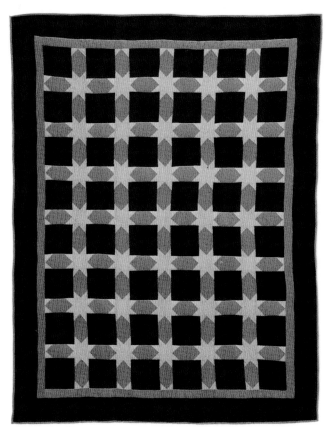

108. *Eight Point Stars, 1920s. Glazed cotton, 78 x 75. Ohio. Judi Boisson Antique American Quilts, New York.*

109. *Stars and Stripes, late 1920s-early 1930s. Cotton, 64 x 80. Walnut Creek, Ohio. Collection of Catherine H. Anthony.*

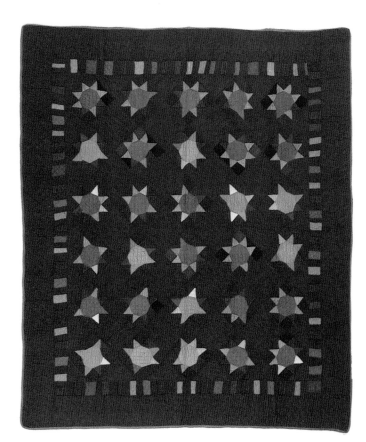

110. *Star Variation, c. 1930-40. Cotton, crepe, 84 x 70. Wayne County, Ohio. The Darwin D. Bearley Collection.*

111. *"Star Medallion," c. 1910. Cotton, 73 x 77. Elkhart County, Indiana. Judi Boisson Antique American Quilts, New York. Similar in concept to the Tumbling Blocks Pattern, the stars in this quilt are created from diamonds, but the hexagons between stars are solid pieces.*

112. *String Star or Crazy Star, c. 1915-20. Cotton, wool, 81 x 80. Elkhart County, Indiana. Joseph M. B. Sarah.*

Jacob's Ladder

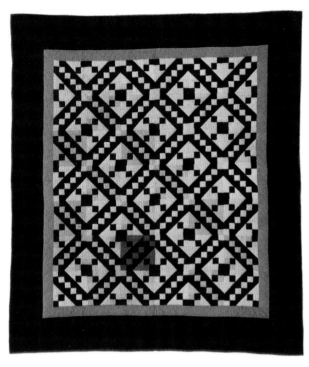

The Jacob's Ladder pattern was brought into the Amish community from outside. Its religious roots perhaps made it desirable to Amish women.

Jacob's Ladder depicts the ladder from the Old Testament story of Jacob's vision of angels ascending and descending from heaven to minister to him on earth.

Colors must be carefully arranged to execute this pattern correctly. The pattern is a series of four nine patch blocks and triangles arranged with light and dark fabrics to form continuous diagonals across the quilt surface.

Quilting on the pieced portion of this quilt is generally done in straight lines with more elaborate quilting on the borders.

113. Jacob's Ladder, c. 1920. Cotton, 68 x 80. Probably LaGrange County, Indiana. Rebecca Haarer. One isolated blue patch wandered into the making of an otherwise subdued color scheme.

Detail of above quilt. One patch of singular color is common in old Amish quilts.

Plain Quilts

"Plain quilts" seems a wrong term for these vibrant bedcovers. And yet a parallel can be drawn between this pattern (or lack of it) and the Amish way of life. At first glance both seem severe and almost drab. Only careful scrutiny reveals fullness and refined simplicity.

In these bedcovers is evidence that quilts were more finely done than function alone would require. Their rich spreads of extravagant quilting go way beyond the stitches necessary to keep the top, lining, and backing intact.

Here is sheer appreciation for the skill and beauty of quilting. A woman who undertook such a project was certainly no novice with the quilting needle. Such a venture undoubtedly provides a creative outlet for her skilled hands. This channeling of creative energies into a functional object fits the Amish principles of humility, frugality, and simplicity.

115, 117. Plain, c. 1910. Cotton, 89 x 66. Reno County, Kansas. Mrs. Mary Bontrager. Exquisite quilting covers this quilt. It is reversible (see facing page), one side being black with blue and green inside borders; the other green with blue and black inside borders.

Quilting motifs can be found in many aspects of rural life. This spiderweb, stretched within the pasture fence, reflects a medallion pattern frequently quilted into plain quilts.

118. Center Square, c. 1880. Wool, 83 x 83. Lancaster County, Pennsylvania. Jay M. and Susen E. Leary. The pieced design and central quilting is plain, but the border is elaborately quilted. The feather quilting motif ends with a tiny heart design.

119. Center Square, c. 1890. Wool, 78 x 84. Lancaster County, Pennsylvania. Jay M. and Susen E. Leary.

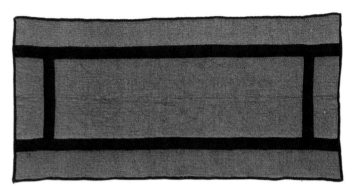

120. *Plain, or Double Inside Border, 1910. Cotton, 69 x 59. Ohio. Judi Boisson Antique American Quilts, New York. Six feather wreaths fill the interior of the quilt, and fiddlehead ferns are quilted on the border.*

121. *Plain, c. 1900. Wool, cotton sateen, 32 x 66. Holmes County, Ohio. William B. Wigton. This shape suggests the quilt was probably made for a hired man's bed.*

122. *Plain, March 31, 1946 quilted in center. Cotton, 65 x 77. Holmes County, Ohio. Collection of Catherine H. Anthony. A bold, sharp, pieced design is softened with curved quilting lines.*

Excerpts from a Grandmother's Diary

This diary represents the life of an Amish woman throughout the year. Many of the entries were first published as news items in Amish publications. Names and places were changed to protect the identities of the people involved.

"Sadie's Diary" was originally compiled by the staff of The People's Place in Intercourse, Pennsylvania where it now hangs as a wall mural.

January 5	Yesterday Amos Stoltzfus attended the funeral of Abner King of New York State. He died of a heart attack if he was informed right.
January 12	I took in the quilting at the Ephrata Clothing Center.
January 21	Martha wrote that they butchered a beef Tuesday.
January 24	Snow piled high on the barnhill. The men had to shovel their way to get supplies.
February 2	Sam Zooks had a singing on Sunday p.m. for the benefit of the visitors.
February 4	Lizzie made fresh doughnuts all morning. She makes the best.
February 12	Eli discouraged by hog prices.
February 15	Cousin David A.'s had a get-together for some families who lost children in accidents. Some came as far as Indiana.
February 27	Abe's crowd was here ice skating. They made hot dogs on the ice.
March 1	Eli and Daudy were with a van load of Fisher relatives to Cumberland County to help build a hog barn at Joe's.
March 10	This morning we had some excitement when I discovered a skunk in the cow barn!
March 14	Yesterday was the sale of John F. Yoders. Lizzie and I helped with the chicken soup.
March 18	Peas are finally in. An extra row this year.
March 26	Children flying kites after school in the meadow these days.
April 4	Aaron Jr. lost his best work horse. Somehow it must have stumbled down a bank in the cow lane and got under a barb fence and couldn't get up.
April 11	We took supper with Bishop Junie Stoltzfuses after giving Jonas Fisher a surprise visit in the p.m.
April 17	Plowing going good. Neighbor with tractor says it's too wet to get in the fields but our men having no problem.
April 25	The boys hauled the grill out of the wash house and we had grilled sausage for supper. Was a bit nippy to eat outside.
May 7	Rachel came to help with planting the flower garden. Her new bread recipe hits the spot!
May 13	Fresh asparagus, new rhubarb with tapioca and oranges, and the last of the roosters.
May 14	The corn's in! The men worked from dawn till dark for five days. Amos and Elam took turns staying home from school.
May 29	School picnic. Lizzie says several families from Honey Brook moving to Missouri. Joe Esh's might be going.
June 1	I'm trying not to eat too many strawberries. They have too much acid for my arthritis.
June 14	We did up 109 quarts of peas. Daudys helped.
June 20	Eli and Abe went to the liability meeting at Christ Millers in Mary County, MD.
June 29	Weather warm and humid again. Where did spring go? Warm weather is hard on J.J. Miller's Johnny with his condition.
July 3	Yesterday afternoon lightning struck close and knocked Jonas A. Smucker down but he got up by himself, and 2 of Jake B's girls were in the cellar and it gave them a hard jolt.

These Amish boys have congregated on the front porch of their school The roof was on fire earlier in the day because the wood stove fire had gotten too hot.

Ice skating is a wonderful winter pastime for many Amish. It's a time to let ice hockey and crack-the-whip add some zest to cold winter afternoons.

July 14	Black raspberries are at an end; sweet corn is on the menu, string beans are plentiful, also weeds in spite of the dry weather.
July 23	Wheat is cut and is on shock. Some farmers started to thrash.
July 30	The 21 qts. apricots we canned from the neighbor's tree will save us some peach canning.
August 7	Clover got washed again today. Has been hard to put up hay at times.
August 14	The last two days were spent in painting the school house inside and out, except the stucco. Had a few extra men at the table.
August 21	Did up tomato juice today with Lizzie. 56 quarts!
August 22	Surprise visit from O'Brien family from New Jersey. Learned to know them last summer at Junie's.
September 8	Church services today were held in shed at Sammy Riehls with a large attendance.
September 16	Mrs. James B. Hamilton, my roommate when I was in hospital, here for supper tonight. Her husband died in November.
September 27	There was a bad accident last evening around 10. A car without lights on the wrong side of the road drove head-on into Levi Kauffman's horse, killing it almost instantly. It threw Levi 20 feet across the car, breaking his pelvis.
October 4	Today a pair of dark frame plastic glasses with bifocals were found along Railroad Avenue in a black case.
October 12	John Lapps had a circle letter get-together last week after the meeting.
October 18	Eli and the boys working late on the corn. Eli's back tired again.
October 23	Helped make snitz pie for church at Aaron Jr's Sunday.
October 29	Small game season opened today. What a racket!
November 1	On Halloween morn a farm hand came to stay with Aaron Jr's., missing his sister Rebecca's birthday by 39 minutes. He will answer to the name of Jacob, named after Lizzie's father.
November 3	Laura Petersheim had a quilting today to give to our teacher (non- Amish).
November 12	Today was the wedding at Eli B. Fishers of their oldest daughter Barbara to Samuel E. Zook, son of Pre. Dan Zook. Several hundred ate at dinner, even more for supper.
November 22	Another wedding, our sixth this month. Cousin Junie Beiler's Sarah hitched to Larry Bontrager from Ohio. They met when Sarah went to help her aunt last year.
December 7	Little Lydia Smoker is sick with fever and earache so she can't go to school.
December 17	Daudy's are going along to the school program. Children working hard on memorization. It tickles me the way Amos is determined.
December 24	It's snowing tonight, really coming down. Looks like we'll have a white Christmas.
December 26	Second Christmas. Joes came over on the sleigh and Lizzie helped me with a meal. Duck and oyster filling. Cookies galore. A happy time for all.
December 31	Another year. "Are we thankful enough the way we have it?"

As the year goes round so do the seasons. Amish farmers are able to begin plowing earlier in the spring than their tractor-driving neighbors. Because horses are lighter in weight than tractors, they can enter the fields before it is as dry as a tractor requires.

Cultivating corn is a precise job, but one often given to young children since it does not require exceptional strength.

Corn binders cut stalks of corn off at ground level and tie them in bundles. These loads of corn are then chopped and put into silos for the livestock throughout the winter. When the silos are filled, the corn is left to dry. Shell corn is then ground and mixed into short feed for cows.

Baskets

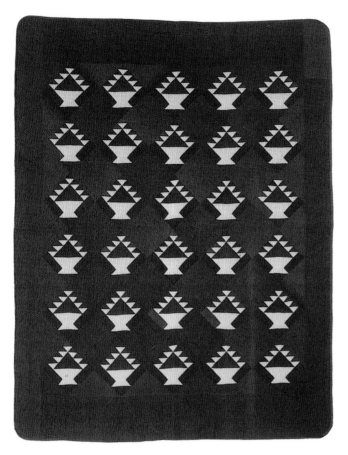

Amish Basket quilts come mainly from the Midwest where there was a comparatively more open approach to quiltmaking than among the Pennsylvania Amish. Baskets were popular in general society, and the adoption of this pattern by Amish women is somewhat unusual, as Amish quilts tend to avoid the realistic reproduction of an object. There are, however, lovely examples of this design worked by Amish quilters.

Basket patterns use a variety of geometric shapes to create the finished image. Adequate and proper contrasting of fabrics is necessary to enhance the basket design. Where curved handles are a part of the basket, they are appliquéd after the Basket block is completed.

The basket, as a design motif, is sometimes quilted on the borders of other quilt patterns. But it is seldom used as a quilting design on a pieced Basket quilt.

On a quilt top the basket blocks are usually alternated with solid blocks of the same size which are quilted with full, flowing lines. Borders provide additional space to display quilting expertise.

128. Baskets, c. 1910. Cotton, 86 x 66. Ohio. Judi Boisson Antique American Quilts, New York. Several shades of blue are contrasted with the hollow baskets. Tulips are quilted in the alternate plain blocks.

Baskets are common containers around Amish farms. Carrying produce from garden to house or from garden to market is often done in baskets.

130. Baskets, dated March 21, 1915 and 1945. Cotton,
84 x 61. LaGrange County, Indiana. Rebecca Haarer.
Baskets stand out sharply against a black background.

132. Baskets, c. 1930s. Cotton, 78 x 65. Dover, Delaware. Judi Boisson Antique American Quilts, New York.

131. Baskets, 1920s. Wool, 80 x 80. Lancaster County, Pennsylvania. Paul and Lorraine Wenrich.

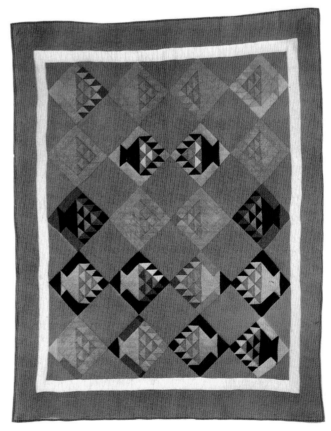

133. Baskets, c. 1915-20. Cotton, wool, 74 x 62. Nappanee, Elkhart County, Indiana. Norma L. Singleton. Fabric contrast or lack of it varies the appearance of the basket shapes.

134. Baskets, dated 1908. Cotton, 66 x 84. Montour County, Pennsylvania. Donna and Jonathan Speigel. A careful blending of subtle colors results in a lovely understated quilt.

135. Cactus Basket or Star Basket, 1940. Cotton, 75 x 92. Amherst, Wisconsin. Collection of Catherine H. Anthony. Perky baskets appear the same at first glance but study shows subtle differences in the fabrics of the inside petals.

136. Baskets, c. 1925. Glazed cotton, 92 x 67. Holmes County, Ohio. Judi Boisson Antique American Quilts, New York. Baskets are pieced and handles appliquéd for this pattern. Note the name embroidered on the inside border.

Crazy Quilt

137. *Crazy Patch, c. 1900-10. Wool, 80 x 88. Mifflin County, Pennsylvania. William and Connie Hayes. The interior of this quilt is knotted and borders are quilted.*

Moving is a concept common in the history of the Amish. Migrations continue to occur as they look for space and peace from the larger world. The pattern of this moving van is not unlike the composition of the Crazy quilt.

An old, old quilt pattern, the Crazy quilt hints of a time when frugality was an inescapable way of life. The Crazy quilt is a collection of scraps and snippets of left-over fabrics or remains of worn-out clothing stitched together with little regard for similarity in shape, size, or color. The result is a wonderful hodgepodge of color and likely a quilt with memories in each patch.

Crazy quilts, although a random collection of shapes and sizes of scraps, are not without an overall plan. The quilt may have a crazy patchwork design over the entire top, or it may be worked in a series of crazy blocks sewn together in a clear-cut pattern, creating order and cohesiveness in the quilt top as a whole.

This is not a time-saving quilt. Any minutes saved by not having to cut patches are soon absorbed in the fancy embroidery work done evenly along the seams of the patches, often in a thread of contrasting color. Occasionally, some fancy embroidery work even appears in the center of one of the larger patches. Perhaps this quilt served as a testing ground for young girls who were learning various embroidery techniques.

Because of the assortment of fabric types and the additional weight of the quilt top (crazy patches are assembled over another piece of fabric), these quilts are often knotted or tied (layers are connected with heavy thread at regular intervals) rather than quilted. Quilting becomes tedious and laborious when going through layers of heavy fabrics.

However, there are outstanding examples of Crazy quilts with superb quilting. Many of these have a crazy patch alternating with a solid patch which is filled with quilting designs. This variety also frequently has wide borders covered with elegant quilting.

139. *Crazy Patch, c. 1900. Cotton, wool, 74 x 88. Mifflin County, Pennsylvania. William B. Wigton. A Crazy quilt with a very specific plan, this quilt is modern in its look.*

140. Crazy, c. 1915. Wool, 77 x 79. Lancaster County, Pennsylvania. Privately owned. A beautiful sampling of embroidery stitches outlines each crazy patch. They are set together in an orderly fashion with beautifully quilted plain patches.

141. Crazy, c. 1920. Cotton, wool, 79 x 79. Lancaster County, Pennsylvania. Jay M. and Susen E. Leary. Tiny grapes and grape leaves are quilted on the inside border. Exquisite embroidery decorates the crazy patches.

143. Scrap Crazy (tied comforter), c. 1925. Denims, cottons, 49 x 71. LaGrange County, Indiana. Rebecca Haarer. This quilt is made mostly of work pants and shirt materials.

142. Contained Crazy (comforter), c. 1900-10. Wool, cotton flannel, 81 x 67. Arthur, Illinois. Rebecca Haarer.

144. Crazy, c. 1900. Cashmere, cotton, 77 x 72. Berks County, Pennsylvania. Anna Lois Umble. The maker of this Crazy quilt had an overall scheme.

Fan

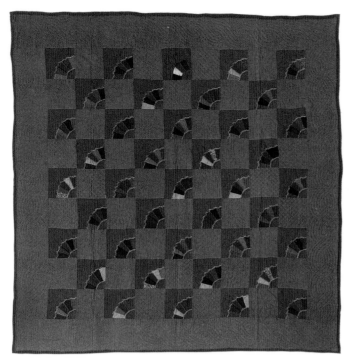

145. Fan, 1904. 79 x 80, Berks County, Pennsylvania.
Anna Lois Umble. One patch was done without the addition of embroidery around the fan.

*New growth coming from the old is a universal theme. It
is also found in the Amish community, both in nature and
the church. The Fan pattern is reflected in the reel of this
binder as it sheaves the wheat.*

A bright and cheerful quilt, the Fan is a pattern used
largely by Amish women of the Midwest who borrowed it from their neighbors. But its organic quality
makes it especially appropriate for these rural farm
women. When fans are set in a quilt, all slanting in one
direction, they resemble bright flowers leaning toward
and drinking in the sunshine. When the blocks are
tipped so that the fans stand upright they look like a
mass of butterflies in flight. When patches are set opposite each other they remind one of the agitation of a
butter churn, and when all four points are assembled
together the fans form a wheel.

The Fan quilt may be a combination of piecing and
appliquéing, or it may be completely pieced. When the
former method is used, the fans are first pieced, then
appliquéd onto a background square. This means of
construction is commonly used when the edge of the
fan is scalloped.

Embroidery around the edges of the fans is an additional feature on some Amish Fan quilts. Quilting sur-
rounds the fan design and decorates the borders.

147. Fan, dated 1927. Cotton, sateen, 76 x 85. Elkhart
County, Indiana. Diana Leone. Several pieces of black
velvet add richness to this vibrant quilt.

148. Fan, dated 1904. Cotton, wool, 74 x 63. Topeka, LaGrange County, Indiana. Rebecca Haarer. Light colored fans look feathery soft against their dark background.

149. Fan, dated 1943. Cotton, wool, 81 x 81. Lancaster County, Pennsylvania. Jay M. and Susen E. Leary. Quilted roses fill the border and spaces above the fans.

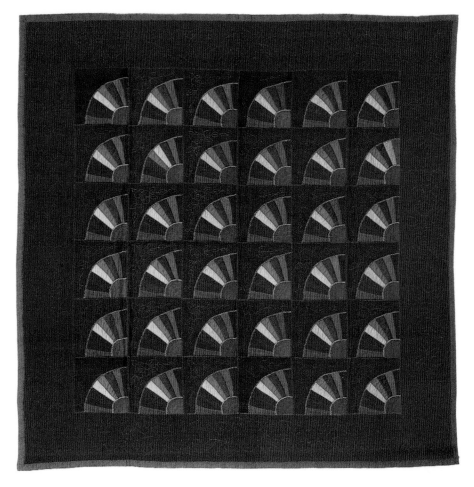

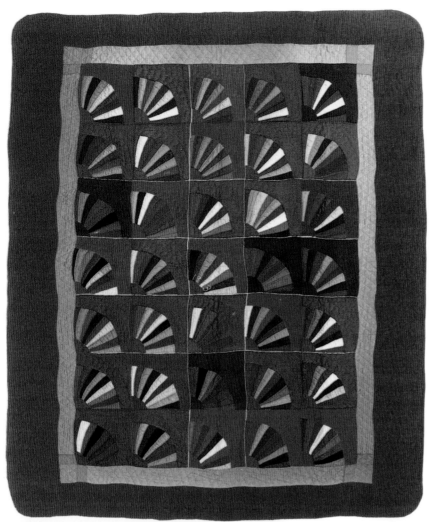

150. Fan, dated 1913. Cotton, wool, 64 x 76. Shipshewana, LaGrange County, Indiana. Rebecca Haarer. The date is prominently displayed in the center of this quilt. Note the different treatment of corners on the inside border.

151. Fan, c. 1900. Wool, 83 x 70. Mifflin County, Pennsylvania. Judi Boisson Antique American Quilts, New York. Bright yellow and blue fans occupy the corners with assorted colors in the center.

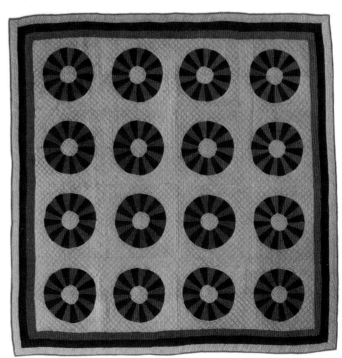

152. Circular Fans, 1890s. Worsted wool, 76 x 78. Holmes County, Ohio. Judi Boisson Antique American Quilts, New York.

Ocean Waves

Ocean Waves is a pattern frequently seen in Midwestern Amish quilts but rarely used by the Pennsylvania Amish. The pattern exemplifies its name with small triangles creating movement and currents in the lines of the quilt.

Because of their limited travel and the landlocked locations of Amish settlements, the makers of these quilts likely never saw ocean waves. Despite that, the many variations of this pattern capture the mix of quiet and storm that bespeaks the ocean.

In general, Midwestern Amish quilters used brighter colors and more diverse patterns but paid less attention to the details of quilting than did Pennsylvania Amish quilters. In Ocean Waves the colors are generally quite bright. Yellow, a frequent choice for this pattern, appears less frequently among Pennsylvania Amish quilts but is common in the Midwest. As is typical of many Midwestern quilts, the borders and bindings of Ocean Waves are often narrower than on Pennsylvania quilts. Furthermore, instead of the elaborate feathered quilting often found on Pennsylvania borders, Midwestern quilting often uses the more simple and easily executed cable design.

153. Ocean Waves, dated August 20, 1919. Cotton, 72 x 84. Holmes County, Ohio. Judi Boisson Antique American Quilts, New York. The gray background seems to perk up the colors in the interior of the quilt.

The orange, slow-moving-vehicle symbols on the rear of these buggies look like the triangles on an Ocean Waves quilt. This hitching post has attracted a diversity of Amish buggies.

155. Ocean Waves, c. 1930. Cotton, 89 x 74. Holmes County, Ohio. Judi Boisson Antique American Quilts, New York.

156. Ocean Waves, c. 1930-40. Cotton, 76 x 69. Holmes County, Ohio. Judi Boisson Antique American Quilts, New York. Touches of bright yellow and several other light fabrics add spark to this quilt. A narrow inner border frames the pieced design.

157. Ocean waves, c. 1940s. Cotton, 71 x 78. Holmes County, Ohio. Judi Boisson Antique American Quilts, New York. The blue-green background on this quilt seems especially appropriate for the Ocean Waves pattern.

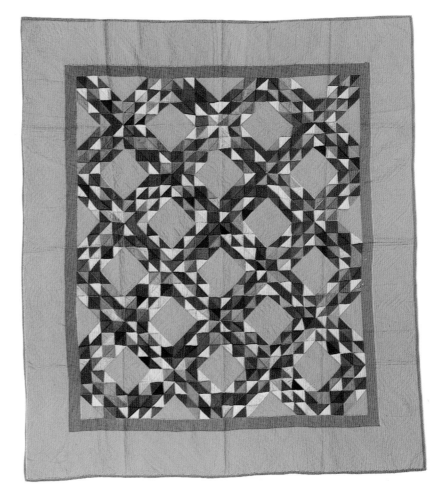

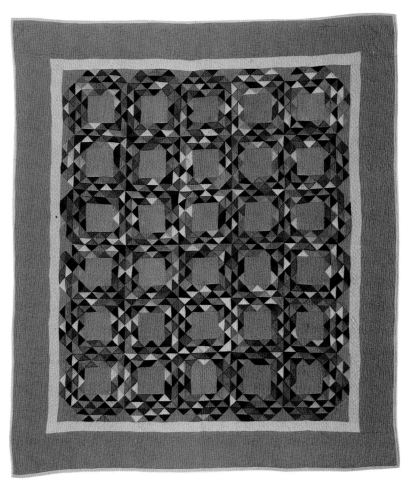

158. Ocean Waves, dated February 10, 1934. Cotton, 80 x 92. Elkhart County, Indiana. Rebecca Haarer. A pattern typical of Midwestern Amish, this quilt shows the use of yellow and lavender not frequently used by Amish in eastern Pennsylvania.

159. Ocean Waves Variation—"Zigzag Diamond," c. 1910. Cotton, 70 x 78. Holmes County, Ohio. Judi Boisson Antique American Quilts, New York.

Roman Stripe

Roman Stripe is a pattern used mainly by Midwestern Amish quilters. A quilt of very simple construction, it may also be referred to as Shadows. In it, square blocks are equally divided with one half being a solid fabric and the other half being a series of diagonal strips ending with a triangle. The strips of brightly colored fabric are usually arranged in a random fashion. Although simply constructed, the overall effect of this pattern is an almost shocking burst of color and energy.

The arrangement of the quilt blocks can totally change the impact of the top. Blocks may be set in the quilt with each triangle pointing in the same direction. Another arrangement with the blocks put together in a zig-zag fashion creates the image of jagged streaks of lightning. And if the blocks are placed with four triangles coming together a diamond is formed. Many other possibilities exist and have been tried by the creative quilter.

160. Roman Stripe, dated 1934. Wool (small piece of velvet in center), 82 x 84. Topeka, LaGrange County, Indiana. Rebecca Haarer. Use of a brown background makes this a quilt with a feeling of warmth, made by Susie Miller for her daughter as a wedding gift.

Sharp and easy angles of farm architecture could well be the inspiration for some quilt patterns. Parallel and alternating diagonal lines reflect both quilt lines and barn lines.

162. Roman Stripe, dated 1906. Wool, 81 x 62. Holmes County, Ohio. The Darwin D. Bearley Collection.

A Quilting

For a people who choose to do without radio, TV, movies, and many types of entertainment enjoyed by the larger society, visiting is vital. Visiting happens regularly and spontaneously. Unannounced guests are always welcome. Even if a visit happens to be near mealtime, the company is heartily invited to stay and eat. Families often spend Sunday afternoons or evenings with relatives or friends. It is the slower pace of the Amish lifestyle that allows time for the simple pleasures of human interaction. Gathered friends may play games together or, more likely, talk about events in each other's lives.

Quilting Mix Work and Visiting

A quilting is an all-day occasion to do some fun "work"—and visit. It is generally hosted by a woman who has one or more quilts to quilt. She may choose to make it a "sisters day," whereupon she invites all her sisters, or she may issue a broader invitation to specific friends and neighbors. Quiltings take place through the year but they are more frequent during less busy seasons on the farm.

"Putting In" the Quilt

The first job to be done (if the hostess has not already completed it) is "putting in" the quilt. That involves stretching the back, lining, and top of the quilt tautly in the frame. The most common type of frame allows quilters to work on all four sides of the quilt at the same time. It is a simple structure with four strips of wood held together by C-clamps. The top and bottom ends of the quilt back are pinned or basted to a strip of heavy fabric which has been tacked along the edge of two of the frame's wooden strips. The back is then tightly stretched between these two strips and the remaining two wooden strips are laid along the sides of the quilt back. The pieces of wood are clamped at the corners, thus making the quilt back a tight, flat surface. The frame, now stretched to its proper size, is then laid across the backs of four chairs making it an appropriate height for quilting. Next, the lining is laid on the quilt back and pinned securely on all sides. And finally the top, with its tracings for quilting designs, is stretched over the back and lining and pinned tightly in place. The bedcover is ready to be quilted.

A Quilting Pecking Order

A typical quilting will involve anywhere from six to twelve women. Seating positions around the quilting frame are often good-naturedly negotiated since no one wants to sit next to and be outshone by the best or fastest quilter! And less experienced quilters choose to sit where there are straight lines to quilt since they are more easily managed than curved lines.

The women, sitting around all four sides of the frame, begin quilting at the outer edge and work toward the center as far as they are able to reach. When all women along the top and bottom of the frame have

Children often accompany their mothers to a quilting. They may also be asked to keep a supply of threaded needles on hand for the quilters. The underside of the quilting frame makes a delightful playhouse for the future seamstresses.

Quilting templates are often made from scrap pieces of cardboard. After the design is cut away, the pattern is traced on the quilt top and then covered with tiny stitches.

quilted to their maximum stretch, the quilt is ready to "roll." The clamps at the four corners of the frame are released and the finished sections of the quilt are gently rolled onto the wood until the unquilted surface is brought to the edge. "Rolling" can take place only from the two ends of the frame. Therefore, when the quilters along the side reach their maximum they must either find and squeeze into a new position at the ends, begin another quilt in another frame, or find something else to do. Those who choose the latter frequently help the hostess prepare lunch.

Eating Belongs with a Quilting

The noon meal is compensation for the time and effort supplied by the invited quilters. It is a highlight of the day. The hostess prepares a full-course meal and services it with pride. Kitchen helpers may be women who were invited to the quilting but would rather not quilt. For them, being in the kitchen is as enjoyable as being around the frame. However, if a woman is assigned to kitchen duty when she would rather quilt, it can be humbling. This sometimes happens to teenaged girls whose stitches are not yet tiny or neat enough to meet the hostess' quilting standards. It is an honor for young girls to be invited to quilt at a quilting. Quilting resumes again after lunch. Women are free to come and go as they are able. Some stay the whole day. Others come for only a few hours.

A Strengthening Time

A quilting is more than a work day. It is an occasion to share household tips, garden hints, home remedies, child rearing information, and the latest news about marriages, births, and deaths. Such a gathering of women with common backgrounds, interests, and goals provides a chance for them to talk at length about their daily lives. A quilting reminds these women of the support they have and gives them a break from daily routine. For hard-working farm women, such an event can be a refreshing one-day vacation.

Quilting for Others

Quiltings are not only held in private homes. The Amish, though separate from the larger world, are not unaware of global needs. Amish women readily participate in quiltings held by the Mennonite Central Committee, a world-wide relief organization that sends food, clothing, and personnel all over the world. Amish women also lend their skills to community projects. Many volunteer fire companies hold quiltings several times a year to produce quilts to sell at their benefit auctions. Since the Amish rely on the services of their local fire companies, they support them actively as volunteer firefighters and contribute time and energy to their quiltings and benefit suppers.

When a quilting day is ended and the quilt completed, it stands as a tangible symbol of a group effort. It portrays not only the skill of these women, but also the strong supportive love that envelops this community and keeps it vibrant and alive despite the pressures of the modern world.

This detail shows five typical quilting designs: 1) pumpkin seed, 2) cross hatch, 3) cable, 4) fan, and 5) feather.

Tumbling Blocks

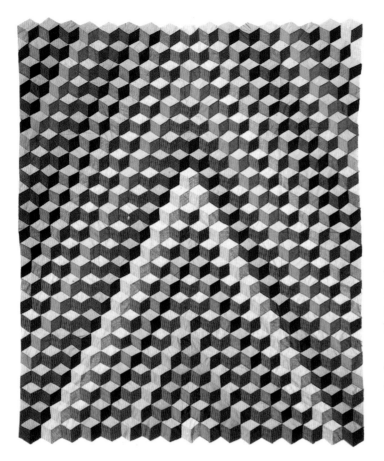

The Tumbling Blocks or Baby Blocks is a simple quilt but one with an intriguing interplay of color and apparent dimension. One can gaze at the Tumbling Block quilt for some time before all of its patterns emerge. By using a single diamond shape and the varied placement of colors, a quiltmaker can create an optical illusion of cubes, hexagons, stars, and diamonds. Occasionally the arrangement of colors also produces a large overall design on the quilt surface.

To achieve the illusion of stacked cubes one must have at least three fabrics in varying intensities of color—one dark, one medium, and one light. The diamonds must be arranged in a hexagon formation with the dark, medium, and light fabrics being used in the same positions throughout the quilt. If diamonds are simply arranged in a random fashion a star is likely to be the dominant emerging pattern.

Quilting stitches generally follow the outline of the diamonds on the pieced top. Surrounding borders are quilted in more fanciful designs.

166. Tumbling Blocks—Pyramid Variation, c. 1930-40. Cotton, rayon (worsted wool-cotton blend), 85 x 99. Ohio. Judi Boisson Antique American Quilts, New York. This is only a quilt top but shows a very successful achievement of a design within a pattern.

Families work together in all aspects of farm life. Here father and sons work beside each other loading straw, an image similar to Tumbling Blocks.

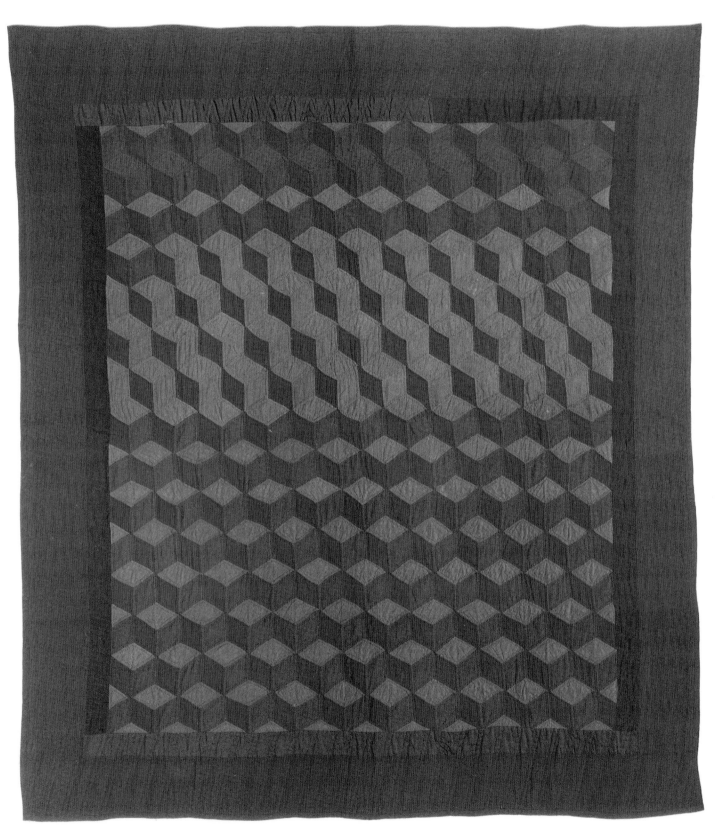

*168. Tumbling Blocks, c. 1930. Cotton, 74 x 67. Ohio.
Judi Boisson Antique American Quilts, New York. Well
organized stacks of cubes form the body of this magnificent quilt.*

*169. Tumbling Blocks, c. 1940s. Cotton,
83 x 76. Kokomo, Indiana. Rebecca Haarer.*

*170. Tumbling Blocks, c. 1925. Cotton, 70 x 79.
Holmes County, Ohio. Judi Boisson Antique
American Quilts, New York. Dark, rich colors
give this quilt depth. Note the combination of
clamshell and diamond motifs quilted on the
border.*

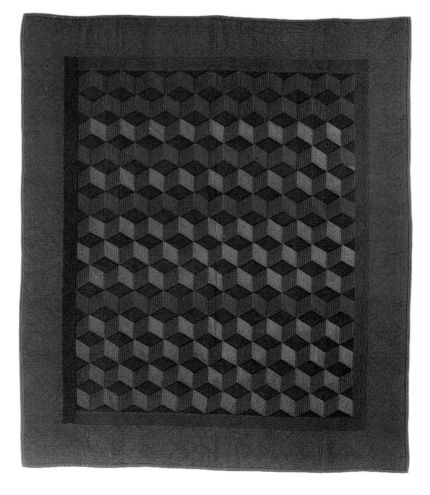

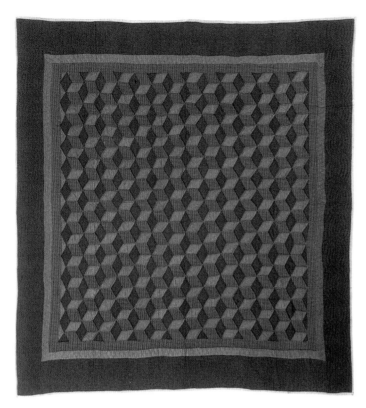

171. Tumbling Blocks (Baby Blocks), c. 1925. Cotton, 80 x 74. Geauga County, Ohio. The Darwin D. Bearley Collection. Effective use of three colors (plus the binding) makes this a successful illusion.

172. Tumbling Blocks (Baby Blocks), c. 1930. Cotton, 80 x 98. LaGrange County, Indiana. Collection of Catherine H. Anthony. Red in combination with two shades of blue give the illusion of stacked cubes.

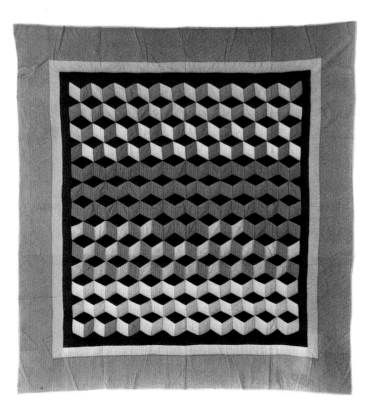

173. Tumbling Blocks, dated November 2, 1929. Cotton, 71 x 75. LaGrange County, Indiana. Rebecca Haarer.

Bow Tie

174. Bow Tie Variation, c. 1900. Cotton, wool, 66 x 82. Loudenville, Ohio. Judi Boisson Antique American Quilts, New York. Bow ties are not as easily seen in this arrangement of the pattern.

Dress regulations within the various Amish groups are generally quite severe. Black outerwear is common. Black felt hats are worn by the men and boys in cold weather; straw hats in hot. Bow ties are found only on Amish quilts, and not on Amish men!

It is fascinating to observe that a group who chooses to avoid the wearing of men's ties makes the Bow Tie quilt pattern with such flair. Obviously there is much creative freedom permitted in quiltmaking. Although considered unnecessary and attention-getting as a clothing accessory, the bow tie as a design is not viewed as wrong if it is used within clear boundaries.

This is a delightful pattern with sprightly little bow ties nearly dancing across the quilt surface. Most often they are arranged in diagonal, vertical, or horizontal rows. On occasion they are set at angles to form a circle on the quilt top.

Possibly an alteration of the basic Four-Patch, the Bow Tie is much more difficult to construct because of the tiny square in the center of the tie. This requires that the four surrounding squares have one corner trimmed diagonally. When piecing, this angled corner must be set in against the bow tie, a task not easily achieved by beginners.

Quilting generally outlines the ties and becomes more plentiful on the one or more borders framing them.

176. Bow Tie, dated 1919. Cotton, 70 x 84. Nappanee, Elkhart County, Indiana. Rebecca Haarer. Set in straight horizontal rows, the ties seem to be arranged for some performance.

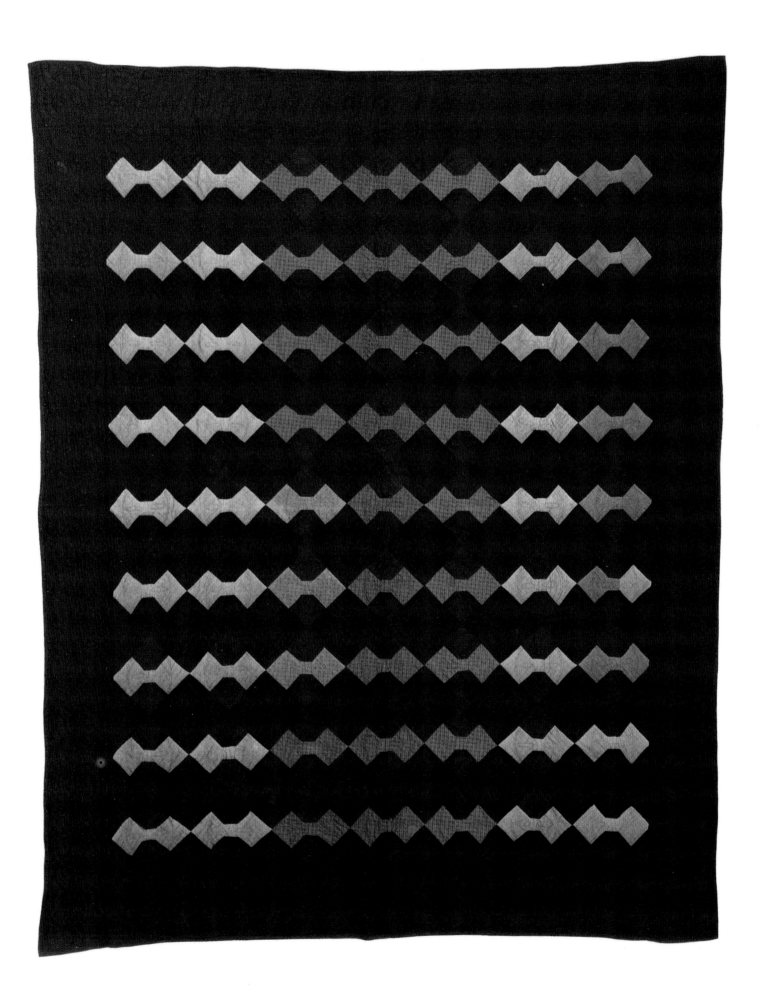

177. Bow Tie, c. late 1940s. Cotton, 75 x 68. Holmes County, Ohio. Nancy Meng. Tiny four-patches form the corners of the inner border. One bow tie in the corner is facing in the opposite direction.

178. Bow Tie, c. 1930. Cotton, 78 x 71. Elkhart County, Indiana. Joseph M. B. Sarah. Trailing tulips fill the inner border on this well organized quilt. Shades of black vary in some patches.

179. Bow Tie, c. 1910-20. Cotton, 68 x 84. Collected in LaGrange County, Indiana. Rebecca Haarer. Quilted hearts filled with a floral design cover the border of this two-color quilt.

Robbing Peter to Pay Paul

This pattern, known to quilters in general, was likely borrowed by an Amish woman from a non-Amish quilter friend. The quilt is often done in only two colors which enhances the power of the finished design.

Robbing Peter to Pay Paul is a logical label for this design: a section of one patch is robbed to fill a gap in the next. The positive and negative aspect of this pattern creates a sharp, clear circular design on the quilt top.

Curved lines make this a pattern for a quilter with experience, since a pieced pattern with curved lines increases the potential for puckers and buckles. Curved edges must be very accurately cut and sewn to achieve a smooth, flat finish.

Quilting designs are stitched on the borders and in the larger patch between circles. Other pieced sections are simply outlined with quilting.

180. Robbing Peter to Pay Paul, 1905-10. Cotton, 68 x 74. Nappanee, Elkhart County, Indiana. Rebecca Haarer. Light and dark fabrics provide excellent contrast in this pattern of positive and negative space.

181. Robbing Peter to Pay Paul, c. 1910-15. Cotton, 82 x 66. LaGrange County, Indiana. Joseph M. B. Sarah. The smooth lines of this curved pattern must have been crafted by a master quiltmaker.

Monkey Wrench

182. Monkey Wrench, c. 1924. Cotton, 83 x 69. Elkhart County, Indiana. Rebecca Haarer.

The Monkey Wrench quilt is also called Hole in the Barn Door. Is there any question about why?

Another name for the Monkey Wrench design is Hole in the Barn Door. Both are apt descriptions for the pattern created by this combination of geometric shapes.

There are not sharp lines drawn between domestic tasks and farm tasks in an Amish home. Women are generally aware of and part of decisions made concerning the farm operations. Nor is it unusual to see women helping in the fields, milking cows, and tending chickens.

Perhaps this quilt pattern is a statement of the overlap in domestic chores, farm work, and the often more pleasurable task of quiltmaking. The Monkey Wrench (pipe wrench) is a tool found on any farm. One never knows when an implement will need minor repairs during planting or harvest season. And perhaps the Hole in the Barn Door label was inspired by an imaginative woman who saw the possibility of a quilt pattern in the cut-out of the stable door, designed to provide ventilation for farm animals.

The design is achieved through the use of triangles and squares or rectangles to form a square patch. These patches may be set straight or tipped on an angle in the quilt top. When set on an angle, the blocks are set alternately with solid squares of fabric which lend themselves well to a fancy quilting design. The blocks are usually framed by one or more borders filled with flowing quilting.

184. Monkey Wrench, 1911. Cotton, 82 x 72. LaGrange
County, Indiana. Rebecca Haarer. Blocks have been
pieced and arranged in symmetry throughout this quilt.

185. Hole in the Barn Door, c. 1915-20. Cotton, 82 x 69. Ohio. The Darwin D. Bearley Collection. Beautiful quilting fills in alternate patches of this pieced design.

186. Hole in the Barn Door Variation, c. 1910. Wool, 72 x 84. Arthur, Illinois. Rebecca Haarer. Likely a scrap quilt, this one uses a myriad of colors throughout.

187. Combination Eight Point Star-Hole in the Barn Door, dated January 27, 1942. Cotton, 88 x 76. Emma, LaGrange County, Indiana. Rebecca Haarer. This quilter successfully combined two patterns into one. It was made by Mrs. Menno Yoder who made several such quilts—one for each of her seven children.

Carolina Lily

188. *North Carolina Lily, c. 1920-30. Cotton, 75 x 77.
Holmes County, Ohio. The Darwin D. Bearley Collection.
Pattern, colors, borders, binding, and quilting make this a
real showpiece.*

It is rare to find the Carolina Lily pattern among Amish quilts. Its occasional presence indicates that a few Amish women were captivated by its beauty and did create quilts of this design.

The Amish have a high respect for nature and its gifts. Living close to the soil makes them more conscious of the earth's bounty and beauty. But because the Amish take seriously the Old Testament commandment against making graven images, they have traditionally kept from reproducing realistic images from nature. But, as in all of life, there are exceptions. And so occasionally, the Carolina Lily image appears.

The lilies and baskets of this pattern are pieced triangles, squares, and rectangles. Stems and handles are appliquéd, a technique seldom used in antique Amish quilts.

This is a showy pattern, and, if a quiltmaker went to the trouble of piecing it, she was likely to cover it with extravagant quilting designs. There is ample space between flower baskets and on the borders to absorb this exuberant work.

189. *Carolina Lily, 1883-93. Cotton, 76 x 76. Davidsville,
Somerset County, Pennsylvania. Romaine S. Sala. The
papers hand-stitched on the corners of this quilt read as
follows: "Romaine's quilt pieced and quilted by G Pa
Kaufmans Mother Christian Johns Kaufman" and "This is
Nora's quilt."*

Shoo-fly

190. *Shoo-fly Variation, dated January 9, 1913. Cotton, 72 x 84. LaGrange County, Indiana. Rebecca Haarer.*

A visitor to an Amish home need not be there long to discover the outstanding culinary skills of these plain people. Their food is basic, plentiful, and, for the most part, home-grown. Since the Amish remain largely an agrarian, hard-working people, foods tend to be heavier and richer than many more sedentary urban- and suburbanites can handle. Cream, butter, eggs, meat, vegetables, and even fruit are readily accessible on many farms. They are therefore used in cooking, creating a delightful spread on the farm kitchen table.

One of the well-known pies associated with the Amish is shoo-fly pie. It is a sweet rich dessert with a gooey molasses bottom topped with spicy cake and baked in a flaky pie crust. Because the pie is so sweet it is said to have attracted flies during the baking process. Hence the name shoo-fly.

Since the Amish are well-known for both delights it seems appropriate that a quilt should bear the name of this notorious dessert, although no visual connection is apparent. The block is a basic nine-patch with some of the blocks halved to create triangles. The same pattern is also known as a Fence Row by some quilters. Patches are generally framed with one or more borders providing plenty of space for the skilled quilter.

191. *Shoo-fly, c. 1925. Wool, cotton sateen, 68 x 72. Mifflin County, Pennsylvania. William B. Wigton. Quilted cloverleafs fill alternate plain patches, and hearts cover the inner border on this bedcover.*

*192. Fence Row, 1908. Cotton, 84 x 72. Nappanee,
Elkhart County, Indiana. Rebecca Haarer. The background fabric is pieced and varies slightly in shade, but
that only seems to add to the overall beauty of the quilt.*

Bear Paw

The inspiration of the Bear Paw pattern is said to have come from frontier days when bear tracks were commonly found in the snow or mud of wooded farmland. An encounter with wildlife was a daily possibility and was captured in this quilt design. The pattern was borrowed by the Amish community and used largely by Midwestern Amish quilters. A slight variation of the pattern is also known as Cross and Crown. This name carries the religious significance of Jesus' death on the cross and the crown of thorns that he wore.

The pattern looks complex because of its jagged edges, but the shapes make construction quite simple. Triangles forming the bear's toes are sewn together to form squares. The squares are connected to a larger square, and rectangles form the connecting cross pieces.

This design's realistic look is achieved when strongly contrasting colors are used, making the paw stand out sharply against the background. Quilting generally outlines the paw shape and decorates alternate squares as well as the borders.

193. Cross and Crown, c. 1925. Cotton, 87 x 64. Elkhart County, Indiana. Rebecca Haarer. This variation of the Bear Paw design places the outer triangles in an alternate direction.

194. Bear Paw, dated 1939. Cotton, 85 x 71. Ohio. Judi Boisson Antique American Quilts, New York. The sawtooth inner border echoes the jagged Bear Paw design.

195. Bear Paw, c. 1915. Cotton, 72 x 64. LaGrange County, Indiana. Joseph M. B. Sarah.

196. Bear Paw, dated 1893. Cotton, 85 x 69. Loudenville, Ohio. Judi Boisson Antique American Quilts, New York. Quilting designs are not elaborate but are very extensive and excellently crafted. The red inner border and binding give life to this quilt.

Crown of Thorns

The Amish are a people deeply committed to God. However, most of these groups are not openly expressive about their faith. In general, Old Order groups do not proselytize. The groups are growing in number mostly because of their large families. It is significant that a high percentage of young people choose to join and remain in the Amish church.

Crown of Thorns is one of the few Amish quilts with distinctively religious connections. It directs one's thinking to the Passion and suffering of Christ. The Amish commitment to discipleship even to death remains strong. Theirs is a spirit of humility and awe before God the Creator and a willingness to give up "worldly" distractions so as to follow the teachings of Jesus more closely. The Amish are at peace with their convictions but do not look down on outsiders whose understandings lead to a different way of life.

The Crown of Thorns pattern is a series of triangles and squares making construction simple. However, the visual impact of the quilt is much more complex. Ornate quilting is reserved for non-pieced blocks and borders.

197. Crown of Thorns, c. 1920. Cotton, 76 x 88.
Collected in LaGrange County, Indiana. Rebecca Haarer.

Some quilt patterns are possibly taken from biblical themes. This single row of corn stalks also reminds one of the Crown of Thorns motif.

199. Crown of Thorns, c. 1930. Cotton sateen, 80 x 94.
Holmes County, Ohio. Collection of Catherine H.
Anthony.

Pinwheel

200. Pinwheel Variation, dated February 12, 1925. Cotton, 76 x 66. LaGrange County, Indiana. Rebecca Haarer. This variation is also called Twin Sisters.

The windmill turns effortlessly in the breeze creating power to pump water to Amish houses and barns. The Amish have drawn fine but distinct lines on energy use.

They do not see electricity itself as wrong, but they do believe that purchasing it from local power companies links them physically to the larger world. Furthermore, such easy availability of electricity would present them with temptations that could undermine their family and community life—radio and television, for example, are seen as threatening.

By choosing to live without electricity, the Amish have become inventive in finding alternatives. They use gas, diesel, and pneumatic power to operate their refrigerators, kitchen appliances, and power tools. They live without electric lights, perhaps the greatest inconvenience modern Americans would feel in an Amish home. Instead, the Amish use gas lamps which provide bright and adequate light, but must be pumped, lit, and carried from room to room in the house. That choice in itself keeps a family physically together, evening after evening.

The Pinwheel quilt looks like the spinning blades of a windmill and is a gentle reminder of this less hurried and separate way of life. Although the pattern is used by many quiltmakers, it seems to have a special link to the Amish. Triangles and rectangles form the pattern of blades, and correct usage of color gives the illusion of movement. Pieced blocks are often alternated with solid blocks which encourage an energetic quilting caper. Borders are also clean open spaces waiting for the skilled artistry of the quilter.

201. Crazy Ann, dated March 1915. Cotton, 86 x 78. Topeka, LaGrange County, Indiana. Rebecca Haarer. This Pinwheel variation has initials embroidered in the bottom right corner.

202. Pinwheel, dated 1929. Wool, 76½ x 67½. Elkhart
County, Indiana. Donna and Jonathan Speigel. Tulip
designs are quilted on the plain patches between the
pieced blocks.

Contentment within Limitations

Being in the world but not of the world is a concept understood and practiced by the Amish in a radical way. This separateness is evidenced in their mode of dress, different language, and independent school systems. They maintain these lines through a strong community and personal accountability to the brotherhood.

Most North Americas find their sense of personal worth in their jobs and their accomplishments. They thrive on a strong spirit of competition. But in the Amish world, values are different. Personal fulfillment is found within the group. Individualism is not erased, but it is tempered by the goals and purposes of the community of faith. The good of the community is placed above one's personal gain. Being at peace with limitations is crucial to being Amish. Yet it seems that it is these very disciplines that inspire their creativity. Witness the ways the Amish have been inventive in order to maintain their lines of separateness without causing paralyzing hardships for themselves.

Living Without Electricity

Most Amish do not use electrical power from their local utility company. But that does not mean they are without energy. Many Amish are dairy farmers who must keep their milk cool while it waits to be picked up by a tank truck. So most use diesel driven refrigeration units, thus bypassing the need for electricity from high tension lines.

Increasingly more and more equipment is being attached to these diesel motors. In some communities it is common to rig up an air compressor to the motor. Air lines are run to the barn, shop, house, and well. Adapters have been designed by Amish craftsmen to permit drills, lathes, and many other kinds of hand and stationary equipment to be pneumatically powered. An air line to the bottom of the farm well supplies water to the house and barn. And in the house, mixers, blenders, and washing machines may be energized by the same air compressor connected to the diesel motor that cools the bulk milk tank.

On farms without air compressors, water may be pumped by a windmill to a reservoir. This reservoir is often an up-ended tank train car placed at the top of the barn hill or some other point of high elevation. Simple gravity then supplies water to the barn and household.

Again, any generalization overlooks exceptions. Some Amish do use their local electrical company, while others continue to reject the use of diesel motors for cooling milk.

The Amish consider children to be a gift from God. They learn the joy, obedience, and difficulty of the Amish way from the time they are born.

Strong Lines Create Energy Within

Many outsiders find these inventions to be grossly inconsistent. But to understand these people one must not forget the Amish community's intent—to draw clearly defined lines that provide solidarity for the group and separation from the world.

Belonging to a group with well-defined rules could seem stifling. And yet when perimeters are outlined, members find freedom to move around within them. When they agree with and understand the guidelines, they tap their own ingenuity to find resourceful ways to be content. The Amish farmer does not envy his non-Amish neighbor who plows with a tractor. He knows a tractor is not an option. He sets his mind to enjoy farming the Amish way. His responsibility is to be a good steward of God's earth. And his perception of how to accomplish that task has been formed within the context of a group who supports and shares his values.

Finding Beauty in the Simple

The Amish have developed a characteristic of contentment. They enjoy the basics of life without thinking about the ruffles. For example, their food is usually prepared in standard, sturdy ways. They haven't nurtured a romance with fancy cuisine. Instead, robust food in plentiful quantity is the rule.

Nor is decorating a major concern of Amish women. This does not mean they have no aesthetic appreciation. Amish homes frequently contain beautifully hand-

The Amish caution on modern technology has resulted in their own collection of inventions. Here is a hydraulic plow, complete with padded seat, which remains within the church regulations that stipulate steel wheels.

painted chairs and chests. Most women own a set of decorated china, and pieces of it are often displayed on a buffet or server when it is not in use. Handpainted mottos hang on bare walls. In general, homes are meticulously clean and tidy.

Even in the clothing that Amish women make for themselves and their families, although it follows a prescribed pattern, there is evident a sense of pride in doing a task well.

Children, who grow up without television and few mass-produced, store-bought toys, learn early to have fun with their imaginations and many brothers and sisters. A farm—and animals—offer many possibilities for play.

The Amish world is not perfect. For instance, Amish families struggle with relationships and economic tensions like their non-Amish neighbors. But the Amish do not need to face their problems in isolation. They have each other for strength and understanding.

On Amish farms, young and old, male and female help with field and garden work. It is common to see women in command of a team of horses and mules in the field.

Friendship or Album Quilt

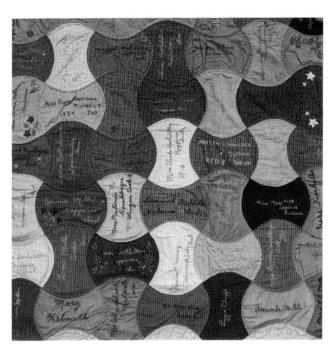

206. Detail of Plate 208 on facing page.

There is security and joy in belonging to a people. The community gathers at important times: at barn raisings and quiltings, at weddings, funerals, and other special occasions. Here people are getting ready to go home after a Sunday morning worship service.

There are few gifts more gratefully received than a Friendship quilt. It consists of quilt patches (sometimes simple square patches, sometimes pieced designs or shaped patches) that are distributed to friends of the recipient. Usually the planning of the quilt is done by one person who decides the number and size of the patches to make an adequate quilt. Each patch is signed by its maker in embroidery stitching. In fact, frequently the patches are filled with embroidered designs, especially if the block is a plain square. Finished blocks are then assembled and quilted, often at a quilting where many of the patchmakers are present. The finished quilt is then given to their mutual friend.

The occasion for the making of a Friendship quilt may be monumental or quite incidental. Sometimes they are made by parents and/or students for a terminating school teacher. Frequently a young Amish girl about to be married will hand out patches to her friends to embroider and sign. She will then host a quilting to finish the quilt in celebration of her coming marriage.

The two square-patch Friendship quilts shown here were made by the community of two sisters following the death of their mother when the girls were quite young. This gesture was a tangible sign of caring and support by the surrounding families.

The third quilt shown here in the Spools design is made of a series of patches gathered over a period of two years by an Amish woman. She sent paper templates to Amish friends in other communities and asked them to cut a patch, sign it, and return it to her. The result was a unique collection of colors and fabrics which she then pieced and quilted. What a lovely remembrance of friends far away! The quilt includes patches from Indiana, Illinois, Ohio, Wisconsin, and Pennsylvania.

208. Friendship, pieced 1933-34, quilted 1937. Cotton, 85 x 68. Nappanee, Elkhart County, Indiana. Susan Wickey. Made of a collection of patches from several states, this quilt represents long-distance friendships. The patches were collected over a two-year period by Susan Mast. She pieced the quilt, and then had a quilting for neighborhood friends.

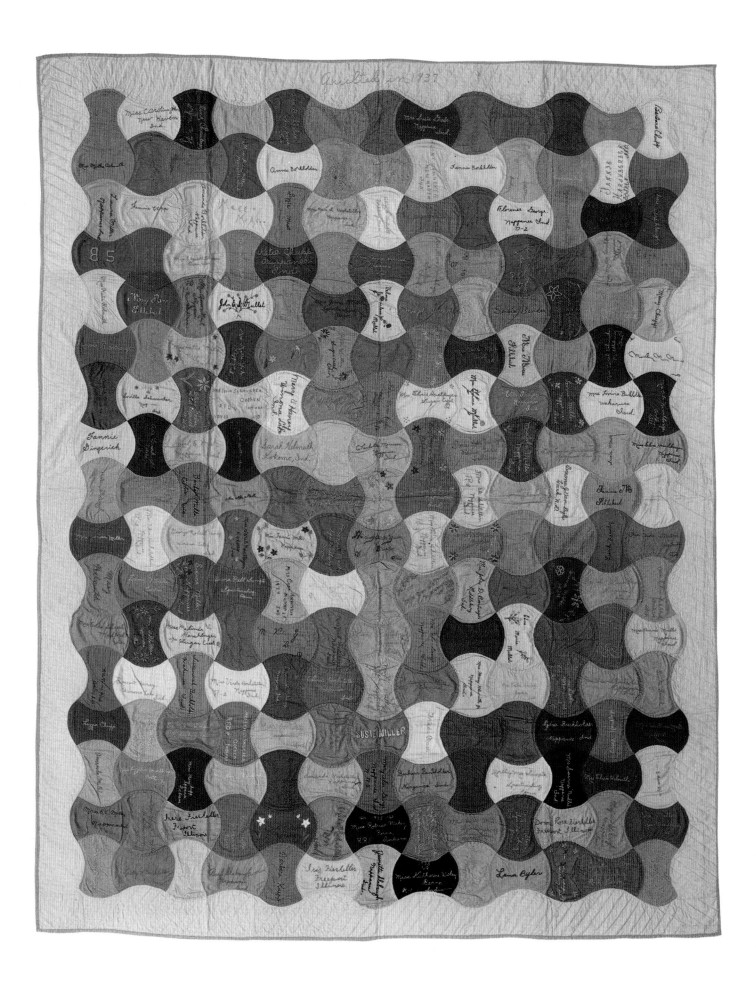

209. Friendship, dated 1939. Cotton, 74 x 87. Nappanee, Elkhart County, Indiana. Mrs. Mary Bontrager.

210. These patches, made by the same woman, can be found on the two quilts pictured above and below. The quilts were made for two young sisters after the death of their mother.

211. Friendship, dated 1939. Cotton, 74 x 87. Nappanee, Elkhart County, Indiana. Rebecca Haarer.

Rail Fence

The Rail Fence uses only one basic shape in its construction—the rectangle. Patches are stitched together to form a square, and then pieced at alternating right angles to each other. It is an unusually simple quilt, but with the careful use of color, intriguing patterns emerge on the finished quilt top.

Quilting lines are generally simple. Pieced patches are usually outlined or quilted in straight lines with more elaborate stitching used on the border(s).

The Rail Fence is not unique to Amish quilters. It is easy to imagine, however, that women on farms with their maze of fences would be attracted to this pattern.

Perhaps the simple beauty of the Rail Fence quilt hints at the simplicity of living within clear, well-defined boundaries.

212. Rail Fence, c. 1930. Cotton, 84 x 76. Loudenville, Ohio. Judi Boisson Antique American Quilts, New York. Because of its visual images this pattern is sometimes known as "Streak of Lightning."

213. Rail Fence, c. 1920. Cotton, 80 x 68. LaGrange County, Indiana. Joseph M. B. Sarah.

109

Garden Maze

214. *Rolling Stone in Garden Maze, c. 1910-20. Cotton, 67 x 78. Collected in Elkhart County, Indiana. Harry Brorby.*

Men help in the family garden by preparing the soil. Here two sons help ready the garden for planting while the team rests in the shade, waiting for another stint in the fields.

Garden Maze describes a pattern of square fabric blocks, each surrounded by elaborate sashing. The two narrow borders that outline each square connect neighboring squares and intersect between their corners. Although the inside square could be left empty, it is commonly filled with a pieced design. The pieced design and the surrounding maze are usually contained within a quilted border.

The Garden Maze quilt is as neat and orderly as an Amish garden. Few gardeners surpass the meticulous care given by Amish growers. Rows are straight and neat. Flowers often surround the garden edge giving it a burst of bright color. Weeds are nipped in the bud and plants are carefully tended. For many women, spring fever and garden fever come hand in hand, and they eagerly await the chance to work in the soil.

Although gardening is thoroughly enjoyed by many Amish families, it is not just a hobby. Preservation of food occupies a large part of women's energies throughout the summer, and, by the onset of winter, their larders are full of canned, pickled, and preserved vegetables, relishes, jams, fruits, and meats.

Quilting takes a back seat to those seasonal requirements. But in the fall and winter when days are spent indoors, quilting resumes at full force. It is a happy balance, enjoyed and incorporated into their more relaxed tasks.

216. *Cups and Saucers in Garden Maze, c. 1919. Cotton, wool, 83 x 68. LaGrange County, Indiana. Rebecca Haarer. The Garden Maze is the sash work surrounding the smaller pieced designs.*

Railroad Crossing

The Railroad Crossing pattern, when used by Amish quilters, is found mainly among Midwestern Amish. This pattern varies extensively. The "crossings" become the main focus when a series of narrow horizontal strips resembling railroad ties are assembled. In other variations the main emphasis is on the space between the "crossings," which is broken into a collage of brightly colored triangles. The entire pieced top is framed with one or more borders.

Although the Amish primarily use horse-drawn carriages, they are permitted to use public transportation. Many Amish take advantage of local bus routes and use trains for extended travel.

It is also common for them to hire a van and driver for a fee, who then serve much like a taxi, with the family or families having direct control of their own route. This allows them to make stops for visiting or shopping en route to their destination. In areas with high concentrations of Amish, there are usually several persons who offer van service. For short trips to town or to a doctor where use of the carriage is not practical, it is not unusual for the Amish to hire their non-Amish neighbors to drive them.

217. Railroad Crossing, dated 1928. Cotton, 86 x 61. Holmes County, Ohio. The Darwin D. Bearley Collection. This variation uses a pinwheel patch in the center of each block surrounded by stacked triangles. A zigzag inner border adds to the drama of this quilt.

218. Railroad Crossing, c. 1920. Cotton, 75 x 79. Holmes County, Ohio. Judi Boisson Antique American Quilts, New York. Unusually light colors are used throughout this quilt. Although the patches vary, each one's color scheme was obviously planned.

219. *Railroad Crossing Variation, dated March 5, 1943. Cotton, 66 x 84. Denton, Ohio. Judi Boisson Antique American Quilts, New York.*

220. *Railroad Crossing Variation, c. 1925-30. Cotton, 92 x 76. Elkhart County, Indiana. Joseph M. B. Sarah. The consistent arrangement of strips on this pattern show careful planning. A touch of yellow in the pattern is highlighted by the narrow yellow border framing the piecework.*

Double Wedding Ring

The Double Wedding Ring is a design of great complexity and openness requiring much of its maker. Its light, airy feeling is achieved by interlocking pieced rings surrounding circular fields that invite intricate quilting. The pattern must have been borrowed by Amish quiltmakers seeking a real challenge in piecing. The Double Wedding Ring pattern is difficult to execute because all sides of the patch are curved. This requires precision in both cutting and piecing so that the finished top will lie flat without gathers or puckers.

Quilting generally outlines the angled pieces within the rings, plus creates an additional design inside each ring. Amish Double Wedding Ring quilts generally have borders that also contain generous quilting.

It is easy to understand the popularity of this design in general society. It is an appropriate choice for a wedding gift. However, in Amish circles, jewelry of all kinds, including wedding bands, is not permitted. So the Amish quiltmakers' fascination with this pattern must have been because of its complexity.

Although the Amish do not use wedding rings, they view marriage as a serious commitment, made for life. Divorce is almost unheard of among Amish groups. Marriages last because of the support system provided by a couple's families and church. They do not marry and rear children in isolation. They are nurtured and tended by a closely knit group of concerned friends who share a common faith-life.

Farmsteads often house three generations, and, although privacy is maintained by the third generation having separate quarters, grandparents, parents, and children have a great deal of interaction. One's closest neighbors are often family or other church members. Together they share in life's joys and sorrows.

221. Double Wedding Ring, 1953. Cotton, 82 x 88. Arthur, Illinois. Rebecca Haarer. The white background and scalloped edges indicate that this is a later quilt. Although the date marks the quilt as later then most collected antique Amish quilts, it is included here as an example of a less conservative approach to color.

Interlocking circular images are found in many places around the farm. Resembling the Double Wedding Ring pattern, the wheels of this implement serve important functions on Amish farmsteads.

223. Double Wedding Ring, dated 1952. Cotton, 73 x 93. Holmes County, Ohio. Judi Boisson Antique American Quilts, New York. Bright colors stand out vividly against a black background. Pieced diamonds form a containing inner border. Spiderweb quilting designs fill the centers of the rings. Although a later quilt, it is done in colors typical of earlier Amish quilts in this pattern.

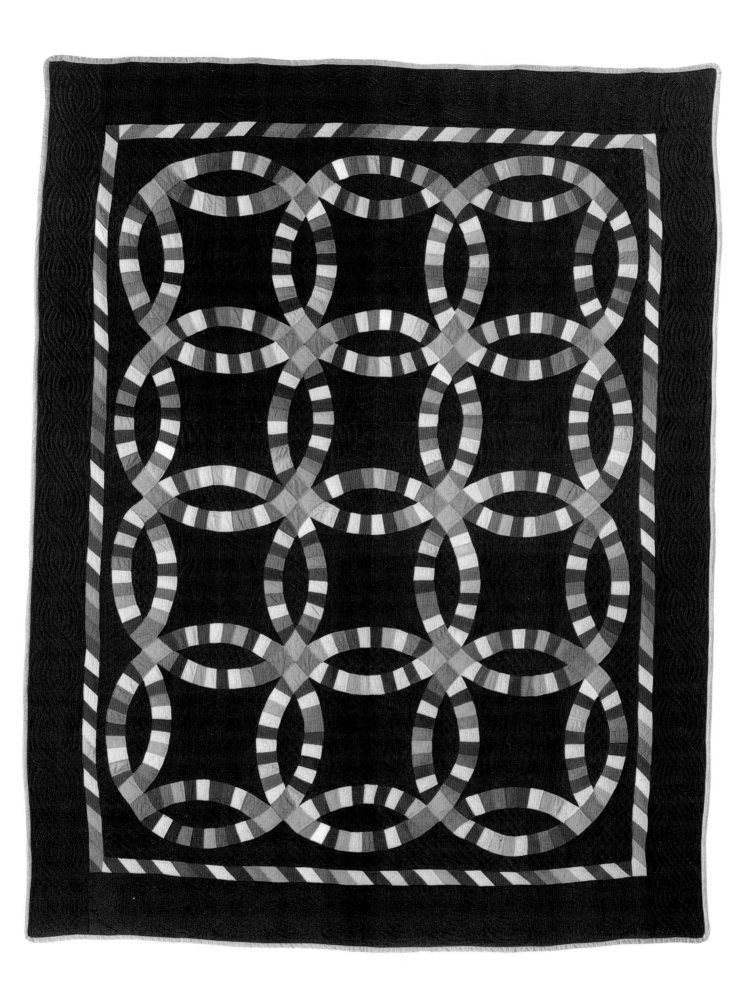

115

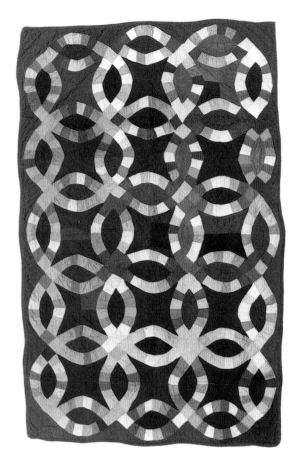 

224, 225. Reversible Double Wedding Ring, c. 1910. Cotton, 78 x 51. Ohio, Judi Boisson Antique American Quilts, New York. This unusual quilt has a pieced pattern on both sides. Note the quilted rings visible on the patchwork back (above right).

226. Double Wedding Ring-Diamond Border, 1920. Cotton, 72 x 82. Ohio. Judi Boisson Antique American Quilts, New York. These brightly colored rings are contained inside a pieced diamond border. The black background serves as a stark contrast to the colors of the small patches.

Diagonal Triangles

Triangles have always seemed to delight quilters. The angles and sharp points give a quilt vibrance and energy. Triangles appear in numerous complex patterns but are perfectly capable of standing alone. In the Diagonal Triangles pattern, light and dark triangles are pitted against each other, forming jagged diagonal lines that shoot across the quilt top.

This quilt sparkles without fancy quilting. Most of its borders are filled with the typical Amish patterns of flowing quilting designs. The pieced body of the quilt generally has its triangles outlined in quilting stitches, or simple straight lines are quilted across its top.

227. *Diagonal Triangles, 1929. Cotton, 76 x 70. Holmes County, Ohio. Judi Boisson Antique American Quilts, New York. Several streaks of red give real zest to this dramatic quilt.*

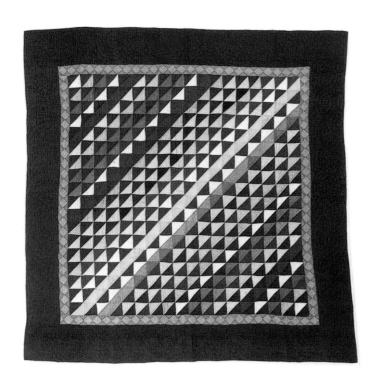

228. *Diagonal Triangles, 1920-30. Cotton, 70 x 71. Holmes County, Ohio. Judi Boisson Antique American Quilts, New York. An inner border of pieced diamonds outlines the sharp diagonal lines.*

Drunkard's Path

Perhaps because the name has a negative connotation, perhaps because there are so many ways to organize it, this quilt has been called by an assortment of titles. Drunkard's Path is also known as Solomon's Puzzle, Old Maid Puzzle, Rocky Road to Kansas, Love Ring, None-Such, World Without End, and more.

No matter its name or arrangement it is a fascinating pattern. The blocks are a combination of positive and negative space. The section cut out of one patch creates a space to be filled by the adjoining patch. The result is a staggering path of patches across the quilt.

Piecing requires skill here because each patch has a curved edge. Care must be taken so that curves are smooth and flat. Assembly of the pieced blocks also demands clear thinking so that a consistent overall pattern is formed.

Quilting stitches generally follow the lines of the pieced design, giving the quilt an additional dimension. Empty space between patches and on borders provides additional space for quilting designs.

229. Drunkard's Path, c. 1935-40. Cotton, 79 x 86. Collected in LaGrange County, and probably made there. Rebecca Haarer. This is also a friendship quilt. Various patches were likely constructed by the persons whose names are embroidered on them. The patches were then collected and assembled by or for a common friend.

230. Drunkard's Path Variation, c. 1910. Cotton, 80 x 75. Ohio. Judi Boisson Antique American Quilts, New York. This assemblage of Drunkard's Path patches is also known as "World Without End" or "Ocean Waves."

*231. Drunkard's Path, 1920-30. Cotton, 84 x 80. Withee,
Wisconsin. Judi Boisson Antique American Quilts, New
York. The addition of a sawtooth inner border brings
angularity to an otherwise curved design.*

Other Quilts

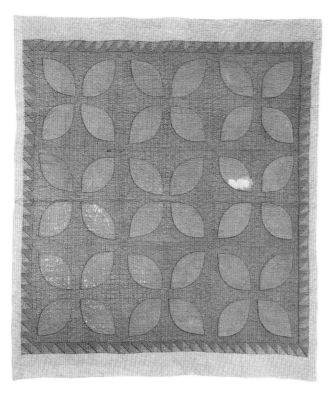

It is impossible to speak of the Amish in general and, at the same time, to give an accurate portrayal of specific Amish groups. They are a living, vibrant people with great diversities.

The same is true of Amish quilts. One cannot categorize Amish quilts in a definitive way. There are always those exceptions, those one-of-a-kind quilts, the unnamed patterns, and unusual variations.

This final category is an attempt to show a few of those singular quilts. Some are not necessarily unusual, just less frequently found or collected. Others are one-of-a-kind quilts that demonstrate the real zest for life and vivid imagination that have inspired so many beautiful bedcovers.

Like the Amish themselves, these quilts cannot be labeled and shelved. They must be understood in their context. These creative bedcovers—or works of art—become more startling when seen as a part of the very fabric of Amish life. Only then can they begin to tell their stories.

232. Leaves, 1910. Cotton, 84 x 74. Loudenville, Ohio. Judi Boisson Antique American Quilts, New York. This quilt is unusual among Amish quilts both in pattern and technique. Most Amish quilts are pieced, whereas this design is appliquéd.

233. Pocket Scrap Quilt (knotted comforter), c. 1930-40. Cotton, 84 x 73. Mifflin County, Pennsylvania. The Darwin D. Bearley Collection. This quilt came from a community of Amish where pockets were not permitted on workshirts. These store-bought shirts were revised at home. The pockets form the pattern on this knotted comforter.

234. Original design: Scrap Quilt, c. 1900-1925. Cotton, 93 x 78. Missouri or Kansas. Nancy Merig. This one-of-a-kind quilt exemplifies the spirit of imagination that has inspired so many beautiful Amish bedcovers.

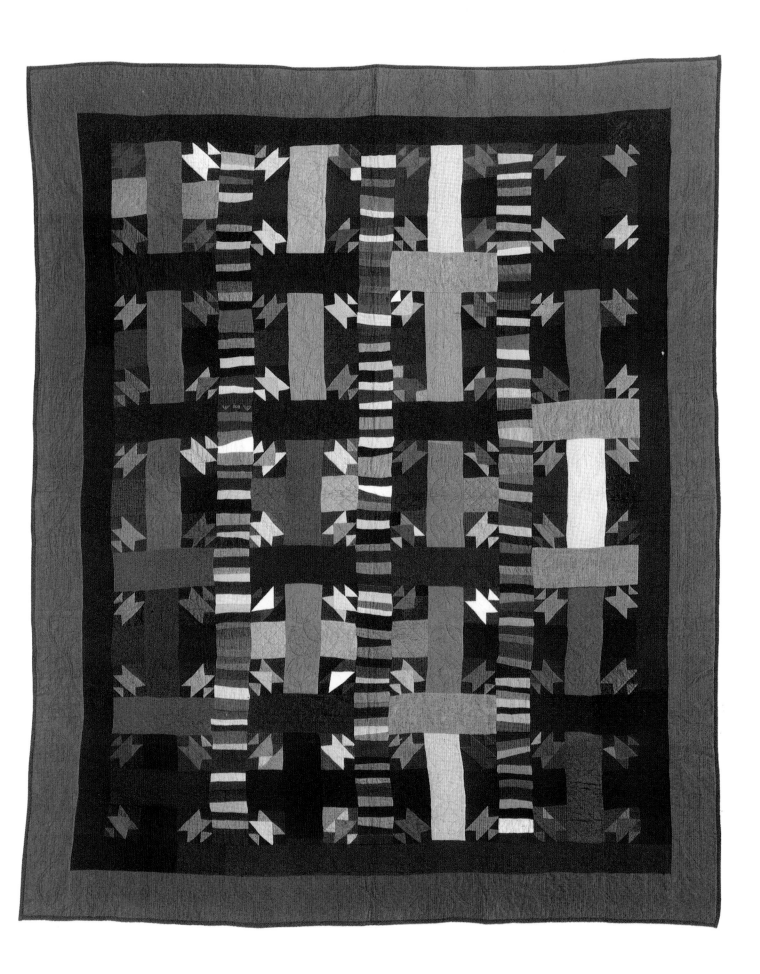

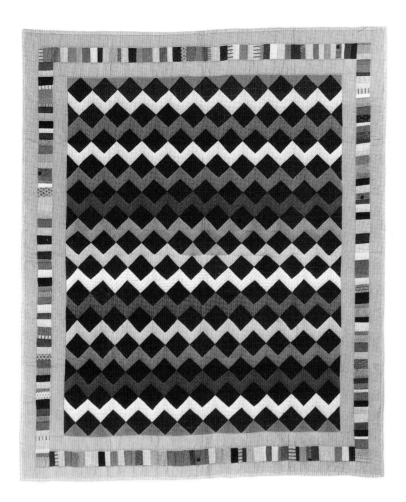

235. Zigzag, c. 1930. Cotton, 82 x 70. Elkhart County, Indiana. Joseph M. B. Sarah. A few snippets of printed fabric crept into the pieced border of this otherwise more typical quilt. It was made from scraps given by non-Amish friends.

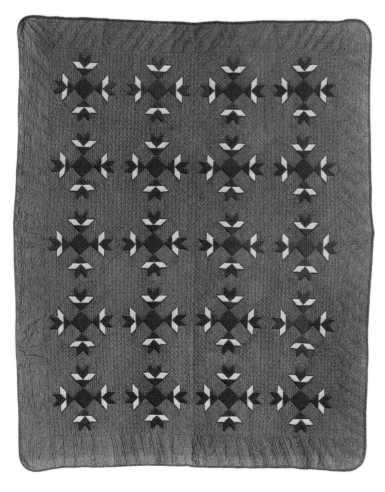

236. Goose Tracks, dated 1871. Cotton, 79 x 64. Judi Boisson Antique American Quilts, New York. Tiny diamonds and closely quilted straight lines add dimension to this sprightly pattern.

237. Crosses and Losses, c. 1900-10. Cotton, 64 x 82. Ohio. William B. Wigton. Strong borders contain the agitation created by brightly colored patches with sharp points.

238. Broken Dishes, c. 1925-30. Cotton, 71 x 62. Ohio. The Darwin D. Bearley Collection. This quilter apparently ran out of border fabric before the job was completed. She simply added a piece of black.

239. Rolling Stone, c. 1915. Cotton, wool, 59 x 72. Middlebury, Elkhart County, Indiana. Mary Ann Ryman. Although all shapes are geometric, the finished patch gives the illusion of rounded edges.

240. Wild Goose Variation, c. 1920-30. Cotton, 68 x 74. LaGrange County, Indiana. Faye and Don Walters. Triangles in a multitude of colors create various shapes in combination with each other.

241. King's Cross Variation, c. 1930. Wool and cotton, 73 x 68. Kalona, Iowa. Kemp and Pat Beall. A simple design done in a myriad of colors creates a spectacular quilt.

242. Tree of Life, c. 1900. Wool, 81 x 65. Arthur, Illinois. Nancy Meng. Although showing signs of age, this quilt speaks to the exceptions in every rule. Few Amish women used this pattern as it would be considered a realistic representation of a tree.

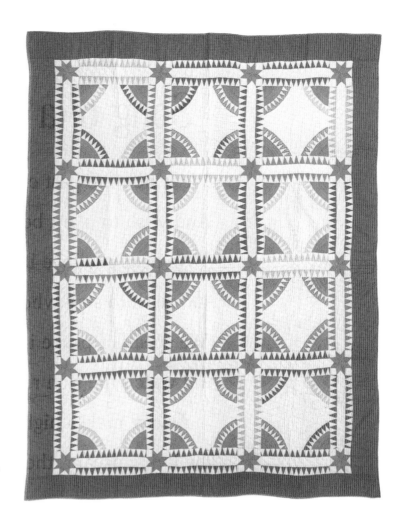

243. New York Beauty, c. 1920-30. Cotton, 70 x 88. Ohio. Judi Boisson Antique American Quilts, New York. A very rare pattern among Amish quilts, this one must have been the work of an extremely adventuresome quilter. She must also have been quite skilled.

244. Bachelor's Puzzle, c. 1925. Cotton, 83 x 70. Collected in Ohio. The Darwin D. Bearley Collection. This pattern is also known as Indiana Puzzle. The white zigzag inner border adds to the turbulent feel of the quilt.

AMISH QUILT
PATTERNS

Introduction

The magic of antique Amish quilts captures admirers everywhere. This book offers patterns, step-by-step instructions, and color suggestions for reproducing many favorite antique Amish quilts.

Why the Interest in Antique Amish Quilts?

Perhaps it is the simplicity and peace visible in the lives of the people who made them that has made Amish quilts so fascinating. Perhaps the combination of energy and restraint in these quilts' simple geometric patterns gives them such broad appeal. Perhaps in a modern, fast-moving technological age people grasp for links with the past to find stability. Whatever the reasons, there are increasing numbers of people interested in Amish quilts.

Many old quilts from the larger Amish settlements of eastern Pennsylvania and the Midwest have already been purchased from private homes by museums and collectors. It happened slowly at first, but in the last decades of the 20th century Amish communities were ravaged by "door knockers"—persons who stopped unannounced at Amish farmsteads, offering to buy old quilts.

Some homes had old quilts stolen from them while the family was away at church. That made the Amish community uneasy, so some owners decided to sell their quilts before they were stolen. Some wanted to sell but wished to wait until the market drove the prices higher. Others wanted to keep their quilts and got weary of questions. But most did not understand the unusual demand.

Within the Amish community, values and commitments are taught and passed on to the next generations through a way of life. Consequently, for the Amish a tangible symbol of their past is not important or sought after because their basic values are firm; they do not have a sense of losing their past. In fact, for them a *new* quilt seems to be more valuable than an old one. And so, many antique quilts left homes, with their sellers happy to have the cash instead.

For those outside the Amish community, these old quilts stand as symbols of the past. They speak of a time of long family evenings, winter leisure, and handcrafted works of love. Their bold shapes and dark vibrant colors show stability and freedom within specific limitations.

Many persons continue to search for these works of art from the past. But the quilts are increasingly hard to find. *Amish Quilt Patterns* attempts to provide the next best thing—a way to make a good reproduction. It is possible to create the drama and vibrancy of these prized quilts by making careful fabric selections and choosing a strong pattern and quilting designs.

This book attempts to provide patterns in the proper scale and with easy-to-follow instructions so that anyone can make one of these choice quilts.

We have adapted the patterns to the proper proportions to accommodate today's varying bed sizes.

How to Use These Amish Quilt Patterns

Good planning is the most basic rule in successful quiltmaking. It will minimize many frustrations!

You should know before selecting your fabric which quilt pattern you are going to make, how many colors you will need to complete your choice, and which colors or color families you want to use. Since it is difficult to visualize a grouping of colors and fabrics in a quilt when working with either large bolts or small swatches, it is helpful to sketch a scale model of the quilt onto graph paper, and then use crayons or colored pencils to fill in your choice of colors.

Making a Model

You can get an even more accurate color representation by purchasing small amounts of the fabrics under consideration and cutting them into tiny patches to cover the appropriate areas on the scale model. This is especially helpful when working with those patterns using large geometric shapes. It becomes more tedious when working with patterns involving small patches. Despite that, it is beneficial exercise since it allows the quilter to see in advance whether one fabric is lost or dominant among the others. If, for instance, you are trying to emphasize a particular design within a patch, the surrounding areas will need to provide adequate contrast so the design pattern will stand out. This dimension can be achieved by using light and dark fabrics or contrasting colors.

Choosing Good Fabric

The quality of a quilt is only as good as the quality of each of its components. Therefore, it is essential to choose high quality fabrics for quiltmaking.

Lightweight 100% cotton or cotton/polyester blends are ideal for quiltmaking. In addition, 100% cottons have a dull finish, making them similar to old fabrics. (Cottons blended with synthetics tend to have more luster or sheen.) The fabric should be tightly woven so it does not ravel excessively. If you check its cut edges and find it frays easily, the fabric will be difficult to work with, especially in small pieces.

Test it for wrinkling by grasping a handful and squeezing it firmly. If sharp creases remain when you release the fabric, it will wrinkle as you work with it and will not have a smooth appearance, especially if it is used in large sections on a quilt.

It is wise to wash all fabrics before using them to preshrink and test them for colorfastness.

Selecting "Amish" Colors

Most Amish quiltmakers did not understand the science of color selection and combinations. They followed their intuitions and used what was at hand.

In the past and today, Amish homes are bare by most American standards. Walls are generally painted a plain blue or green. Floors, if carpeted at all, are usually covered with handmade rag rugs. Very little upholstered furniture is used. In short, these people, because of their commitment to simplicity, have traditionally given very little effort to coordinating room decor and accessories.

The same is true of their clothing. The Amish style of dress is prescribed by the church. They are not concerned about the latest styles or fashion colors. Consequently, they are not bound by the surrounding culture's sense of what is proper and what is not.

This freedom from the dictates of society's norms is evident in the color schemes of antique Amish quilts. Frequently, the colors which color theory describes as complementary appear together in Amish quilts. Likely the makers never *knew* they had selected complementary colors, but they could *see* that those colors brought out the best in each other.

Many Amish quilts have accents of black and red, a combination that decorators recognize as a

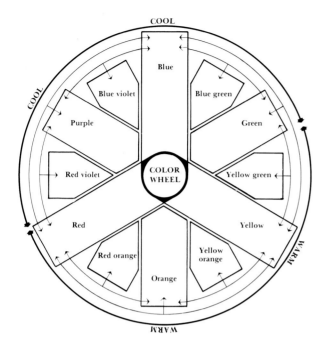

boost for many color schemes. When Amish women emptied their scrap bags they didn't work from a basis of scientific knowledge. They just chose fabrics in relation to each other. Many times the result was a dramatic color scheme that stands up well today.

It would be unfair to imply that all Amish quilts demonstrate masterful use of color. Many are less than pleasingly coordinated. But if you want to capture the unusual power of antique Amish quilt colors, you will likely be most successful if you try to forget what you know about color and use a fresh approach.

There are several guidelines you might follow. The fabrics used in antique Amish quilts were almost always solid colors. Printed fabrics seldom appear. The oldest, most traditional Amish quilts come from eastern Pennsylvania, specifically from Lancaster County. This early settlement tended to be more conservative than some of the groups who later migrated to other areas.

Lancaster Amish primarily used only a part of the spectrum of the color wheel, avoiding warm colors—bright reds, red orange, orange, yellow orange, yellows, and yellow green. The "cool" colors—burgundys, blues, purples, and greens—were the colors they were permitted to use for clothing and also their quilts. Therefore, the more conservative, traditional Amish quilts reflected their community's standards and used a myriad of colors, but only those within the boundaries of that "cooler" spectrum.

Antique Amish quilts made in areas outside eastern Pennsylvania were often more daring in their colors. Yellows and oranges appear frequently in mid-western quilts and those made in Pennsylvania counties other than Lancaster. However, these colors are used in conjunction with the darker hues.

Try, as much as you can, to approach your color selection in an uninhibited way. The closer you can come to that approach, the more likely it is that you can create a quilt that looks authentically Amish.

Experiment with colors in several arrangements before you make a final decision. See how they stand in reference to each other. Some colors highlight one another, and others dull each other.

Don't Forget Black

To approximate "Amish" color choices, use colors of varying intensities and shades. And don't forget black. Black, although dark, can be a spark of life in a color scheme. Several shades of black may be more interesting than only one. The varying shades that appear in old quilts happened because they were often scrap quilts. Substitutions were often made for fabrics that ran out. You should not be afraid to try substituting one or several similar fabrics instead of using the same one throughout the quilt.

Quiltmakers in Lancaster County used black sparingly in their quiltmaking, and thus highlighted other colors in their quilts.

In contrast, quilters in the midwestern Amish communities liked black and used it extensively in their quilts. Frequently they selected black as a background color and used it with pieced blocks of vibrant contrasting colors, thereby creating a dramatic visual impact.

Planning Borders

Notice the role that borders play in traditional Amish quilts. At times they served to increase a quilt's dimensions to an adequate size; at other times they acted as the frame that highlighted the quilt pattern. In certain cases they achieved both at the same time. At any rate, a border is never an afterthought. Many Amish quilts have wide, elaborately quilted borders.

The important factor is that the borders should be proportionate to the interior pattern of the quilt. You will notice that border widths vary from pattern to pattern.

Given with each pattern in this book are templates (and instructions for piecing and connecting individual block units). Trace the templates *accurately* onto a material that will withstand repeated outlining without wearing down the edges.

Cardboard is not appropriate for a template that must be traced repeatedly. More durable materials are plastic lids from throw-away containers; the sides of a plastic milk, water, or bleach jug; old linoleum scraps; or tin. (If you use tin, beware of sharp edges.) You may glue sandpaper to the back of the template to keep it from slipping as you mark the fabrics.

If your template is not accurately traced or cut, you will have a very difficult time making your quilt fit together well.

Before you cut all the quilt's patches, cut enough for just one block using the template you've made. Assemble the patch to test for accuracy. Be sure to sew all seams using exactly ¼-inch seam allowances. If you need to make changes, adjust the template and try again. *Always test the templates by assembling one block before you cut fabrics for an entire quilt top.*

You may make your templates with or without a seam allowance, depending on the method of marking, cutting, and piecing you prefer.

Marking Patches with *Seam Allowances*

This method requires that the template be made with a ¼-inch seam allowance on all sides. The line that you trace onto the fabric becomes the cutting line. The seam line is ¼-inch inside the marked line. The advantage of this method is that you can trace the outline on the top layer of fabric, and then cut through several layers of fabric at the same time. The disadvantage is that when you begin stitching the patches together, you will need to guess accurately the exact location of the ¼-inch seam allowances so that the corners of the patches meet precisely.

Marking Patches without *Seam Allowances*

This method requires that the template be made the actual size of the finished patch. The line that you trace onto the fabric becomes the stitching line. You must imagine the cutting line ¼-inch outside this line. The advantage here is that you have a tracing line to stitch along, almost guaranteeing accuracy in piecing. The disadvantage is that each patch must be marked and cut individually. With this method you cannot stack and cut multiple layers of fabrics. Each quilter must choose which of these methods works best for her/him. The important thing is to maintain accuracy by whatever way you find most comfortable.

It is extremely important to be precise in marking and cutting. A very minute mistake in either step will be multiplied many times over when you try to assemble the quilt. Ultimately, you want to have a smooth flat quilt top. To achieve that, the individual pieces must fit together precisely.

Marking Fabrics

There are many ways to mark fabrics. You may use a regular lead pencil to trace the template. However, on some fabrics, especially dark fabrics, the markings will be very difficult to see.

There are several pencils designed especially for quilters. Some of these make markings that are soluble in cold water, allowing the markings to be easily removed. Some pencils make markings that disappear after a certain period of time. That works well if you use the marked pieces before the time elapses. Whatever you choose, be sure to follow the manufacturer's instructions for the marker's use.

Every quiltmaker should have a good pair of sharp fabric shears. The longer the blade of the scissors, the greater the chances of cutting a continuous straight line. The scissors must be sharp all the way to the point to cut well-defined corners.

A Word About Rotary Cutters and Strip-Piecing

Some quilters prefer to cut patches without templates, using a rotary cutter and a ruler to measure instead. This method can be faster and more accurate, especially if you are cutting simple shapes like squares and rectangles. If you prefer to use this method, be sure to use the same ruler and mat for all measuring. Rulers vary slightly and can create problems with accuracy if you use more than one ruler in a project.

Although we give instructions for the traditional method of connecting individual patches, you may strip-piece instead. To do that, sew strips of fabric together, and then cut patches in units from the already joined strips. This is particularly useful in patterns such as the Nine-Patch or Roman Stripe. For example, to strip-piece a Nine-Patch block, sew three strips of fabric together to form a vertical strip. Cut the strip horizontally to form units of three patches, which are already joined and ready to be sewn together to form the Nine-Patch block.

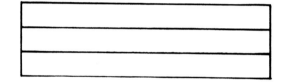

Join fabric into vertical strips.

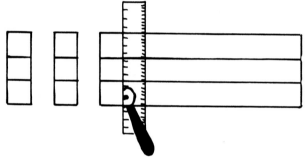

Cut horizontal units.

To strip-piece a Roman Stripe block, sew the strips together, and then cut the triangles.

Join vertical strips of fabric.

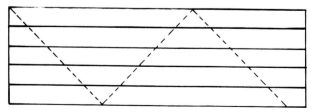

Cut triangle units from joined strips.

Strip-piecing works more efficiently with some patterns than with others. You will need to determine whether or not you want to make it part of your quiltmaking.

Piecing

You may piece a quilt by hand or by machine. Hand-piecing is a more time-consuming and laborious process. Most quilters today choose to piece by machine. However, when you are working with very small pieces and when you need to make several points meet, hand-piecing is the most precise and exact method. This way also allows you to work on the project anywhere, rather than being tied to a sewing machine. If you hand-piece, you can still stitch the borders and the sashing between blocks on the sewing machine to save time.

Hand-piecing is very simple. Pin the patches with their right sides together and with their stitching lines perfectly matched. Using a fine sharp needle, stitch with short running stitches through both layers of fabric. Stitches must be straight, even, and tight to achieve an accurate and strong seam. Check the stitches periodically to be sure they are not causing puckering. Put an occasional backstitch in with the running stitches to tighten the seam without creating puckers. At the end of the patch, backstitch and knot the thread before clipping. Open the patch and check the seam for precision.

When piecing, always begin by assembling the smaller patches, and then build them on to larger pieces to form the quilt block. Combine patches to form straight sewing lines whenever you can.

Avoid having to set in squares and triangles if at all possible, since stitching around corners requires the utmost care to prevent bunching and puckering. When setting in is required, stitch the patches that need to be set against each other only to the ends of their stitching lines. Do *not* stitch through their seam allowances. The seam allowances must be kept free to fit against the seam allowances on the pieces being added.

There are two ways to set in a corner. One is to start at the outer edges of one patch, stitch its full length (stopping at the seam allowance), pivot, and proceed along the other edge. The other method is to begin stitching along the edge at the center or inner corner. Stitch from the inner corner to one outside edge and then go back to the corner and

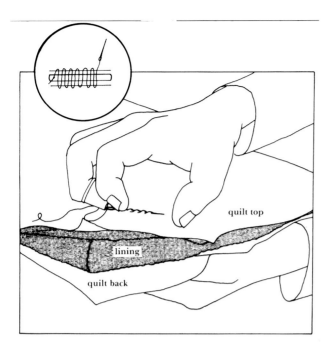

A quilt is a sandwich of three layers—the quilt back, lining or batting, and the quilt top—all held together by quilting stitches.

stitch the remaining edge. Practice both methods and use the one that works best for you.

Machine-piecing is obviously a lot faster. The procedure is basically the same as hand-piecing, but the stitching is done by machine. Pin the patches together accurately. Watch carefully that they do not slip as they go through the machine. Backstitch whenever you begin or end a seam.

When you join units of patches to each other, you will face the problem of what to do with the seam allowances. Seam allowances are a particular menace in two situations: one, if quilting needs to be done through the seam allowances making small stitches virtually impossible; and two, if a seam allowance of a dark fabric is visible underneath a lighter fabric.

It is generally a good idea to lay all seam allowances in the same direction. However, if this creates either of the above problems, make an exception and lay the seam allowance the opposite way.

Preparing to Quilt

Much of the wonder of old Amish quilts is in their quilting. They have been lavished with quilting designs, leaving few open spaces. This tiny, intricate quilting is essential in reproducing the look of an old quilt.

You can mark quilting designs on the quilt top in a variety of ways. See "Marking Fabrics" on page 7 for information about quiltmarking pencils. Remember to mark with something that will not rub off easily, because as you quilt, your hands will move across the surface. At the same time, you want the markings to be completely removable when the quilting is completed, so that unsightly lines do not remain.

If you work with fabric that is light enough to see through, it is easiest to mark by tracing. Outline the quilting designs on paper with a heavy magic marker. Lay the fabric to be marked, wrong side down, on top of the quilting design. Trace with a fabric marker over the lines to stitch.

Although this method is easiest, many fabrics used in Amish quilts are too dark to see the lines through the fabric. Therefore, the design must be traced in an alternate way. You can do this by cutting very thin slashes at intervals on the quilting template. This creates a dot-to-dot effect with the slashes. Lay the template on top of the right side of the fabric and trace the lines onto the quilt top.

Since you will use the templates repeatedly, it is wise to make them of a material more durable than paper. Cardboard or thin plastic are suitable.

You can mark straight lines or crosshatching by laying a ruler on the fabric and tracing along both sides. On large areas, snap a chalk line across the quilt.

When you just want to outline patches, you do not need to mark around them. Simply quilt close to the seam to emphasize the patch.

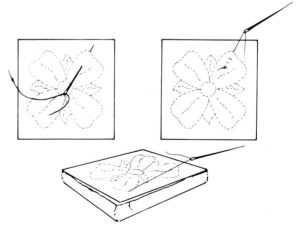

*To both secure the quilting thread at the beginning and to hide the knot, insert the needle through **only** the quilt top about 1 inch from where the quilting will begin, pull the thread through to the knot, and gently tug on the knot until it slips through the fabric and is lodged invisibly underneath the top.*

Quilting is both a descriptive word and an action word. To quilt means to stitch three layers of material together to form a heavier whole. The finished stitches, often done in decorative patterns, are also called quilting.

A quilt is a sandwich of three layers: the quilt back, the lining or batting which adds insulation value, and the top which is often pieced or appliqued. The three layers are held together by the quilting stitches.

Making Tiny, Even Stitches

To quilt, one uses a simple running stitch. Quilting is done most easily and durably with quilting thread, since it is heavier than regular thread and more able to withstand being pulled repeatedly through three quilt layers.

Quilting needles are called "betweens." They are shorter than "sharps," which are considered normal handsewing needles. Betweens come in various sizes which are identified by numbers. Most quilters use a size 7 or 8 to quilt. Some quilters prefer the even smaller size 9 needle. The best way to choose a needle size is to try several, and then use the one that seems most comfortable for you.

A thimble is a must for quilting since the needle must be pushed repeatedly through three fabric layers. The thimble should fit snugly on the second finger of the hand used for pushing the quilting needle.

To begin quilting, cut a piece of quilting thread about one yard in length. Thread the needle and make a single knot at the end of the thread. Then insert the needle through *only* the quilt top, about one inch from where quilting will begin. Pull the thread through to the knot. Gently tug on the knot until it slips through the fabric and is lodged invisibly underneath the top. This will secure the quilting thread at the beginning.

With one hand underneath the quilt and the other on top, push the needle through all three layers until the hand underneath feels a prick. That indicates that you've been successful and stitched through all the thicknesses! (Experienced quilters develop calluses from this repeated pricking.)

Then with the thimble on your upper hand, tilt the needle upward. Use your lower hand to push up slightly from underneath. As soon as the needle point appears again on top, reinsert it through the layers again. Continue this process until three to five stitches are stacked on the needle. Finally, pull the needle and thread through the fabric to create the quilting pattern. The stitches should be snug but not so tight as to create puckering. Continue the process of stacking stitches onto the needle until the thread is used.

When the length of thread is nearly gone, do a tiny backstitch to secure the thread. Insert the needle again through only the top layer, and make a stitch the length of the needle, away from the quilting design. Pull the needle through the surface and snip the thread with the long stitch left buried underneath the quilt top. Thread the needle and begin again.

The goal is to strive for tiny, even stitches. And they come only with practice! Initially, concentrate on making straight, *even* stitches, without worrying too much about their size. Try to have the stitch length be the same on both the top and bottom of the quilt. Holding the needle straight is crucial for achieving straight stitches. Then after you have mastered evenness, try to decrease the size of the stitches.

When quilting curved lines, do not try to stack as many stitches on the needle before pulling it through. No more than two stitches on the needle at a time are best for executing smooth, even curves.

The type of batting or lining used in a quilt will affect its finished look. Polyester batting has a much puffier quality than the lining used in antique quilts. Cotton batting creates a flatter, smoother effect and is available from quilt supply shops. A thin sheet blanket, or something similar, adds weight and insulation value but retains the flat appearance of an old quilt. These thinner materials also make it possible to quilt tiny, even stitches.

Putting the Quilt in the Frame

In order to achieve a smooth, even quilting surface, it is necessary to stretch all three layers of the quilt in a frame. This creates a taut surface conducive to quilting.

The most traditional and probably the most effective frame is the type that is large enough to stretch the entire quilt out at once. This allows for even tension over the whole quilt. These frames are generally used at quiltings when several persons work on the quilt at the same time.

The disadvantages of such a frame are its size and lack of mobility. Since the entire quilt surface is exposed, the frame obviously requires that much floor space. Also, once the quilt is stretched in the frame, it should not be removed until quilting is completed. That usually means that the space is occupied for an extended period of time. Many quilters do not have the space required for such a frame.

Another type of frame accommodates the entire quilt at once, but most of it is rolled on to a long rail along one side of the frame. Only about a three-foot length, along the width of the quilt, is exposed for quilting. As that area is completed, the quilt is rolled on to the opposite rail until the entire quilt is finished.

Still smaller frames are available for quilters with very limited space. These look like giant embroidery hoops which allow the quilt to be quilted in small sections.

A very important procedure before using this type of frame is to baste the entire quilt together through all three layers. Basting should begin at the center and work out towards the edges. Doing this assures that the layers will be evenly stretched while being quilted, and it avoids creating puckers during the quilting process. However, do not quilt over the basting stitches because this makes them extremely tedious to remove later.

Binding the Quilt

The final step in finishing a quilt is adding its binding. The binding covers the raw edges along the four sides of a quilt. Bindings, particularly on antique Amish quilts from Pennsylvania, are generally wider than bindings found on many other quilts.

Since the edge of a quilt receives a lot of wear, the binding is often done with a double thickness of fabric. It is not uncommon for bindings on old quilts to have been machine-stitched in place.

Bindings can be done in several ways. One of the easier methods is to cut strips of fabric that measure four times the width of the finished binding. These strips can be cut either lengthwise or crosswise on the fabric grain. Lengthwise strips do not need to be pieced, but piecing on a binding is not very obvious and can be done without diminishing the beauty of the quilt.

Cut four binding strips, each one measuring the length of one side of the quilt, plus one inch.

Fold each binding strip in half, wrong sides together, so that both raw edges meet. Trim any excess lining and backing from the quilt itself. Pin the shorter two binding strips against the two parallel edges of the quilt top's width, with the raw edges of the binding flush with the raw edges of the quilt.

Machine-stitch in place using a ¼-inch seam allowance. Open the seam so that the folded edge of the binding is now the outer edge of the quilt.

Sew the remaining binding strips onto the other two sides of the quilt, extending out to the folded edge of the attached binding strips. Fold the binding in half again so that the previously folded edge goes around to the back and covers the seam made by attaching the strips. Handstitch the binding in place. Fold corners under so that no raw edges are exposed.

Another method of finishing a quilt, less commonly used on old Amish designs, is to simply wrap excess border fabric from the top, bottom, and sides of the quilt around to the back where it is stitched in place. Or wrap the extra backing fabric forward over the raw edges to the front, where you can stitch it in place on the quilt top.

Most old Amish quilts used a cut binding. It was frequently in a color which contrasted with the border and was new to the color scheme of the interior of the quilt.

After your binding is completed, it is a good idea to initial and date your quilt so that it can be identified by future generations. You can sign and date it with embroidery on a lower back corner. Or you may choose to quilt your initials and the date in a lower back corner.

How to Assemble Your Quilt

DIAGRAM 1

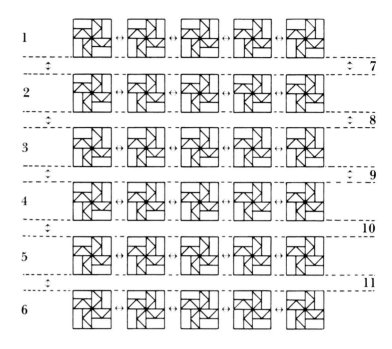

DIAGRAM 2

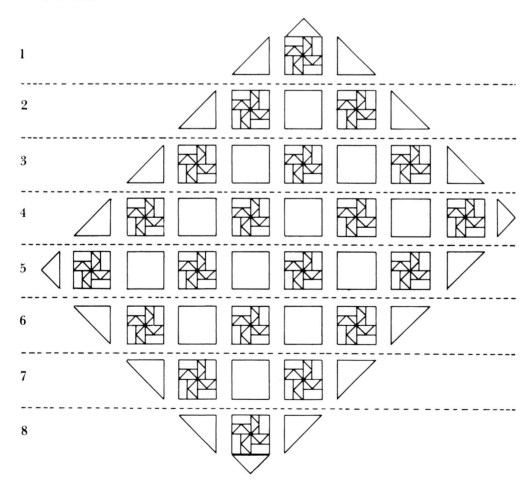

Border Application Diagram

(Border templates are designated with different letters in the quilt patterns that follow. Adapt these instructions for the pattern you have chosen.)

ASSEMBLY INSTRUCTIONS: STEP 1—Sew Blocks B to top and bottom of Unit A. STEP 2—Sew Blocks C to sides of Unit A/B. STEP 3—Sew Blocks D to top and bottom of Unit A/B/C. STEP 4—Sew Blocks E to sides of Unit A/B/C/D.

When corner blocks are used, sew them to the ends of the last border pieces (E), and then add the border and blocks as a complete section.

STEP 1

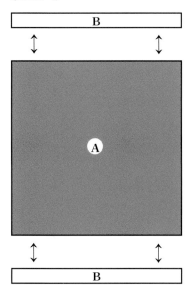

STEP 2

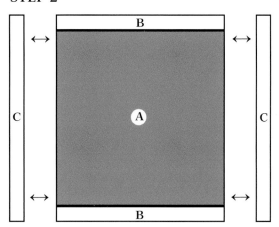

STEP 3

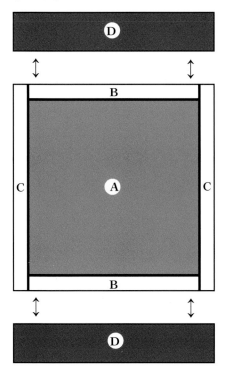

STEP 4

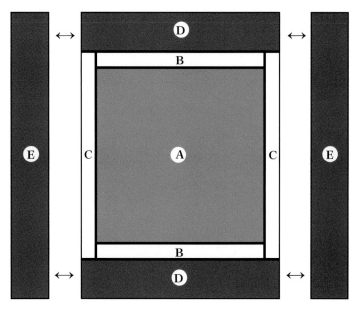

Center Diamond

Approximate size—96" x 96"

Variation 1

Measurements given with seam allowances.

- A — 25½" x 25½"; cut 1
- B — 6¾" x 25½"; cut 2
- C — 6¾" x 6¾"; cut 4
- D — 6¾" x 25½"; cut 2
- E — 27⅜" x 27⅜"; cut 2 squares;
     then cut in half diagonally
- F — 7" x 53½"; cut 2
- G — 7" x 7"; cut 4
- H — 7" x 53½"; cut 2
- I — 15½" x 66½"; cut 2
- J — 15½" x 15½"; cut 4
- K — 15½" x 66½"; cut 2

Fabric Requirements

- ▪ — 1⅝ yds.
- ▫ — 3 yds.
- ☐ — 4¾ yds.
- ▦ — 4⅞ yds.

Backing—8 yds.

Batting—101" x 101"

Assembly Instructions:

1. Sew one Template B to Template A. Sew the other Template B to the other side of Template A.

2. Sew one Template C to the one end of Template D. Sew the other Template C to the opposite end of Template D. Repeat with the second set of Templates C and D.

3. Sew one C,D unit to the A,B unit. Sew the other C,D unit to the A,B unit.

4. Sew one Template E to each side of the main unit.

5. See paragraph 2 of the Border Application Diagram, page 13, for instructions about how to assemble Templates G, H, I, J, and K.

Variation 1

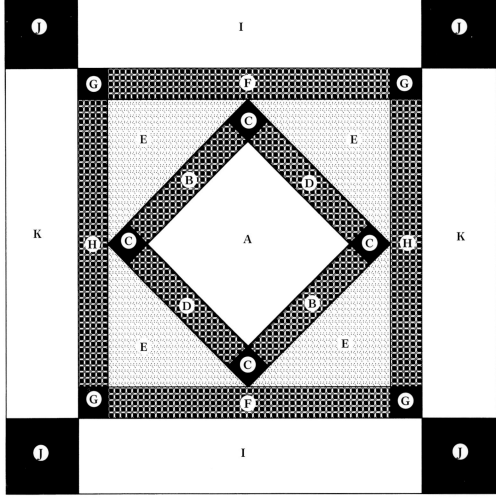

Variation 2

Measurements given with seam allowances.

- A — 37½" x 37½"; cut 1
- B — 27⅜" x 27⅜"; cut 2 squares; then cut in half diagonally
- C — 7" x 53½"; cut 2
- D — 7" x 7"; cut 4
- E — 7" x 53½"; cut 2
- F — 15½" x 66½"; cut 2
- G — 15½" x 15½"; cut 4
- H — 15½" x 66½"; cut 2

Assembly Instructions:

1. Sew 4 Template B's to A on 4 sides.
2. Follow instructions for the Border Application as explained and shown on page 13, to assemble Templates C through H.

Fabric Requirements

- ■ — 1⅜ yds.
- □ — 5¼ yds.
- ▨ — 3 yds.
- ▨ — 1½ yds.

Backing—8 yds.

Batting—101" x 101"

Variation 2

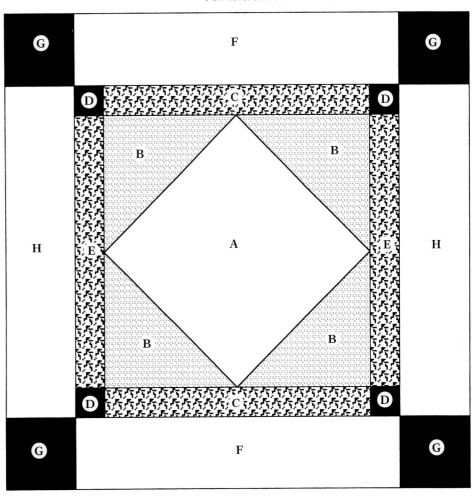

141

Variation 3

Measurements given with seam allowances.

A — 12³⁄₈" x 12³⁄₈"; cut 1
B — Template given; cut 72
C — Template given; cut 72
D — 5¹⁄₄" x 26⁵⁄₈"; cut 2
E — 5¹⁄₄" x 17¹⁄₈"; cut 2
F — 27³⁄₈" x 27³⁄₈"; cut 2 squares;
      then cut in half diagonally
G — Template given; cut 128
H — Template given; cut 128
I — 7³⁄₄" x 51¹⁄₄"; cut 2
J — 7³⁄₄" x 65³⁄₄"; cut 2
K — 12¹⁄₄" x 73¹⁄₂"; cut 2
L — 12¹⁄₄" x 96¹⁄₂"; cut 2

Fabric Requirements

 — 9³⁄₄ yds.

— 5¹⁄₂ yds.

Backing—8 yds.

Batting—
    101" x 101"

Template B and C

Variation 3—Sawtooth Diamond

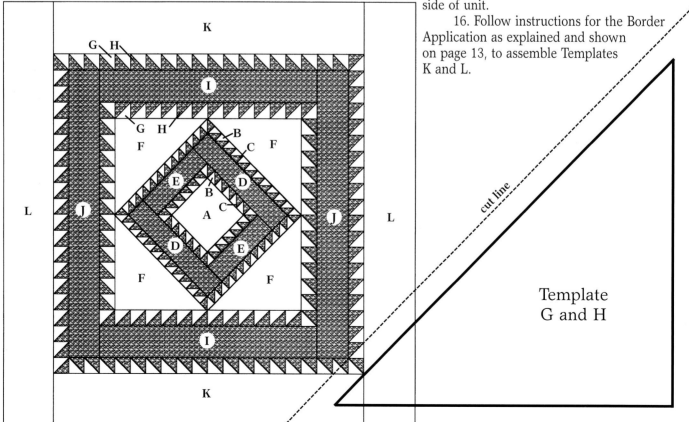

Assembly Instructions:

1. Sew long side of Template B to long side of Template C to form a square block. Sew 2 strips of 5 blocks, 2 strips of 7 blocks, 2 strips of 11 blocks, and 2 strips of 13 blocks.

2. Sew one strip of 5 blocks to end of Template A. Sew the other strip of 5 blocks to other side of Template A.

3. Sew one strip of 7 blocks to side of main unit. Sew other strip of 7 blocks to other side of main unit.

4. Sew Template D to the one end of main unit. Sew the other Template D to the other side of main unit.

5. Sew Template E to the one end of main unit. Sew the other Template E to the other side of main unit.

6. Sew one strip of 11 blocks to end of main unit. Sew the other strip of 11 blocks to other side of main unit.

7. Sew one strip of 13 blocks to end of main unit. Sew other strip of 13 blocks to the other side of main unit.

8. Sew 4 triangle F's to 4 sides of main unit.

9. Sew long side of Template G to long side of Template H to form square. Sew 2 strips of 12 blocks, 2 strips of 14 blocks, 2 strips of 18 blocks, and 2 strips of 20 blocks.

10. Sew one strip of 12 blocks to one end of main unit. Sew the other strip of 12 blocks to other side of unit.

11. Sew one strip of 14 blocks to one end of main unit. Sew the other strip of 14 blocks to other side of unit.

12. Sew Template I to the one end of main unit. Sew the other Template I to the other side of main unit.

13. Sew Template J to the one end of main unit. Sew the other Template J to the other side of main unit.

14. Sew one strip of 18 blocks to one end of main unit. Sew the other strip of 18 blocks to the other side of unit.

15. Sew one strip of 20 blocks to one end of main unit. Sew the other strip of 20 blocks to the other side of unit.

16. Follow instructions for the Border Application as explained and shown on page 13, to assemble Templates K and L.

Template G and H

142

Sunshine and Shadow

Approximate size—96" x 96"

Variation 1

Measurements given with seam allowances.

- A — Template given; cut 137
- B — Template given; cut 136
- C — Template given; cut 136
- D — Template given; cut 136
- E — Template given; cut 136
- F — Template given; cut 136
- G — Template given; cut 136
- H — Template given; cut 136
- I — $6\frac{1}{2}$" x $57\frac{1}{2}$"; cut 2
- J — $6\frac{1}{2}$" x $69\frac{1}{2}$"; cut 2
- K — $14\frac{1}{2}$" x $69\frac{1}{2}$"; cut 2
- L — $14\frac{1}{2}$" x $14\frac{1}{2}$"; cut 4
- M — $14\frac{1}{2}$" x $69\frac{1}{2}$"; cut 2

Assembly Instructions:

1. Sew Template A to Template B. Sew Templates C, D, E, F, G, and H to A/B to form strip. Continue sewing strips of patches in order as shown in diagram.

2. Sew together strips of patches to form block that is $57\frac{1}{2}$" x $57\frac{1}{2}$".

3. To assemble Templates I through M, follow instructions for the Border Application as explained on page 13.

Fabric Requirements

- ■ — $1\frac{1}{4}$ yds.
- □ — $2\frac{3}{8}$ yds.
- ▨ — $\frac{1}{2}$ yd.
- ▨ — $\frac{1}{2}$ yd.
- ▨ — $4\frac{3}{8}$ yds.
- ▨ — $\frac{1}{2}$ yd.
- ▨ — $\frac{1}{2}$ yd.
- ▨ — $\frac{1}{2}$ yd.

Backing—$8\frac{1}{8}$ yds.

Batting—101" x 101"

Variation 1

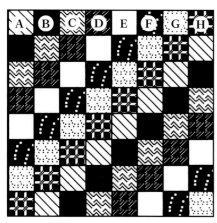

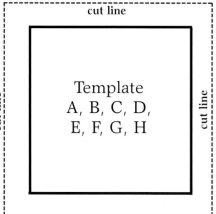

Template
A, B, C, D,
E, F, G, H

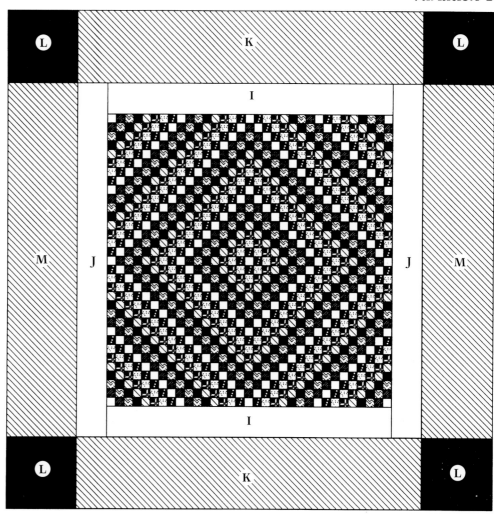

Variation 2

Measurements given with seam allowances.

- A — Template given; cut 5
- B — Template given; cut 16
- C — Template given; cut 28
- D — Template given; cut 40
- E — Template given; cut 52
- F — Template given; cut 64
- G — Template given; cut 76
- H — Template given; cut 88
- I — Template given; cut 8
- J — Template given; cut 92
- K — $6\frac{5}{8}$" x 25"; cut 2
- L — $6\frac{5}{8}$" x $37\frac{1}{4}$"; cut 2
- M — $6\frac{1}{2}$" x $52\frac{1}{2}$"; cut 2
- N — $6\frac{1}{2}$" x $64\frac{1}{2}$"; cut 2
- O — $16\frac{1}{2}$" x $64\frac{1}{2}$"; cut 2
- P — $16\frac{1}{2}$" x $96\frac{1}{2}$"; cut 2

Assembly Instructions:

1. Sew Template A to Template B. Sew Templates C, D, E, F, G, H, I, and J to A/B to form strip. Continue sewing strips of patches in order as shown in diagram.

2. Sew together strips of patches to form block in center and triangles for corners.

3. Sew one Template K to one side of center block. Sew other Template K to opposite side.

4. Sew one Template L to one side of center block. Sew other Template L to opposite side.

5. Sew a triangle of patches in strips to each side of main unit.

6. See Border Application Diagram on page 13 to complete the quilt and use Templates M through P.

Fabric Requirements

- ■ — $\frac{5}{8}$ yd.
- □ — $5\frac{1}{8}$ yds.
- ▦ — $\frac{3}{4}$ yd.
- ▤ — $\frac{1}{2}$ yd.
- ▨ — $\frac{1}{2}$ yd.
- ▥ — $4\frac{5}{8}$ yds.
- ▧ — $\frac{1}{4}$ yd.
- ▦ — $\frac{3}{8}$ yd.
- ▦ — $\frac{3}{8}$ yd.

Backing—8 yds.

Batting—101" x 101"

Variation 2

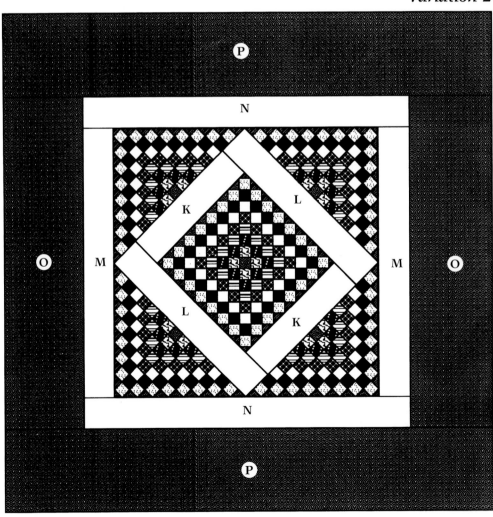

**Templates for
Variation Two**

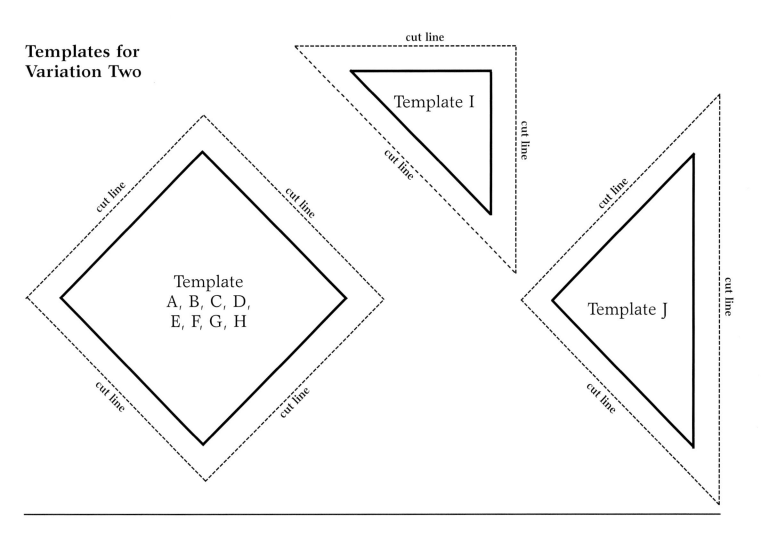

Template I

Template
A, B, C, D,
E, F, G, H

cut line

Template J

**Templates for
Variation Three**

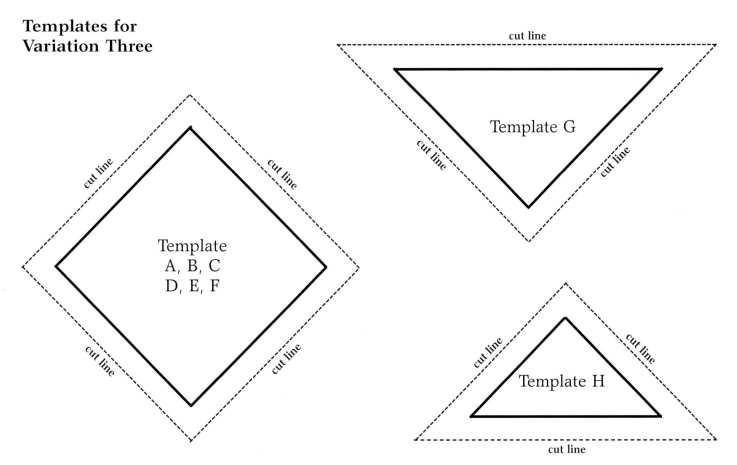

Template
A, B, C
D, E, F

Template G

Template H

Variation 3

Measurements given with seam allowances.

A — Template given; cut 73
B — Template given; cut 84
C — Template given; cut 96
D — Template given; cut 108
E — Template given; cut 120
F — Template given; cut 132
G — Template given; cut 68
H — Template given; cut 4
I — $6\frac{1}{2}''$ x $52\frac{5}{8}''$; cut 2
J — $6\frac{1}{2}''$ x $64\frac{5}{8}''$; cut 2
K — $16\frac{1}{2}''$ x $64\frac{5}{8}''$; cut 2
L — $16\frac{1}{2}''$ x $16\frac{1}{2}''$; cut 4
M — $16\frac{1}{2}''$ x $64\frac{5}{8}''$; cut 2

Fabric Requirements

— 2 yds.

— 1 yd.

— $4\frac{3}{4}$ yds.

— $2\frac{5}{8}$ yds.

— 1 yd.

— $\frac{3}{4}$ yd.

Backing—8 yds.

Batting—101″ x 101″

Assembly Instructions:

1. Sew Template A to Template B. Sew Templates C, D, E, F, G, and H to A/B to form strip. Continue sewing strips of patches in order as shown in diagram.

2. Sew together strips of patches to form block.

3. See Border Application Diagram on page 13 for instructions about how to complete the quilt top, using Templates I through M.

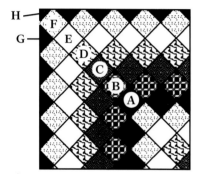

Variation 3

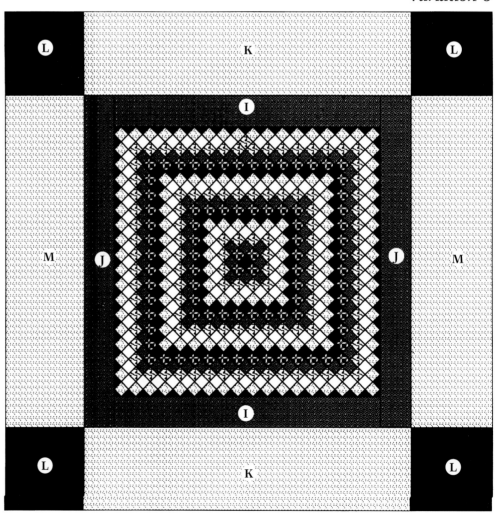

146

Bars

Approximate size—91" x 108"

Variation 1

Measurements given with seam allowances.

- A — 8" x 69"; cut 4
- B — 8" x 69"; cut 3
- C — 5¼" x 53"; cut 2
- D — 5¼" x 5¼"; cut 4
- E — 5¼" x 69"; cut 2
- F — 15½" x 62½"; cut 2
- G — 15½" x 15½"; cut 4
- H — 15½" x 69"; cut 2

Assembly Instructions:

1. Sew one Template A to one Template B. Sew another Template A to unit A,B. Sew another Template B to unit A,B,A. Sew another Template A to unit A,B,A,B. Sew another Template B to unit A,B,A,B,A. Sew remaining Template A to unit A,B,A,B,A,B.

2. See Border Application Diagram on page 13 to complete the borders, using Templates C through H.

Fabric Requirements

- ■ — 2⅞ yds.
- □ — 2 yds.
- ▦ — 2⅛ yds.
- ▨ — 4 yds.

Backing—If using horizontal seams—9 yds.
If using vertical seams—7⅝ yds.

Batting—96" x 113"

Variation 1

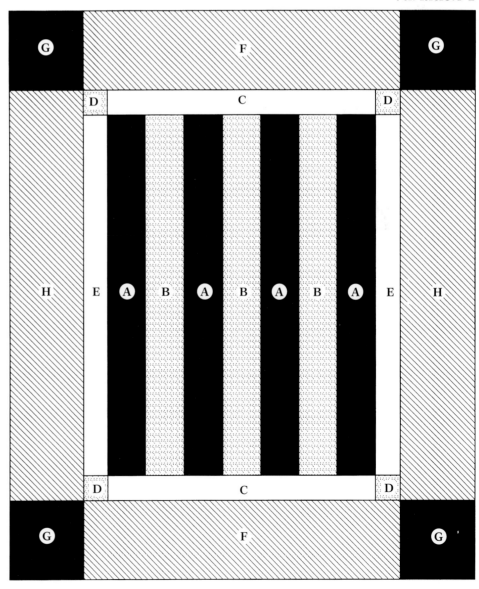

Variation 2

Measurements given with seam allowances.

A — 9¼" x 78½"; cut 3
B — 9¼" x 78½"; cut 4
C — 15½" x 61¾"; cut 2
D — 15½" x 15½"; cut 4
E — 15½" x 78½"; cut 2

Assembly Instructions:

1. Sew one Template A to one Template B. Sew another Template B to unit BA. Sew another Template A to unit BAB. Sew another Template B to unit BABA. Sew another Template A to unit BABAB. Sew remaining Template B to unit BABABA.

2. See Border Application Diagram on page 13 to complete the border using Templates C through E.

Fabric Requirements

— 3⅛ yds.

— 2¼ yds.

— 4 yds.

Backing—If using horizontal seams—9 yds.
If using vertical seams—7⅝ yds.

Batting—96" x 113"

Variation 2

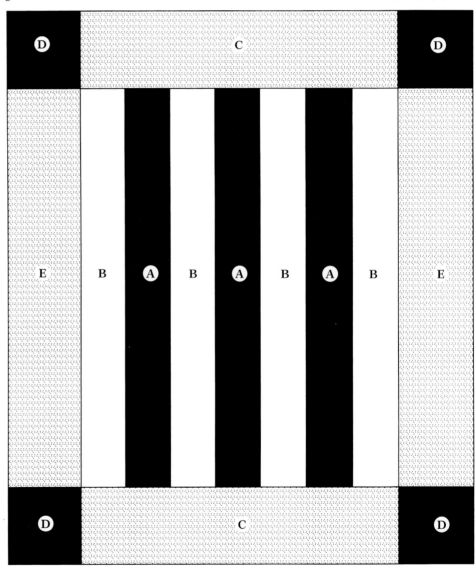

Variation 3

Measurements given with seam allowances.
- A — Template given; cut 240
- B — Template given; cut 240
- C — Template given; cut 240
- D — 9" x 85½"; cut 5
- E — 4" x 68½"; cut 2
- F — 4" x 92½"; cut 2
- G — 8½" x 75½"; cut 2
- H — 8½" x 108½"; cut 2

Assembly Instructions:

1. Sew Template A and Template B to Template C to create a horizontal rectangle. Repeat with remaining Templates A, B, and C.

2. Sew 40 A,B,C units together. Repeat, making a total of 6 strips.

3. Sew one strip to a Template D. Repeat as shown on diagram, until all strips and all Template D's are sewn together.

4. See Border Application Diagram on page 13 to complete the border, using Templates E through H.

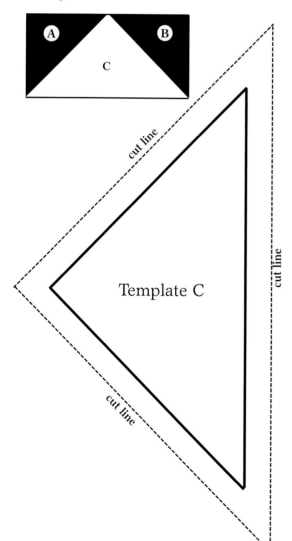

Fabric Requirements

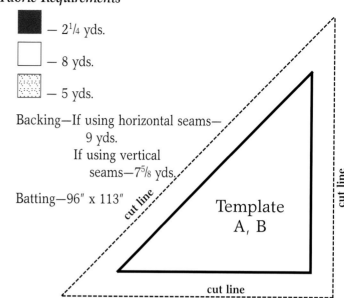

— 2¼ yds.

— 8 yds.

— 5 yds.

Backing—If using horizontal seams—
9 yds.
If using vertical
seams—7⅝ yds.

Batting—96" x 113"

Template A, B

Variation 3—Wild Goose Chase

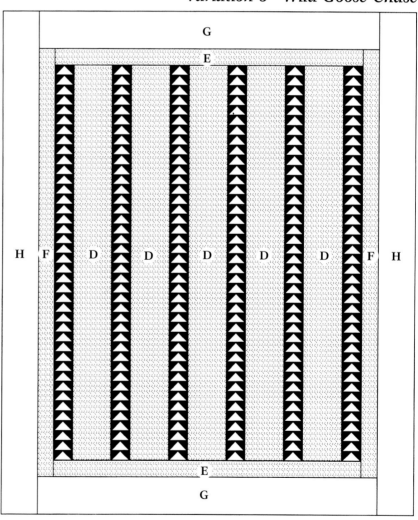

Multiple Patch

Variation 1—91" x 111"

Measurements given with seam allowances.

A — Template given; cut 60
B — Template given; cut 240
C — Template given; cut 240
D — Template given; cut 48
E — $15^3/8$" x $15^3/8$"; cut 2; then cut in half diagonally
F — $11^1/8$" x $11^1/8$"; cut 2; then cut in half diagonally
G — 15" x 15"; cut 6
H — $3^1/8$" x 62", cut 2
I — $3^1/8$" x $87^3/4$"; cut 2
J — $12^1/2$" x $67^1/4$"; cut 2
K — $12^1/2$" x $111^3/4$"; cut 2

Fabric Requirements

 — $2^1/8$ yds.

 — $5^1/8$ yds.

 — $6^1/4$ yds.

 — $3^3/4$ yds.

Backing—If using horizontal seams—
$9^1/4$ yds.
If using vertical seams—
$7^5/8$ yds.

Batting—96" x 116"

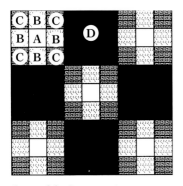

Assembly Instructions:

1. To create a Multiple Patch Block:

A. Sew a Template C to end of Template B. Sew another Template C to the other end of Template B. Repeat, to make 2 strips.

B. Sew a Template B to end of Template A. Sew another Template B to the other end of Template A.

C. Sew Unit C/B/C to one side of B/A/B. Sew another Unit C/B/C to opposite sides of B/A/B, to form a Multiple Patch block.

D. Sew a Multiple Patch Block to each end of a Template D to create a Strip 1. Repeat, to make 2 Strip 1's.

E. Sew a Template D to each end of a Multiple Patch Block to create a Strip 2.

F. Create a Big Block by sewing a Strip 2 between two Strip 1's.

2. Repeat 11 more times, to create 12 Big Blocks.

3. Follow the diagram, How to Assemble Your Quilt, on page 12.

4. When your patches are sewen together, follow the Border Application Diagram on page 13, to use Templates H through K.

Variation 1

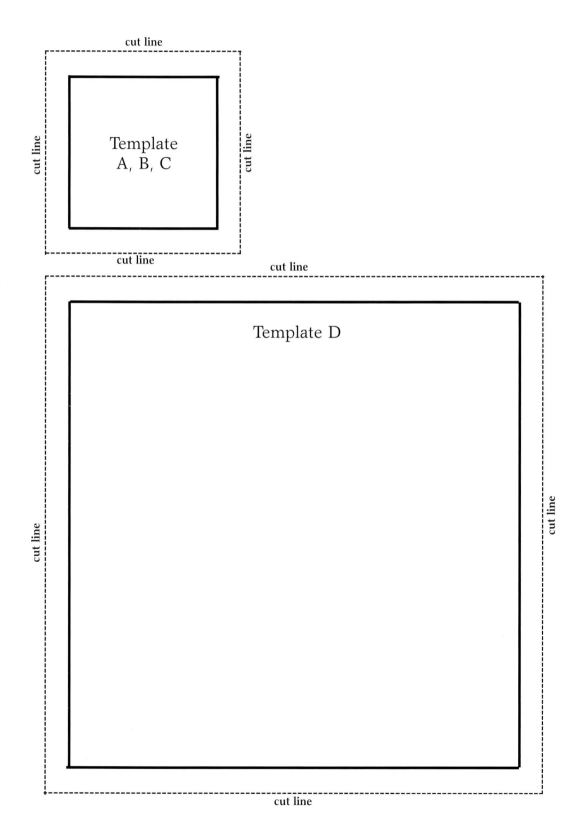

cut line

cut line

cut line

Template
A, B, C

cut line

cut line

Template D

cut line

cut line

cut line

Variation 2—94" x 110"

Measurements given with seam allowances.

A — 2½" x 2½"; cut 160
B — 2½" x 2½"; cut 160
C — 4½" x 4½"; cut 80
D — 8½" x 8½"; cut 40
E — 3½" x 64½"; cut 2
F — 3½" x 86½"; cut 2
G — 12½" x 70½"; cut 2
H — 12½" x 110½"; cut 2

Fabric Requirements

— 1⅛ yds.

— 2 yds.

— 3⅛ yds.

— 5¾ yds.

Backing—If using horizontal seams—
9⅛ yds.
If using vertical seams—
7⅞ yds.

Batting—100" x 116"

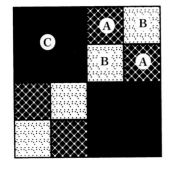

Assembly Instructions:

1. To create one Multiple Patch Block:

   A. Sew Template A to end of Template B. Repeat 4 times to create 4 strips.

   B. Sew Unit B/A to Unit A/B to form block. Repeat to make 2 blocks.

   C. Sew Template C to block. Repeat to make 2 strips.

   D. Sew two strips together to form block.

2. Repeat entire process 39 more times. (40 blocks total.)

3. Follow the diagram, How to Assemble Your Quilt, Diagram 2, on page 12.

4. When your patches are sewn together, follow the Border Application Diagram on page 13 to use Templates E through H.

Variation 2

152

Irish Chain

Variation 1—94″ x 110″

Measurements given with seam allowances.

- A — 11³/₄″ x 11³/₄″; cut 10
- B — 2³/₄″ x 2³/₄″; cut 160
- C — 2³/₄″ x 2³/₄″; cut 330
- D — 2³/₄″ x 2³/₄″; cut 240
- E — 4″ x 63¹/₂″; cut 2
- F — 4″ x 86¹/₄″; cut 2
- G — 12¹/₂″ x 70¹/₂″; cut 2
- H — 12¹/₂″ x 110¹/₄″; cut 2

Fabric Requirements

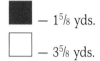

- ■ — 1⁵/₈ yds.
- □ — 3⁵/₈ yds.
- ▨ — 9³/₈ yds.

Backing—If using horizontal seams—9¹/₈ yds.
If using vertical seams—7⁷/₈ yds.

Batting—100″ x 116″

Assembly Instructions:

1. To create one Irish Chain Block 1:

    A. Sew together Row One, working from left to right.

    B. Sew together Row Two, working from left to right.

    C. Sew together other 5 rows in Block 1.

    D. Sew Row One to Row Two.

    E. Sew Row Three to other side of Row Two.

    F. Repeat with remaining 5 rows.

2. Repeat process for Block 1, 9 more times (10 blocks total).

3. To create one Irish Chain Block 2:

    A. Sew together Row One, working from left to right.

    B. Sew together the first blocks in Rows 2, 3, 4, 5, and 6.

    C. Sew together the last blocks in Rows 2, 3, 4, 5, and 6.

    D. Sew these two strips to either side of Template A.

    E. Sew together Row Seven, working from left to right.

    F. Sew Row One to top of main block and Row Seven to bottom of main block.

4. Repeat process for Block 2, 9 more times (10 blocks total).

5. Follow the diagram, How to Assemble your Quilt, Diagram 1, on page 12.

6. When your patches are sewn together, follow the Border Application Diagram on page 13 to use Templates E through H.

Block 1

Block 2

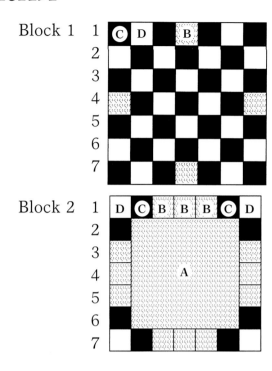

Variation 1

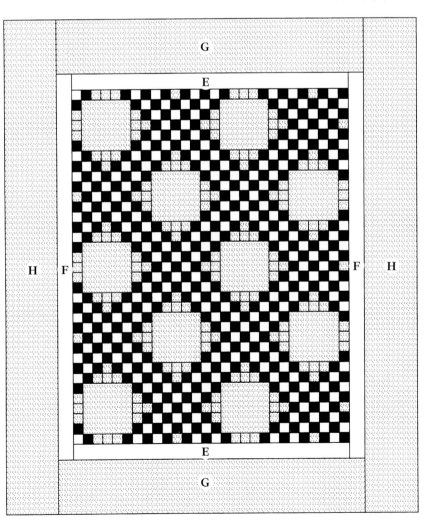

153

Variation 2—98" x 112"

Measurements given with seam allowances.

- A — 2½" x 2½"; cut 270
- B — 2½" x 2½"; cut 360
- C — 2½" x 2½"; cut 120
- D — 10⅞" x 10⅞"; cut 9; then cut in half diagonally
- E — 8" x 8"; cut 2; then cut in half diagonally
- F — 10½" x 10½"; cut 20
- G — 3" x 71¼"; cut 2
- H — 3" x 90⅜"; cut 2
- I — 11½" x 76¼"; cut 2
- J — 11½" x 112⅜"; cut 2

Fabric Requirements

— 2 yds.

— 11 yds.

— 5⅛ yds.

Backing—If using horizontal seams—9⅜ yds.
If using vertical seams—8⅛ yds.

Batting—103" x 118"

Assembly Instructions:

1. To create one Irish Chain Block:

   A. Sew together Row One, working from left to right. Make a second Row One.

   B. Sew together Row Two, working from left to right. Make a second Row Two.

   C. Make one Row Three.

   D. Sew one Row One and one Row Two together.

   E. Sew Row Three to other side of Row Two.

   F. Continue with remaining 2 Rows.

2. Repeat 29 more times (30 blocks total).

3. Follow the diagram, How to Assemble your Quilt, Diagram 1, on page 12.

4. When your patches are sewn together, follow the Border Application Diagram on page 13 to use Templates E through H.

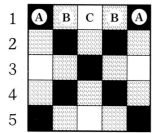

Block 1

Variation 2

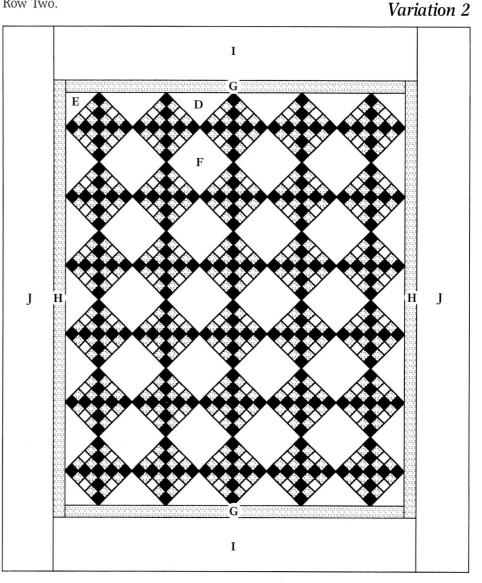

154

Log Cabin

Approximate size—97" x 109$\frac{1}{2}$"

Measurements given with seam allowances.

A — 3" x 3"; cut 42
B — 1$\frac{3}{4}$" x 3"; cut 42
C — 1$\frac{3}{4}$" x 4$\frac{1}{4}$"; cut 42
D — 1$\frac{3}{4}$" x 4$\frac{1}{4}$"; cut 42
E — 1$\frac{3}{4}$" x 5$\frac{1}{2}$"; cut 42
F — 1$\frac{3}{4}$" x 5$\frac{1}{2}$"; cut 42
G — 1$\frac{3}{4}$" x 6$\frac{3}{4}$"; cut 42
H — 1$\frac{3}{4}$" x 6$\frac{3}{4}$"; cut 42
I — 1$\frac{3}{4}$" x 8"; cut 42
J — 1$\frac{3}{4}$" x 8"; cut 42
K — 1$\frac{3}{4}$" x 9$\frac{1}{4}$"; cut 42
L — 1$\frac{3}{4}$" x 9$\frac{1}{4}$"; cut 42
M — 1$\frac{3}{4}$" x 10$\frac{1}{2}$"; cut 42
N — 1$\frac{3}{4}$" x 10$\frac{1}{2}$"; cut 42
O — 1$\frac{3}{4}$" x 11$\frac{3}{4}$"; cut 42
P — 1$\frac{3}{4}$" x 11$\frac{3}{4}$"; cut 42
Q — 1$\frac{3}{4}$" x 13"; cut 42
R — 3$\frac{1}{2}$" x 75$\frac{1}{2}$"; cut 2
S — 3$\frac{1}{2}$" x 94"; cut 2
T — 8$\frac{1}{2}$" x 81$\frac{1}{2}$"; cut 2
U — 8$\frac{1}{2}$" x 110"; cut 2

Fabric Requirements

 — $\frac{1}{4}$ yd.

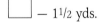 — 1$\frac{1}{2}$ yds.

 — 4$\frac{1}{8}$ yds.

 — $\frac{5}{8}$ yd.

 — $\frac{3}{8}$ yd.

 — 1$\frac{3}{8}$ yds.

 — 3$\frac{1}{4}$ yds.

 — $\frac{7}{8}$ yd.

 — $\frac{7}{8}$ yd.

Backing— If using horizontal seams—
9$\frac{1}{8}$ yds.
If using vertical seams—
8$\frac{1}{8}$ yds.

Batting—102" x 114$\frac{1}{2}$"

Assembly Instructions:

To create The Log Cabin Block:

A. Sew Template B to one side of Template A.

B. Sew Template C to unit A,B.

C. Sew Template D to unit A,B,C.

D. Repeat with strips E through Q, until Log Cabin block is formed.

2. Repeat 41 more times (42 blocks total).

3. Follow the diagram, How to Assemble your Quilt, Diagram 1, on page 12.

4. When your patches are sewn together, follow the Border Application Diagram on page 13 to use Templates R through U.

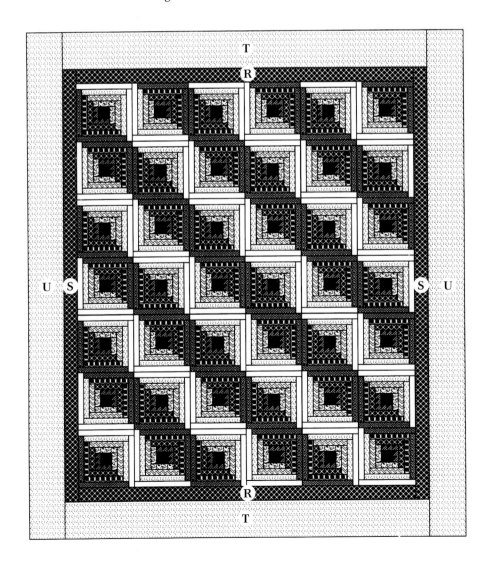

Double T
Approximate size—96¹/₄" x 111"

Measurements given with seam allowances.

A — 4" x 4"; cut 30
B — 2⁵/₈" x 2⁵/₈"; cut 240; then cut in half diagonally
C — 2⁵/₈" x 2⁵/₈"; cut 240; then cut in half diagonally
D — 4³/₈" x 4³/₈"; cut 60; then cut in half diagonally
E — 4³/₈" x 4³/₈"; cut 60; then cut in half diagonally
F — 8³/₈" x 8³/₈"; cut 2; then cut in half diagonally
G — 11³/₈" x 11³/₈"; cut 9; then cut in half diagonally
H — 11" x 11"; cut 20
I — 2¹/₂" x 74³/₄"; cut 2
J — 2¹/₂" x 93¹/₂"; cut 2
K — 9¹/₂" x 78³/₄"; cut 2
L — 9¹/₂" x 111¹/₂"; cut 2

Fabric Requirements

☐ — 7³/₈ yds.

▦ — 7 yds.

▨ — 8³/₄ yds.

Backing— If using horizontal seams—
9¹/₄ yds.
If using vertical seams—
8 yds.

Batting—101¹/₄" x 116"

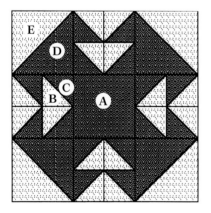

Assembly Instructions:

1. To create one Double T block:

A. Sew long side of Template B to long side of Template C. Repeat 15 more times (16 B/C Units total).

B. Sew 2 B/C strips together as shown in Block below. Repeat 7 more times (8 B/C strips total). Sew 1 B/C strip to another B/C strip. Repeat 3 more times (4 blocks total).

C. Sew long side of Template D to long side of Template E. Repeat 3 more times (4 C/D Units total).

C. Sew 1 E/D Unit to 1 B/C block. Sew another E/D Unit to the opposite side of the B/C block. Repeat.

D. Sew 1 B/C block to Template A. Sew another B/C unit to opposite side of Template A.

E. Sew three strips together to form block.

F. Repeat entire process 29 more times (30 blocks total).

2. Follow How to Assemble Your Quilt, on page 12.

3. Follow Border Application Diagram on page 13 to use Templates I through L.

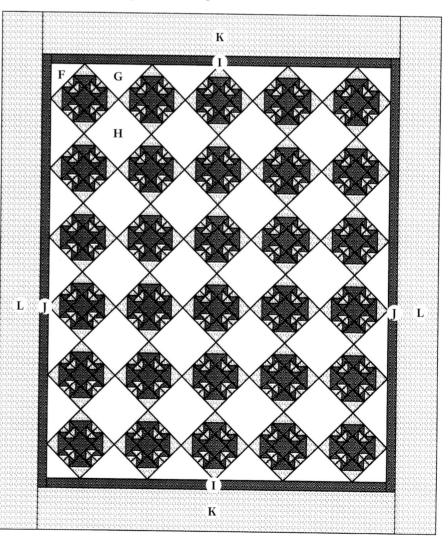

Stars

Variation 1—96$^{1}/_{2}$″ x 109$^{3}/_{4}$″

Measurements given with seam allowances.

A — Template given; cut 128
B — Template given; cut 128
C — Template given; cut 128
D — Template given; cut 128
E — 18$^{1}/_{4}$″ x 18$^{1}/_{4}$″; cut 4
F — 18$^{5}/_{8}$″ x 18$^{5}/_{8}$″; cut 2; then cut in half diagonally
G — 16$^{1}/_{2}$″ x 61″; cut 1
H — 16$^{1}/_{2}$″ x 61″; cut 2
I — 16″ x 108″; cut 2

Assembly Instructions:

1. To form one Star block:

A. Sew Template A to Template B. Sew Template C to Unit A/B. Sew Template D to Unit A/B/C. Sew another Template A to Unit A/B/C/D. Continue until the Unit is A/B/C/D/A/B/C/D. Repeat. (2 strips total.)

B. Sew together a strip of 8 diamonds, starting with B and ending with A. Repeat. (2 strips total.)

C. Sew together a strip of 8 diamonds, starting with C and ending with B. Repeat. (2 strips total.)

D. Sew together a strip of 8 diamonds, starting with D and ending with C. Repeat. (2 strips total.)

E. Sew together 8 strips, as shown, to create large diamond.

F. Repeat entire process 7 more times, to create a total of 8 large diamonds.

2. Sew together 4 large diamonds as shown. Repeat. Sew 2 strips of diamonds together.

3. Insert 4 Template E's into corners.

4. Insert 4 Template F's into sides.

5. Sew Template G to top of center square.

6. Follow Border Application Diagram on page 13 to complete the quilt using Templates H and I.

Fabric Requirements

■ — $^{3}/_{4}$ yd.
□ — 3$^{1}/_{4}$ yds.
▨ — 5$^{1}/_{2}$ yds.
▨ — 2$^{1}/_{2}$ yds.

Backing— If using horizontal seams—9 yds.
If using vertical seams—7$^{3}/_{4}$ yds.

Batting—101$^{1}/_{2}$″ x 114$^{3}/_{4}$″

Variation 1

Template for Variation One

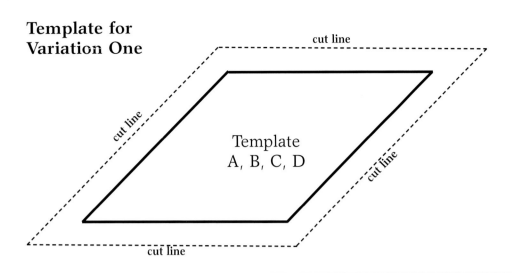

Template A, B, C, D

cut line
cut line
cut line
cut line

Variation 2—98″ x 112″

Measurements given with seam allowances.

- A — Template given; cut 256
- B — Template given; cut 224
- C — Template given; cut 224
- D — Template given; cut 224
- E — Template given; cut 224
- F — $9^3/8$″ x $9^3/8$″; cut 20
- G — $9^3/4$″ x $9^3/4$″; cut 4; then cut in half diagonally
- H — $16^1/2$″ x 61″; cut 1
- I — $16^1/2$″ x 61″; cut 2
- J — $16^1/2$″ x $108^1/2$″; cut 2

Fabric Requirements

- ■ — $^3/4$ yd.
- □ — $4^1/2$ yds.
- ▨ — $5^1/2$ yds.
- ▨ — $2^1/2$ yds.

Backing— If using horizontal seams—9 yds.
If using vertical seams—$7^3/4$ yds.

Batting—$101^1/2$″ x $114^3/4$″

Assembly Instructions:

1. To form one Star block:

A. Sew Template A to Template B. Sew Template C to Unit A/B. Sew Template D to Unit A/B/C. Sew Template E to Unit A/B/C/D. Sew another Template A to Unit A/B/C/D/E. Repeat. (2 strips total.)

B. Sew together a strip of 6 diamonds, starting with B and ending with B.

C. Sew together a strip of 6 diamonds, starting with C and ending with C.

D. Sew together a strip of 6 diamonds, starting with D and ending with D.

E. Sew together a strip of 6 diamonds, starting with E and ending with E.

E. Sew together 6 strips, as shown, to create large diamond.

F. Repeat entire process 31 more times, to create a total of 32 large diamonds.

2. Sew together 8 large diamonds as shown to form center.

3. Insert 8 Template F's into corners and sides of center.

4. Sew together three large diamonds. Repeat 7 times. Insert these units by sewing to Template F's that surround the center star.

5. Insert 3 Template F's into each corner.

6. Insert 2 Template G's into each side, to finish center square.

7. Sew Template H to top of center square.

8. See Border Application Diagram on page 13 to complete border, using Templates I and J.

Template for Variation Two

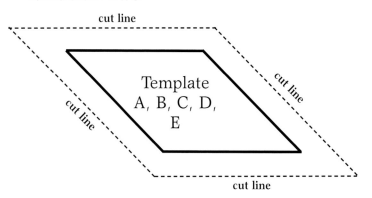

Variation 2—Broken Star

Jacob's Ladder

Approximate size—97$^{1}/_{2}$" x 108$^{3}/_{4}$"

Measurements given with seam allowances.

- A — 2$^{3}/_{8}$" x 2$^{3}/_{8}$"; cut 420
- B — 2$^{3}/_{8}$" x 2$^{3}/_{8}$"; cut 420
- C — 4$^{5}/_{8}$" x 4$^{5}/_{8}$"; cut 84; then cut in half diagonally
- D — 4$^{5}/_{8}$" x 4$^{5}/_{8}$"; cut 84; then cut in half diagonally
- E — 4$^{1}/_{2}$" x 68"; cut 2
- F — 4$^{1}/_{2}$" x 87$^{1}/_{4}$"; cut 2
- G — 11$^{1}/_{2}$" x 76"; cut 2
- H — 11$^{1}/_{2}$" x 109$^{1}/_{4}$"; cut 2

Fabric Requirements

 — 7$^{3}/_{8}$ yds.

 — 7 yds.

 — 8$^{3}/_{4}$ yds.

Backing— If using horizontal seams—9 yds.
If using vertical seams—8$^{1}/_{8}$ yds.

Batting—102$^{1}/_{2}$" x 113$^{3}/_{4}$"

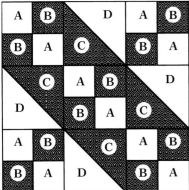

Assembly Instructions:

1. To form one Jacob's Ladder block:

    A. Sew Template A to Template B. Repeat.

    B. Sew together Unit A/B with Unit B/A to form block. Repeat 4 more times. (5 blocks total.)

    C. Sew long side of Template C to long side of Template D. Repeat 3 more times. (4 blocks total.)

    D. Sew A/B Block, to one side of C/D Unit. Sew another A/B Block to opposite side of C/D Unit. Repeat.

    E. Sew C/D Unit to one side of A/B Unit. Sew another C/D Unit to opposite side of A/B Unit.

    F. Sew three strips together to form block.

2. Repeat 41 more times. (42 blocks total.)

3. See How to Assemble Your Quilt, Diagram 1, page 12.

4. Follow Border Application Diagram on page 13 to complete quilt using Templates E through H.

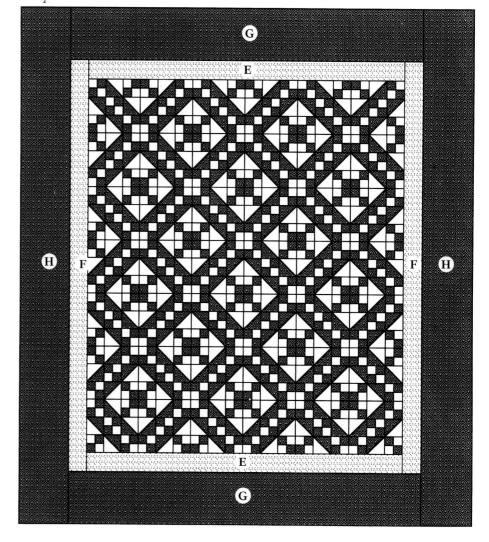

Baskets

Variation 1—94" x 108"

Measurements given with seam allowances.

A — 2⅞" x 2⅞"; cut 70; then cut in half diagonally
B — 2⅞" x 2⅞"; cut 90; then cut in half diagonally
C — 6⅞" x 6⅞"; cut 10; then cut in half diagonally
D — 6⅞" x 6⅞"; cut 10; then cut in half diagonally
E — 2½" x 6½"; cut 40
F — 4⅞" x 4⅞"; cut 10; then cut in half diagonally
G — 10½" x 10½"; cut 12
H — 10⅞" x 10⅞"; cut 7; then cut in half diagonally
I — 8" x 8"; cut 2; then cut in half diagonally
J — 4" x 57"; cut 2
K — 4" x 78¼"; cut 2
L — 15¾" x 64"; cut 2
M — 15¾" x 108½"; cut 2

Assembly Instructions:

1. To form one Basket Block:

A. Sew the long side of Template A to the long side of Template B. Repeat 6 times. (7 blocks total.)

B. Sew the long side of Template C to the long side of Template D.

C. Sew together 4 of the A/B Units to form a horizontal strip.

D. Sew together 3 of the A/B Units to form a vertical strip.

E. Sew Unit C/D to vertical strip of 3 A/B Units.

F. Sew horizontal strip of 4 A/B Units to A/B/C/D Unit to create block.

G. Sew Template B to end of Template E. Repeat.

H. Sew B/E Unit to bottom of large block. Sew second B/E Unit to right of large block.

I. Sew Template F to corner of large unit to create Basket Block.

2. Repeat 19 more times. (20 blocks total.)

3. See How to Assemble Your Quilt, Diagram 2, on page 12.

4. Follow Border Application Diagram on page 13 to complete your quilt, using Templates J through M.

Fabric Requirements

☐ — 15¾ yds.

▨ — 6⅜ yds.

Backing— If using horizontal seams—9 yds.
If using vertical seams—7⅞ yds.

Batting—99" x 113"

Variation 1

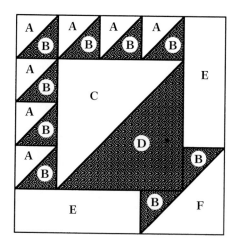

161

Variation 2—94" x 108"

Measurements given with seam allowances.

A — 2⅞" x 2⅞"; cut 60; then cut in half diagonally
B — 2⅞" x 2⅞"; cut 80; then cut in half diagonally
C — 6⅞" x 6⅞"; cut 10; then cut in half diagonally
D — 6⅞" x 6⅞"; cut 10; then cut in half diagonally
E — 2½" x 6½"; cut 40
F — 4⅞" x 4⅞"; cut 10; then cut in half diagonally
G — 2½" x 2½", cut 20
H — 10½" x 10½"; cut 12
I — 10⅞" x 10⅞"; cut 7; then cut in half diagonally
J — 8" x 8"; cut 2; then cut in half diagonally
K — 4" x 57"; cut 2
L — 4" x 78¼"; cut 2
M — 15¾" x 64"; cut 2
N — 15¾" x 108½"; cut 2

Assembly Instructions:

1. To form one Basket Block:

A. Sew the long side of Template A to the long side of Template B. Repeat 5 times. (6 blocks total.)

B. Sew the long side of Template C to the long side of Template D.

C. Sew together 3 of the A/B Units to form a horizontal strip. Repeat to form a vertical strip.

D. Sew Template G to end of one strip.

E. Sew Unit C/D to strip of 3 A/B Units.

F. Sew strip of A/B/G Unit to A/B/C/D Unit to create block.

G. Sew Template B to end of Template E. Repeat.

H. Sew B/E Unit to bottom of large block. Sew second B/E Unit to right of large block.

I. Sew Template F to corner of large unit to create Basket Block.

2. Repeat 19 more times. (20 blocks total.)

3. See How to Assemble Your Quilt, Diagram 2, page 12.

4. Follow Border Application Diagram, page 13, to complete your quilt, using Templates K through N.

Fabric Requirements

☐ — 3⅜ yds.

▦ — 6⅜ yds.

▨ — 7½ yds.

Backing— If using horizontal seams—9 yds.
If using vertical seams—7⅞ yds.

Batting—
99" x 113"

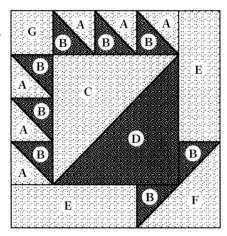

Variation 2

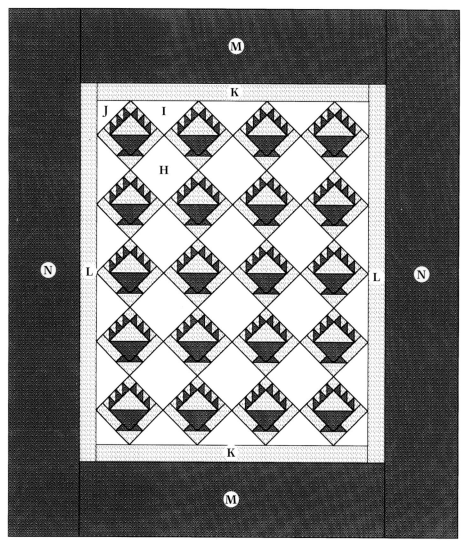

162

Variation 3—94" x 108"

Measurements given with seam allowances.

A — 2⅞" x 2⅞"; cut 60; then cut in half diagonally
B — 2⅞" x 2⅞"; cut 80; then cut in half diagonally
C — 2⅞" x 2⅞"; cut 60; then cut in half diagonally
D — 2⅞" x 2⅞"; cut 30; then cut in half diagonally
E — 6⅞" x 6⅞"; cut 10; then cut in half diagonally
F — 4⅞" x 4⅞"; cut 10; then cut in half diagonally
G — 2½" x 2½"; cut 20
H — 2½" x 6½"; cut 40
I — 10½" x 10½"; cut 12
J — 10⅞" x 10⅞"; cut 7; then cut in half diagonally
K — 8" x 8"; cut 2; then cut in half diagonally
L — 4" x 57"; cut 2
M — 4" x 78¼"; cut 2
N — 15¾" x 64"; cut 2
O — 15¾" x 108½"; cut 2

Assembly Instructions:

1. To form one Basket Block:

A. Sew the long side of Template A to the long side of Template B. Repeat 5 times. (6 blocks total.)

B. Sew the long side of Template C to the long side of Template D. Repeat 2 times. (3 blocks total.)

C. Sew together a horizontal strip of 4 pieces in the following order: Template G, B/A Unit, B/A Unit, B/A Unit.

D. Sew together a horizontal strip of 4 pieces in the following order: A/B Unit, C/D Unit, C/D Unit, Template C.

E. Sew together a horizontal strip of 3 pieces in the following order: A/B Unit, C/D Unit, Template C.

F. Sew together a horizontal strip of 2 pieces in the following order: A/B Unit, Template C.

G. Sew these four horizontal strips together to creat a partial triangle.

H. Sew Template E onto pieced strips to create a block.

I. Sew Template B to end of Template H. Repeat. (2 strips total.)

H. Sew B/H Unit to bottom of large block. Sew second B/G Unit to right of large block.

I. Sew Template F to corner of large unit to create Basket Block.

2. Repeat 19 more times. (20 blocks total.)

3. See How to Assemble Your Quilt, Diagram 2, on page 12.

4. Follow Border Application Diagram on page 13 to complete your quilt, using Templates L through O.

Fabric Requirements

■ — ⅝ yd.
□ — 3⅜ yds.
▨ — 8¼ yds.
▨ — 4¾ yds.

Backing— If using horizontal seams—9 yds.
If using vertical seams—7⅞ yds.

Batting—
99" x 113"

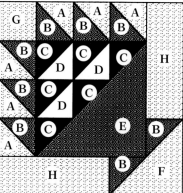

Variation 3

Fan

Variation 1—98″ x 109″

Measurements given with seam allowances.

A — Template given; cut 42
B — Template given; cut 42
C — Template given; cut 42
D — Template given; cut 42
E — Template given; cut 42
F — Template given; cut 42
G — Template given; cut 42
H — Template given; cut 42
I — Template given; cut 42
J — Template given; cut 42
K — 16½″ x 66½″; cut 2
L — 16½″ x 109½″; cut 2

Fabric Requirements

 — 4½ yds.

— ¾ yd.

— ¾ yd.

 — 5⅝ yds.

— 1 yd.

— ½ yd.

— 1 yd.

— ½ yd.

— 1 yd.

— ⅞ yd.

Backing—If using horizontal seams—
9⅛ yds.
If using vertical seams—
⅛ yds.

Batting—103″ x 114″

Assembly Instructions:

1. To create one Fan Block:

A. Sew one Template B to one Template C. Sew Template D to B/C Unit. Continue sewing Templates E through I to Unit B/C/D.

B. Sew Template A to pieced unit.

C. Sew Template J to pieced unit to create block.

2. Repeat 41 more times. (42 blocks total.)

3. See How to Assemble Your Quilt, Diagram 1, page 12.

4. Follow Border Application Diagram on page 13 to complete quilt, using Templates K and L.

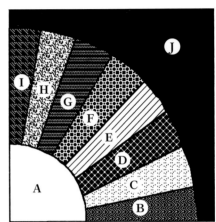

Variation 1

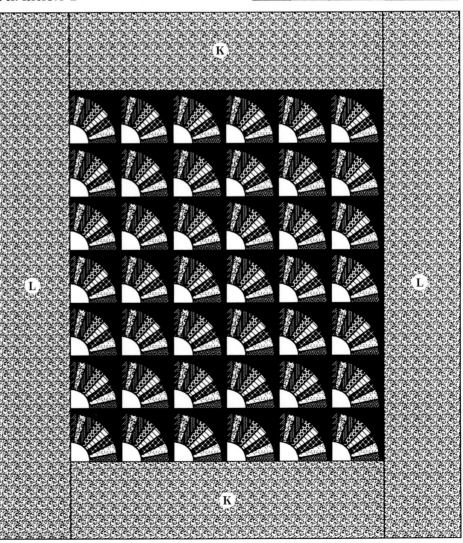

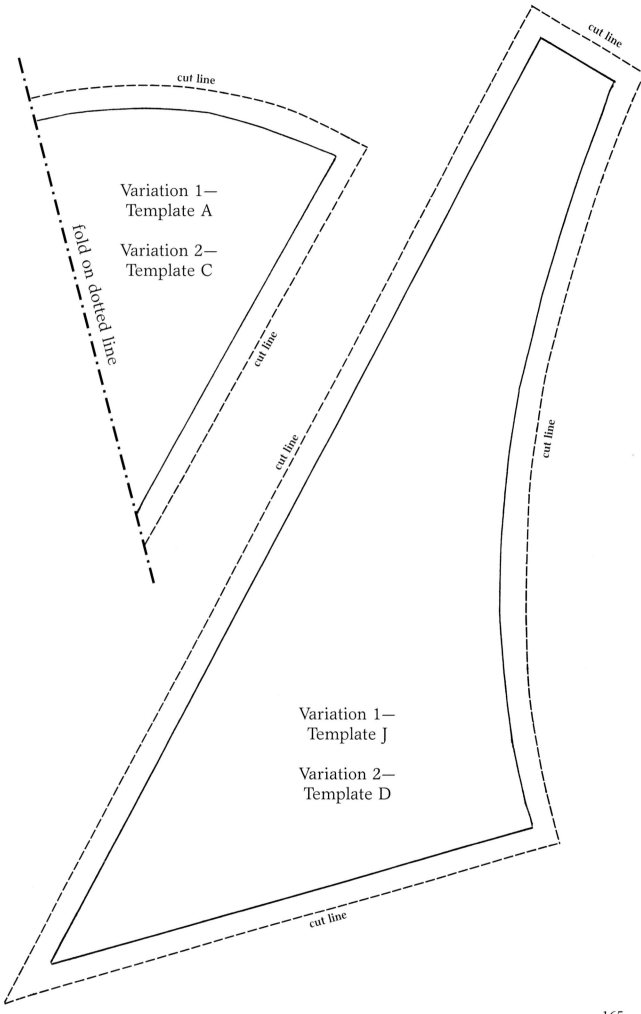

cut line

Variation 1—
Template A

Variation 2—
Template C

fold on dotted line

cut line

cut line

cut line

cut line

Variation 1—
Template J

Variation 2—
Template D

cut line

165

Variation 2—98" x 109"

Measurements given with seam allowances.

A — Template given; cut 168
B — Template given; cut 168
C — Template given; cut 42
E — 16½" x 66½"; cut 2
F — 16½" x 109½"; cut 2

Assembly Instructions:

1. To create one Fan Block:

A. Sew one Template B to one Template A. Sew Template A to B/A Unit. Continue alternating Templates A and B to form the following: A/B/A/B/A/B/A/B.

B. Sew Template C to pieced unit.

C. Sew Template D to pieced unit to create block.

2. Repeat 41 more times. (42 blocks total.)

3. See How to Assemble Your Quilt, Diagram 1, page 12.

4. Follow Border Appilcation Diagram on page 13 to complete your quilt, using Templates E and F.

Fabric Requirements

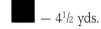 — 4½ yds.

 — ¾ yd.

 — ¾ yd.

Backing—If using horizontal seams—9⅛ yds.
If using vertical seams—8⅛ yds.

Batting—103" x 114"

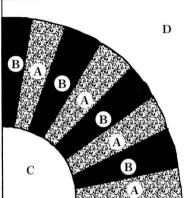

Variation 2

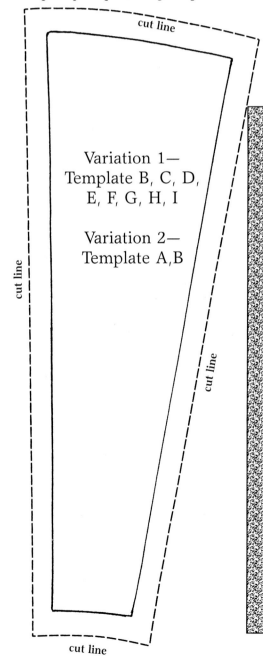

Variation 1—
Template B, C, D,
E, F, G, H, I

Variation 2—
Template A, B

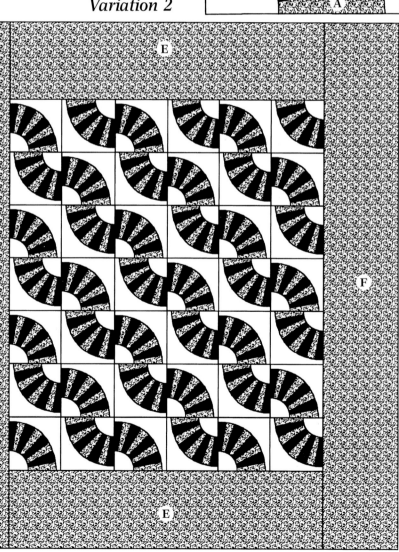

Ocean Waves

Variation 1—90" x 112½"

Measurements given with seam allowances.

A — 8½" x 8½"; cut 17

B — Template provided; cut 1,152 total from 7 different fabrics

C — 8⅞" x 8⅞"; cut 7; then cut in half diagonally

D — 3½" x 69"; cut 2

E — 3½" x 99"; cut 2

F — 8½" x 75"; cut 2

G — 8½" x 115"; cut 2

Fabric Requirements

 — 1½ yds.

 — 5¾ yds.

 — 7½ yds.

 — 1½ yds.

 — 1½ yds.

 — 1½ yds.

 — 1½ yds.

— 1½ yds.

Backing—If using horizontal seams—9⅜ yds.
If using vertical seams—7½ yds.

Batting—95" x 117"

Assembly Instructions:

1. To create one Ocean Wave Block 1:

   A. Create horizontal strip by sewing together 3 Template B's, following numbers 2 through 4.

   B. Sew another Template B to the strip of 3 triangles, to create a large triangle.

   C. Repeat entire process 11 more times. (12 triangles total.)

   D. Sew a triangle to top, bottom, and sides of Template A.

   E. Sew together 2 triangles to form 1 large triangle. Repeat 3 more times. (4 large triangles.)

   F. Sew a large triangle to each side of the patch, to create a large block.

   G. Repeat Steps A through F 16 more times. (17 blocks total.)

2. To create one Ocean Wave Block 2:

   A. Follow steps 1A and 1B, 6 more times.

   B. Sew a triangle to 2 sides of Template C.

   C. Repeat this step 13 more times. (14 triangles total.)

3. See How to Assemble Your Quilt, Diagram 2, page 12.

4. Follow Border Application Diagram on page 13 to complete your quilt, using Templates D through G.

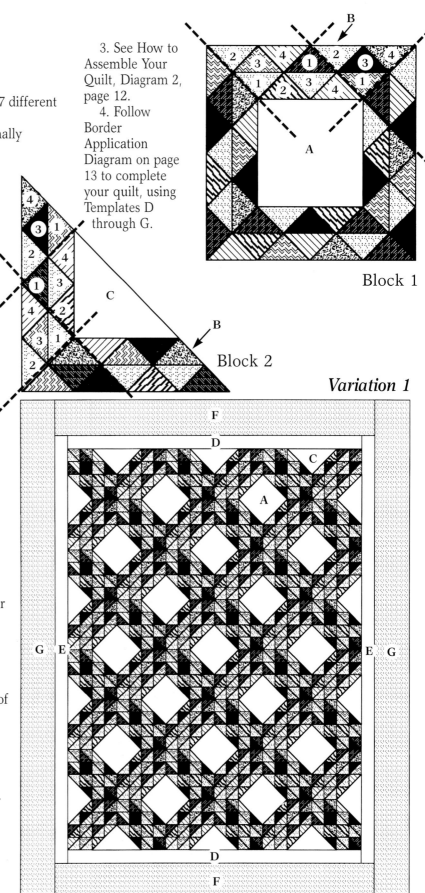

Block 1

Block 2

Variation 1

Template for Variation One

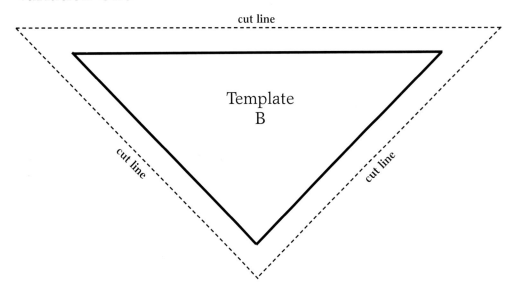

cut line

cut line

Template
B

cut line

Variation 2—90¹/₂″ x 112″

Measurements given with seam allowances.

A — 8″ x 8″; cut 17

B — 2⁵/₈″ x 2⁵/₈″; cut 1,296 from 7 fabrics;
then cut in half diagonally

C — 8³/₈″ x 8³/₈″; cut 7; then cut in half diagonally

D — 4″ x 64¹/₈″; cut 2

E — 4″ x 91⁷/₈″; cut 2

F — 10¹/₂″ x 71¹/₈″; cut 2

G — 10¹/₂″ x 111⁷/₈″; cut 2

Fabric Requirements

 — 1¹/₂ yds.

— 8 yds.

 — 6⁵/₈ yds.

— 1¹/₂ yds.

— 1¹/₂ yds.

 — 1¹/₂ yds.

— 1¹/₂ yds.

— 1¹/₂ yds.

Backing—If using horizontal seams—9³/₈ yds.
If using vertical seams—7¹/₂ yds.

Batting—95¹/₂″ x 117″

Variation 2

168

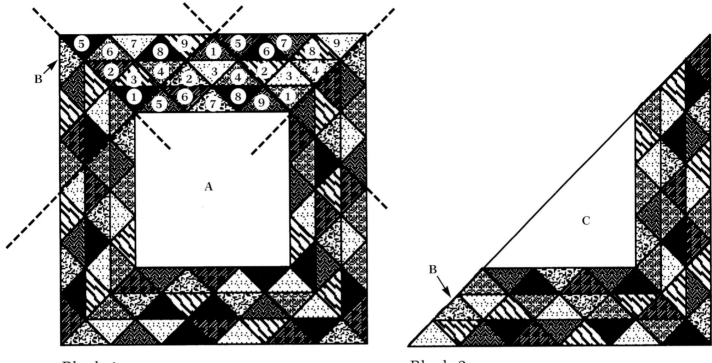

Block 1   Block 2

Assembly Instructions:

1. To create one Ocean Wave Block 1:

A. Create horizontal strip by sewing together 5 Template B's, following Numbers 5 through 9 on Block 1 above.

B. Create horizontal strip by sewing together 3 Template B's, following Numbers 2 through 4 on Block 1 above.

C. Sew bottom of Numbers 5-9 Strip to top of Numbers 2-4 Strip. Sew another Template B to the strip of 3 triangles, to create a large triangle.

D. Repeat entire process 11 more times. (12 triangles total.)

E. Sew a large triangle to top, bottom, and sides of Template A.

F. Sew together 2 large triangles to form 1 very large triangle. Repeat 3 more times. (4 large triangles.)

G. Sew very large triangle to each side of the patch, to create a large block.

H. Repeat Steps A through G 16 more times. (17 blocks total.)

2. To create one Ocean Wave Block 2:

A. Follow steps 1A through 1C 7 times.

B. Sew a large triangle to the one short side of Template C, and another large triangle to the other short side of Template C.

C. Repeat this step 13 more times. (14 triangles total.)

3. See How to Assemble Your Quilt, Diagram 2, page 12.

4. Follow Border Application Diagram on page 13 to complete your quilt, using Templates D through G.

Roman Stripe

Variation 1—98″ x 108″

Measurements given with seam allowances.

- A — Template given; cut 42
- B — Template given; cut 42
- C — Template given; cut 42
- D — Template given; cut 42
- E — Template given; cut 42
- F — $10^7/8$″ x $10^7/8$″; cut 21; then cut in half diagonally
- G — $4^1/2$″ x $60^1/2$″; cut 2
- H — $4^1/2$″ x $78^1/2$″; cut 2
- I — $15^1/2$″ x $68^1/2$″; cut 2
- J — $15^1/2$″ x $108^1/2$″; cut 2

Fabric Requirements

 — $^1/4$ yd.

 — $10^7/8$ yds.

 — $2^1/8$ yds.

 — $1^3/8$ yds.

 — $5^1/8$ yds.

 — $^5/8$ yd.

Backing—
  If using horizontal seams—9 yds.
  If using vertical seams—$8^1/8$ yds.

Batting—103″ x 113″

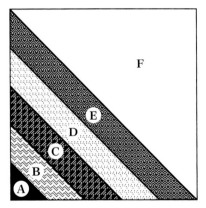

Assembly Instructions:

1. To create one Roman Stripe Block:
   A. Sew Template A to Template B.
   B. Sew Template C to A/B Unit.
   D. Sew Template D to A/B/C Unit.
   E. Sew Template E to A/B/C/D Unit.
   F. Sew Template F to A/B/C/D/E Unit to create block.
   G. Repeat steps 1A through 1F 41 more times.
(42 blocks total.)
2. See How to Assemble Your Quilt, Diagram 1, page 12.
3. Follow Border Application Diagram on page 13 to complete your quilt, using Templates G through J.

Variation 1

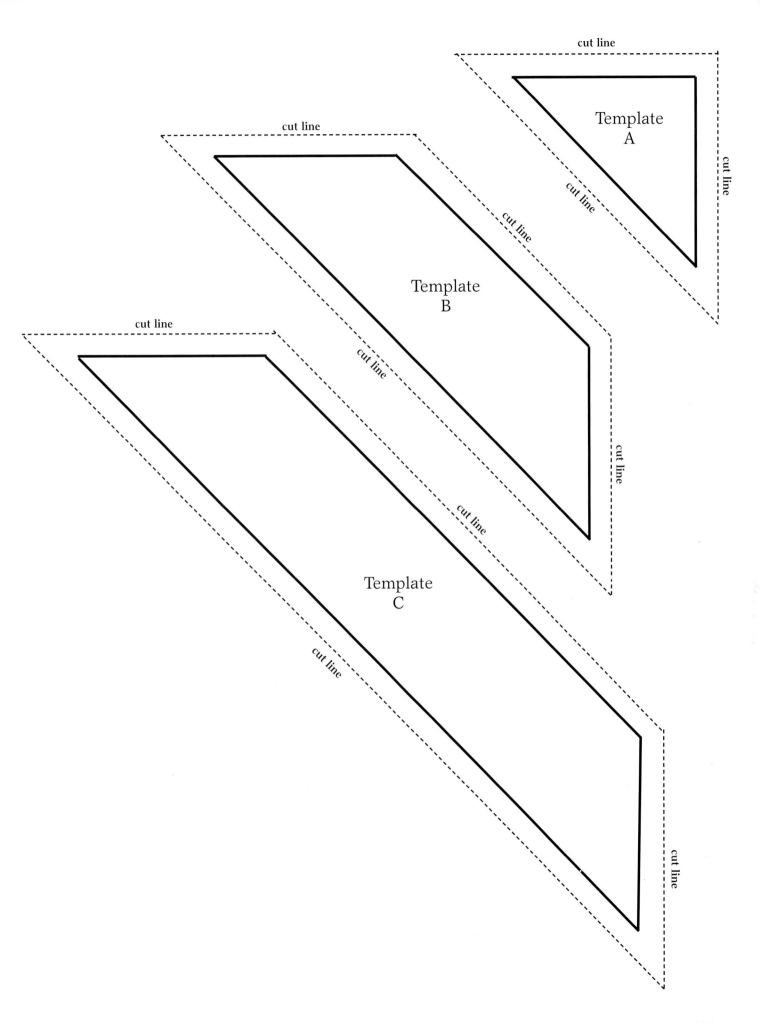

cut line

Template
A

cut line

cut line

cut line

Template
B

cut line

cut line

cut line

cut line

Template
C

cut line

cut line

171

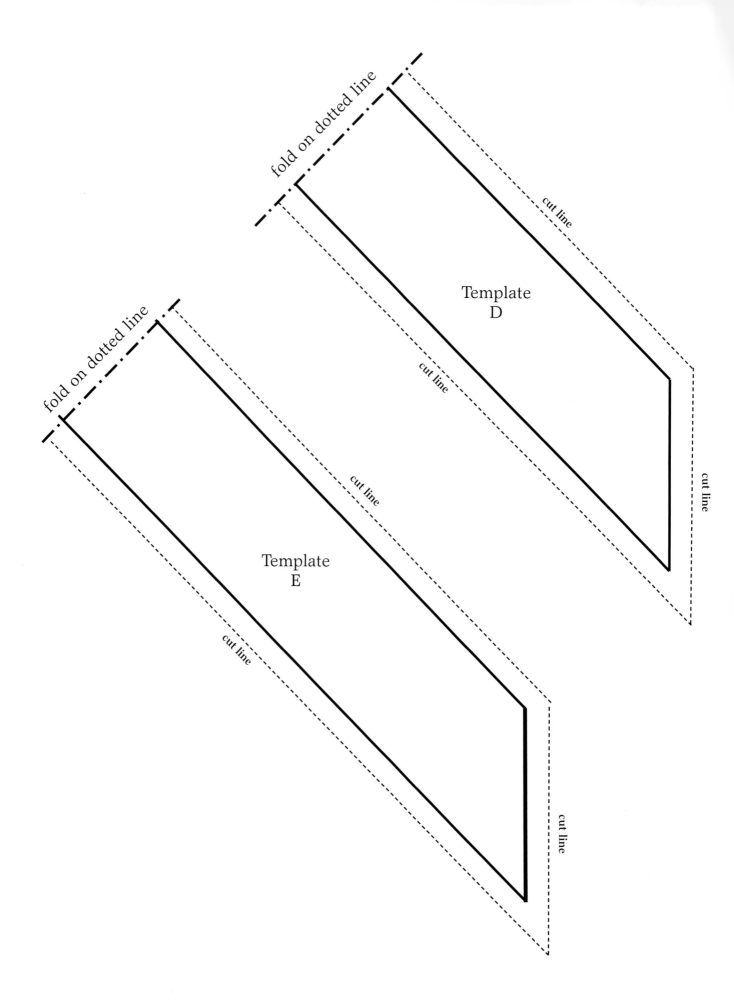

fold on dotted line

cut line

Template
D

cut line

cut line

fold on dotted line

cut line

Template
E

cut line

cut line

Variation 2—98" x 108"

Measurements given with seam allowances.

A — Template given; cut 42
B — Template given; cut 42
C — Template given; cut 42
D — Template given; cut 21 of two different fabrics (42 total)
E — Template given; cut 21 of two different fabrics (42 total)
F — $10^7/8$" x $10^7/8$"; cut 21; then cut in half diagonally
G — $4^1/2$" x $60^1/2$"; cut 2
H — $4^1/2$" x $78^1/2$"; cut 2
I — $15^1/2$" x $68^1/2$"; cut 2
J — $15^1/2$" x $108^1/2$"; cut 2

Assembly Instructions:

1. To create one Roman Stripe Block 1:
   A. Sew Template A to Template B.
   B. Sew Template C to A/B Unit.
   D. Sew Template D to A/B/C Unit.
   E. Sew Template E to A/B/C/D Unit.
   F. Sew Template F to A/B/C/D/E Unit to create block.
   G. Repeat steps 1A through 1F 20 more times. (21 blocks total.)

2. To create one Roman Stripe Block 2:
   Repeat steps 1A through 1F 21 times, using different fabrics for Templates B, D, and E than you used in Block 1.

3. See How to Assemble Your Quilt, Diagram 1, page 12.

4. Follow Border Application Diagram on page 13 to complete your quilt, using Templates G through J.

Block 1

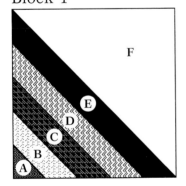

Block 2

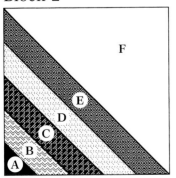

Fabric Requirements

 — $1^7/8$ yds.

— $7^7/8$ yds.

— $3^3/8$ yds.

— $1^3/8$ yds.

— $1^7/8$ yds.

— $1^1/2$ yds.

Backing—
   If using horizontal seams—9 yds.
   If using vertical seams—$8^1/8$ yds.

Batting—103" x 113"

Variation 2

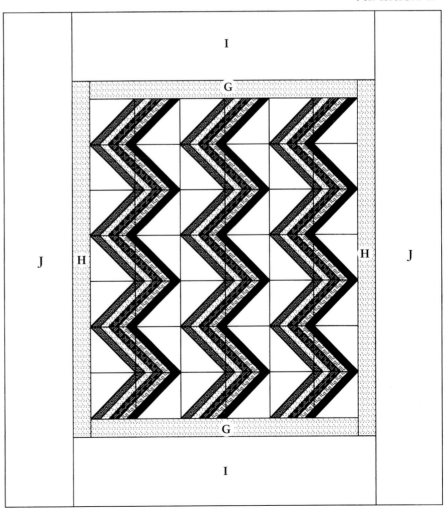

Tumbling Blocks

Approximate size—98" x 107½"

Measurements given with seam allowances.

A — Template given; cut 108
B — Template given; cut 108
C — Template given; cut 93
D — Template given; cut 12
E — Template given; cut 18
F — 3½" x 67½"; cut 2
G — 3½" x 83"; cut 2
H — 13" x 73½"; cut 2
I — 13" x 108"; cut 2

Assembly Instructions:

1. Sew one Template A to one Template B. Sew Template C to the top of A/B Unit. Repeat 92 more times. (93 blocks total.)

2. Sew one Template A to one Template B. Sew Template E to top of A/B Unit. Repeat 8 more times (9 blocks total).

3. Sew one Template B to one Template D. Repeat 5 more times. (6 blocks total.)

4. Sew one Template A to one Template D. Repeat 5 more times. (6 blocks total.)

5. Sew 8 A/B/C Units together to create a horizontal strip. Sew one D/B unit to left end of strip and one A/D unit to right. Repeat 5 times. (6 horizontal strips total.)

6. Sew 9 A/B/C Units together to create a horizontal strip. Repeat 4 times. (5 strips total.)

7. Sew 9 A/B/E Units together to create a horizontal strip.

8. Sew strip from Step 7 to strip from Step 5. Add strip from Step 6. Continue alternating strips from Step 5 and strips from Step 6, until all strips are used.

9. Sew 9 Template E's along bottom of quilt.

10. Follow Border Application Diagram on page 13 to complete your quilt, using Templates F through I.

Fabric Requirements

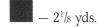 — 2⅛ yds.

☐ — 4½ yds.

▦ — 9 yds.

Backing—If using horizontal seams—9 yds.
If using vertical seams—8⅛ yds.

Batting—103" x 112½"

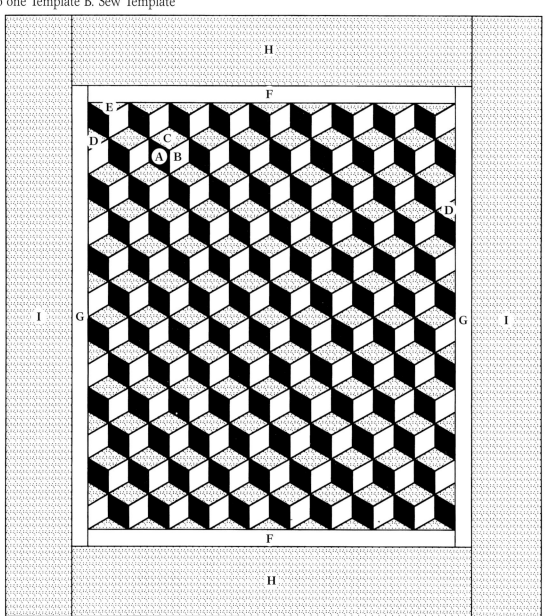

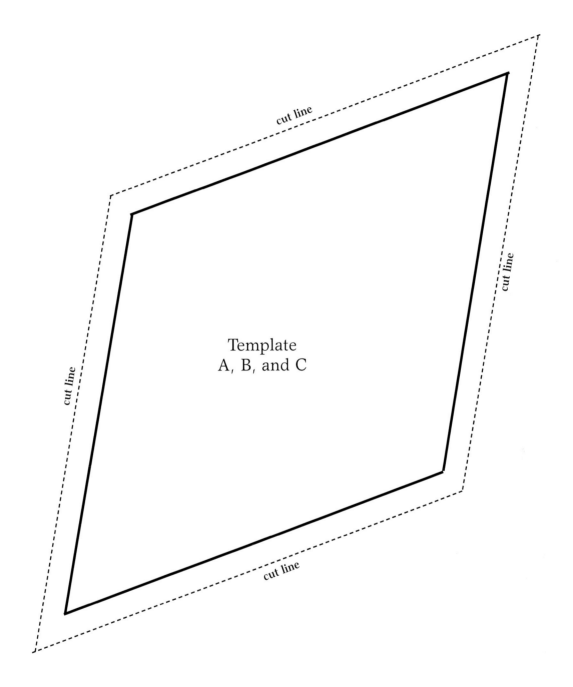

Template
A, B, and C

cut line

cut line

cut line

cut line

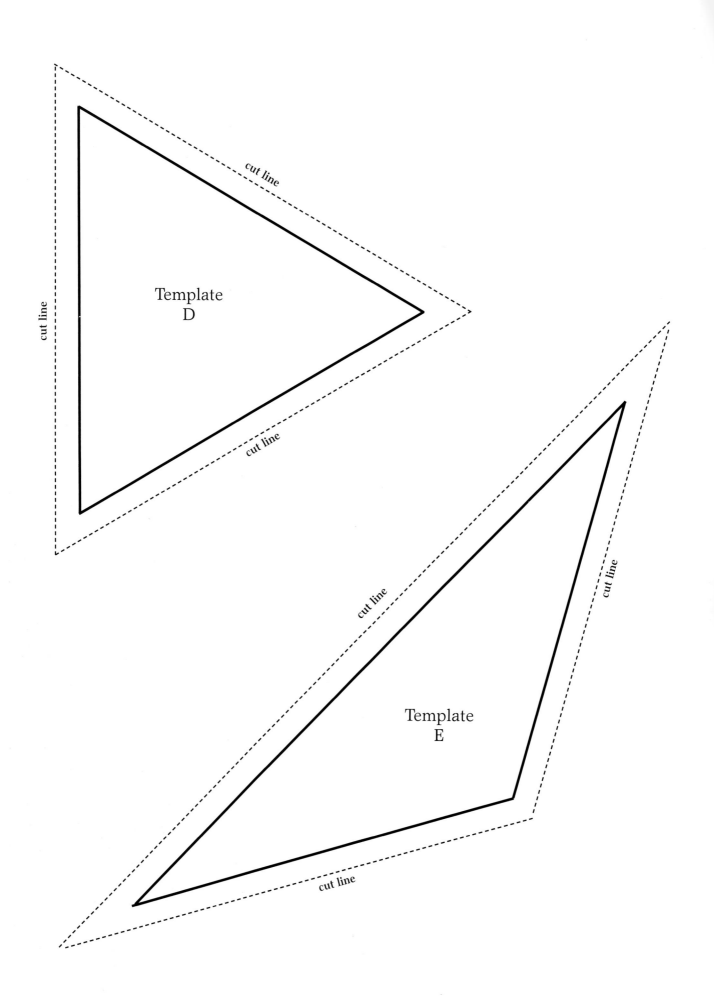

Template
D

cut line

cut line

cut line

Template
E

cut line

cut line

cut line

Rail Fence

Approximate size—96" x 108"

Measurements given with seam allowances.
- A — 1½" x 3½"; cut 672
- B — 1½" x 3½"; cut 672
- C — 1½" x 3½"; cut 672
- D — 3½" x 72½"; cut 2
- E — 3½" x 90½"; cut 2
- F — 9½" x 78½"; cut 2
- G — 9½" x 108½"; cut 2

Fabric Requirements

 — 2⅜ yds.

 — 2⅞ yds.

 — 5⅜ yds.

Backing—If using horizontal seams—9 yds.
If using vertical seams—8 yds.

Batting—101" x 113"

Assembly Instructions:

1. Sew one Template A to one Template B. Sew Template C to A/B Unit. Repeat 671 more times. (672 blocks total.)

2. Sew together A/B/C Units to form strips as shown on diagram below.

3. Sew together strips.

4. Follow Border Application Diagram on page 13 to complete your quilt, using Templates D through G.

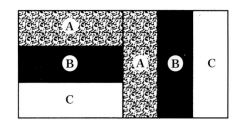

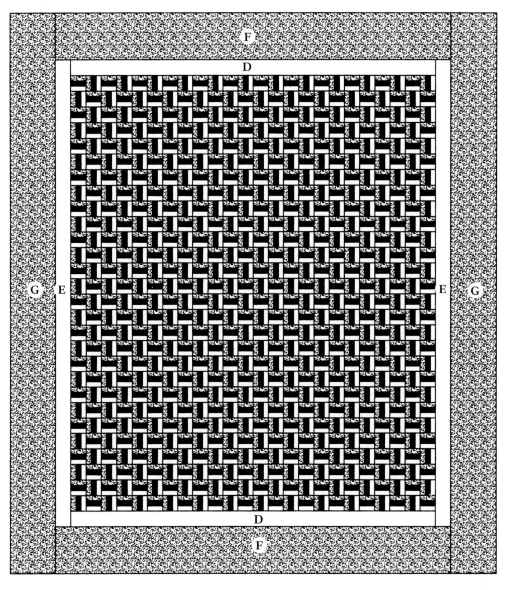

Bow Tie

Variation 1—95″ x 108″

Measurements given with seam allowances.
- A — Template given; cut 120
- B — Template given; cut 480 (240 each of 2 fabrics)
- C — $3\frac{1}{2}$″ x $65\frac{1}{2}$″; cut 2
- D — $3\frac{1}{2}$″ x $84\frac{1}{2}$″; cut 2
- E — $12\frac{1}{2}$″ x $71\frac{1}{2}$″; cut 2
- F — $12\frac{1}{2}$″ x $108\frac{1}{2}$″; cut 2

Assembly Instructions:

1. To create one Bow Tie Block:

   A. Sew one Template B to one side of Template A.

   B. Sew another Template B (of matching fabric to the First Template B) to the opposite side of Template A.

   C. Sew a Template B of different fabric to each of the remaining sides of Template A.

   D. Repeat 119 more times. (120 blocks total.)

2. See How to Assemble Your Quilt, Diagram 1, page 12.

3. Follow Border Application Diagram on page 13 to complete your quilt, using Templates C through F.

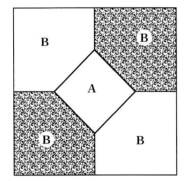

Fabric Requirements

 — $5\frac{3}{4}$ yds.

— $7\frac{3}{8}$ yds.

Backing—If using horizontal seams—9 yds.
If using vertical seams—$8\frac{1}{8}$ yds.

Batting—100″ x 113″

Variation 1

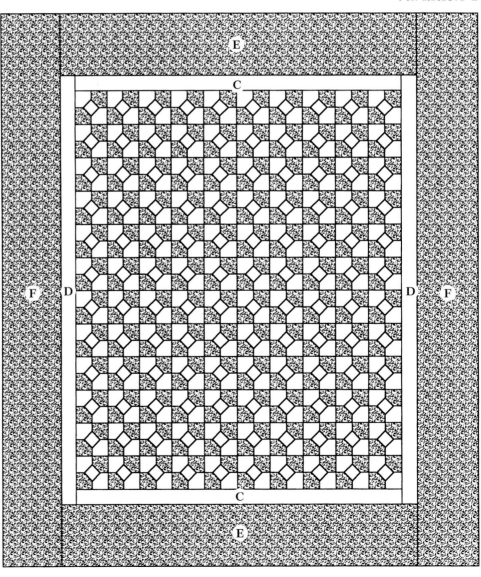

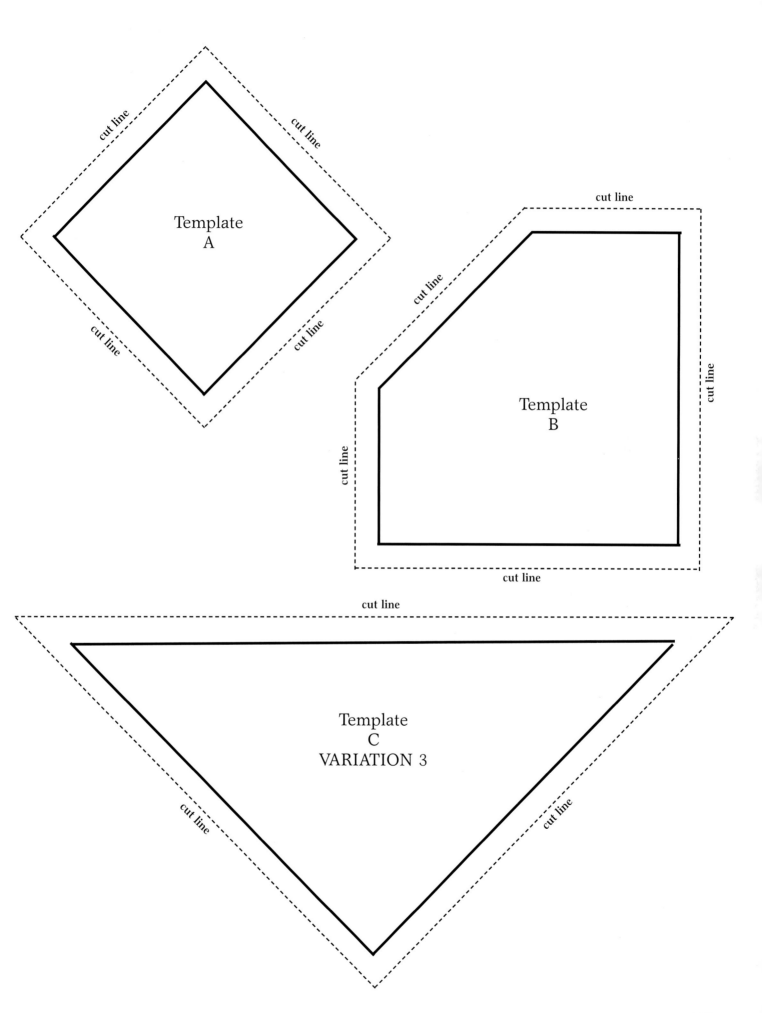

Template
A

cut line
cut line
cut line
cut line

cut line

Template
B

cut line

cut line

cut line

cut line

cut line

Template
C
VARIATION 3

cut line

cut line

179

Variation 2—95" x 108"

Measurements given with seam allowances.

- A — Template given; cut 60
- B — Template given; cut 240 (120 each of 2 fabrics)
- C — 7" x 7"; cut 60
- D — 3$\frac{1}{2}$" x 65$\frac{1}{2}$"; cut 2
- E — 3$\frac{1}{2}$" x 84$\frac{1}{2}$"; cut 2
- F — 12$\frac{1}{2}$" x 71$\frac{1}{2}$"; cut 2
- G — 12$\frac{1}{2}$" x 108$\frac{1}{2}$"; cut 2

Assembly Instructions:

1. To create one Bow Tie Block:

    A. Sew one Template B to one side of Template A.

    B. Sew another Template B (of matching fabric to the first Template B) to the opposite side of Template A.

    C. Sew a Template B of different fabric to each of the remaining sides of Template A.

    D. Repeat 59 more times. (60 blocks total.)

2. See How to Assemble Your Quilt, Diagram 1, page 12.

3. Follow Border Application Diagram on page 13 to complete your quilt, using Templates D through G.

Fabric Requirements

 — $\frac{5}{8}$ yd.

 — 5$\frac{3}{4}$ yds.

— 9 yds.

Backing—If using horizontal seams—9 yds.
    If using vertical seams—8$\frac{1}{8}$ yds.

Batting—100" x 113"

Variation 2

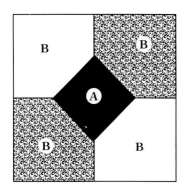

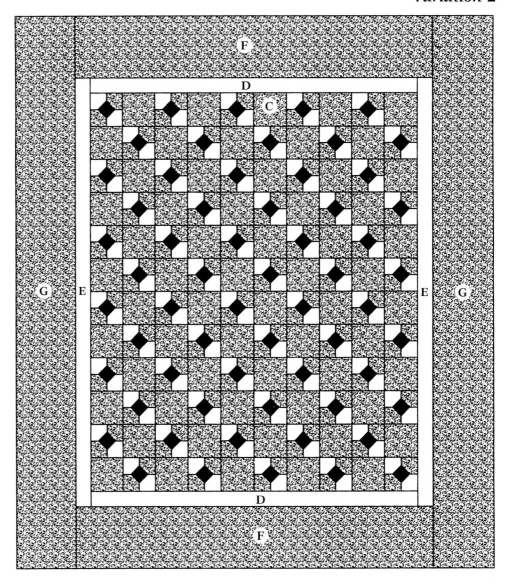

180

Variation 3—92¹/₂″ x 110³/₄″

Measurements given with seam allowances.

- A — Template given; cut 63
- B — Template given; cut 252 (126 each of 2 fabrics)
- C — Template given; cut 4
- D — 7³/₈″ x 7³/₈″; cut 14; then cut in half diagonally
- E — 7″ x 7″; cut 48
- F — 3¹/₂″ x 65³/₄″; cut 2
- G — 3¹/₂″ x 90¹/₂″; cut 2
- H — 11¹/₂″ x 71³/₄″; cut 2
- I — 11¹/₂″ x 113″; cut 2

Fabric Requirements

 — 10 yds.

 — 2³/₈ yds.

 — 4¹/₄ yds.

Backing—If using horizontal seams—9¹/₄ yds.
If using vertical seams—7³/₄ yds.

Batting—97¹/₂″ x 115³/₄″

Assembly Instructions:

1. To create one Bow Tie Block:

   A. Sew one Template B to one side of Template A.

   B. Sew another Template B (of matching fabric to the first Template B) to the opposite side of Template A.

   C. Sew a Template B of different fabric to each of the remaining sides of Template A.

   D. Repeat 62 more times. (63 blocks total.)

2. See How to Assemble Your Quilt, Diagram 2, page 12.

3. Follow Border Application Diagram on page 13 to complete your quilt, using Templates F through I.

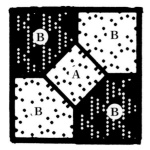

Variation 3

Robbing Peter to Pay Paul

Approximate size—98" x 108"

Measurements given with seam allowances.
  A — Template given; cut 224 (112 each of 2 fabrics)
  B — Template given; cut 56 (28 each of 2 fabrics)
  C — $3\frac{1}{2}$" x $70\frac{1}{2}$"; cut 2
  D — $3\frac{1}{2}$" x $86\frac{1}{2}$"; cut 2
  E — $11\frac{1}{2}$" x $76\frac{1}{2}$"; cut 2
  F — $11\frac{1}{2}$" x $108\frac{1}{2}$"; cut 2

Assembly Instructions:
  1. To create one Robbing Peter to Pay Paul Block:
    A. Sew one Template A to one side of Template B.
    B. Sew another Template A to the opposite side of Template B.
    C. Sew another Template A to each of the remaining sides of Template B.
    D. Repeat 56 times, always using matching fabrics for Template A pieces, and a contrasting fabric for Template B. (55 blocks total.)
  2. See How to Assemble Your Quilt, Diagram 1, page 12.
  3. Follow Border Application Diagram on page 13 to complete your quilt, using Templates C through F.

Fabric Requirements

 — $13\frac{7}{8}$ yds.

 — $11\frac{1}{8}$ yds.

Backing—If using horizontal seams—9 yds.
        If using vertical seams—$8\frac{1}{8}$ yds.

Batting—103" x 113"

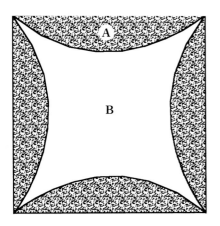

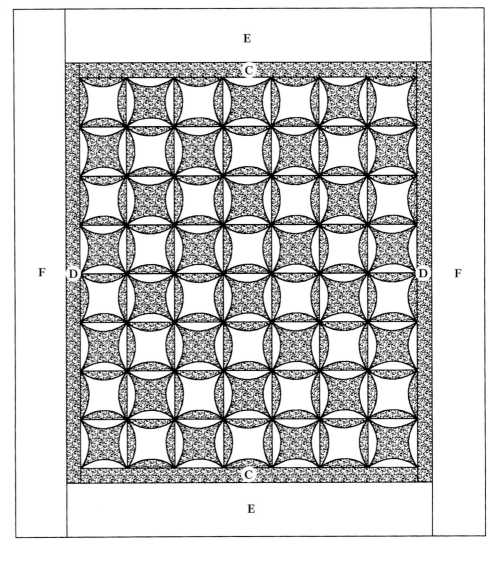

182

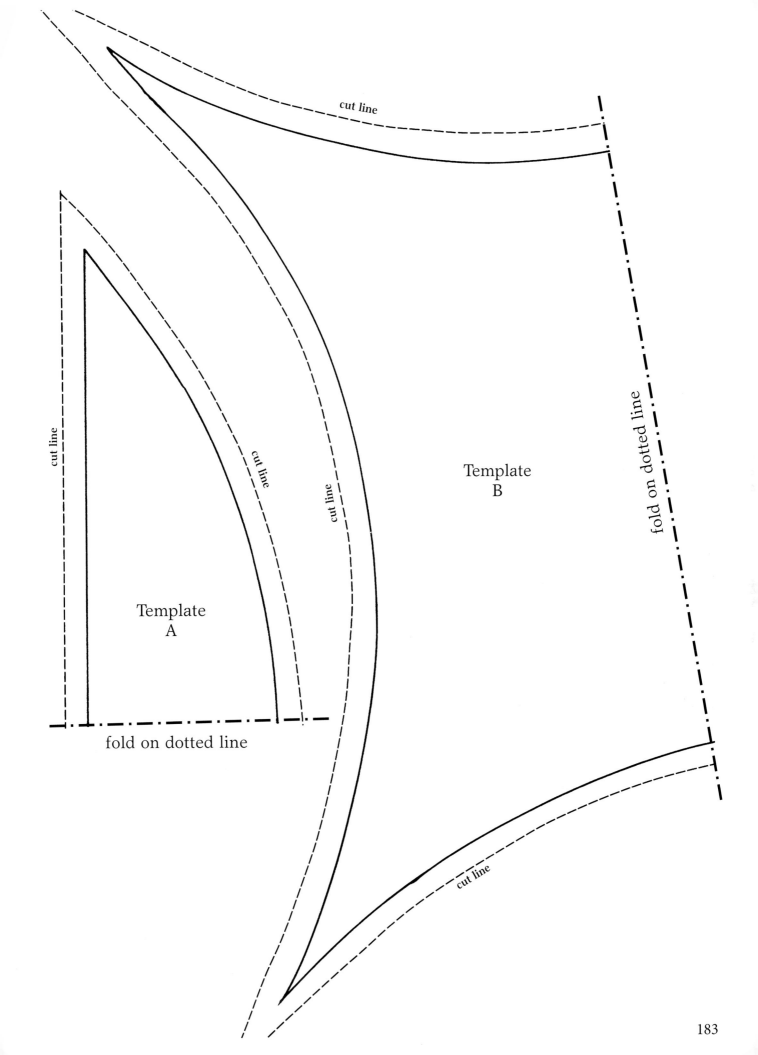

cut line

Template
B

fold on dotted line

cut line

cut line

cut line

Template
A

cut line

fold on dotted line

cut line

Shoo-Fly

Approximate size—94" x 111"

Measurements given with seam allowances.

- A — $4^1/2$" x $4^1/2$"; cut 20
- B — $4^7/8$" x $4^7/8$"; cut 40; then cut in half diagonally
- C — $4^7/8$" x $4^7/8$"; cut 40; then cut in half diagonally
- D — $4^1/2$" x $4^1/2$"; cut 80
- E — $12^1/2$" x $12^1/2$"; cut 12
- F — $12^7/8$" x $12^7/8$"; cut 7; then cut in half diagonally
- G — $9^3/8$" x $9^3/8$"; cut 2; then cut in half diagonally
- H — $3^1/2$" x $68^3/8$"; cut 2
- I — $3^1/2$" x $91^3/8$"; cut 2
- J — $10^1/2$" x $74^3/8$"; cut 2
- K — $10^1/2$" x $111^3/8$"; cut 2

Fabric Requirements

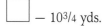 — $10^3/4$ yds.

 — $6^1/2$ yds.

Backing—
  If using horizontal seams—
    $9^1/4$ yds.
  If using vertical seams—
    $7^7/8$ yds.

Batting—99" x 116"

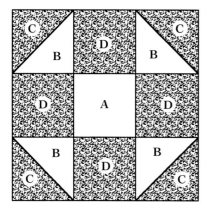

Assembly Instructions:

1. To create one Shoo-fly Block:

A. Sew long sides of Template B and Template C together. Repeat 3 more times. (4 blocks total.)

B. Sew a B/C Unit to opposite sides of Template D. Repeat. (2 horizontal strips total.)

C. Sew a Template D to opposite sides of a Template A.

D. Sew three horizontal strips together as shown on diagram.

E. Repeat steps 1A through 1D 19 more times. (20 blocks total.)

2. See How to Assemble Your Quilt, Diagram 2, page 12.

3. Follow Border Application Diagram on page 13 to complete your quilt using Templates H through K.

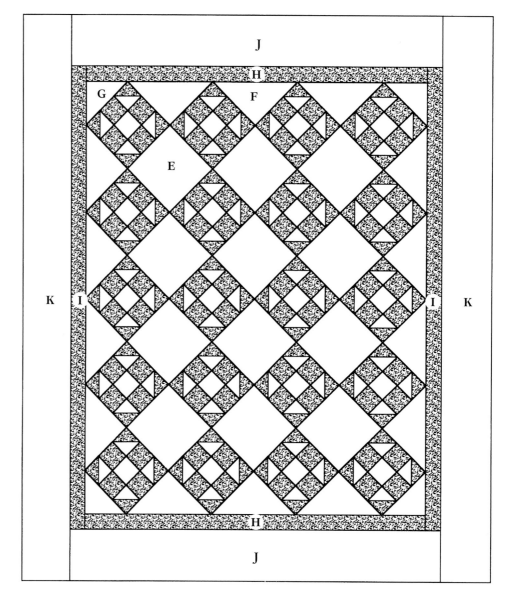

Monkey Wrench

Variation 1—92″ x 108″

Measurements given with seam allowances.

A — 2⅞″ x 2⅞″; cut 100
B — 2⅞″ x 2⅞″; cut 80
C — 5⅞″ x 5⅞″; cut 40; then cut in half diagonally
D — 5⅝″ x 5⅝″; cut 40; then cut in half diagonally
E — 4½″ x 12½″; cut 24
F — 4½″ x 84½″; cut 5
G — 12½″ x 68½″; cut 2
H — 12½″ x 108½″; cut 2

Assembly Instructions:

1. To create one Monkey Wrench Block:

A. Sew long sides of Template C and Template D together. Repeat 3 more times. (4 blocks total.)

B. Sew a Template A to a Template B. Repeat. (2 strips total.)

C. Sew two C/D Units to opposite sides of an A/B Unit. Make a second such strip.

D. Sew a Template A to a Template B. Sew a Template A to the A/B Unit. Sew a Template B to the A/B/A Unit. Sew a Template A to the A/B/A/B Unit.

E. Sew the three strips together as shown on diagram to create block.

F. Repeat steps 1A through 1E, 19 more times. (20 blocks total.)

2. Sew a Template E to top of a block. Repeat 19 more times. (20 blocks total.)

3. Sew together 5 blocks to create strip. Repeat 3 more times. (4 strips total.)

4. Sew a Template E to the bottom of each strip.

5. Sew a Template F to the left of each strip.

6. Sew strips together. Sew a Template F to the right of the final block.

7. Follow Border Application Diagram on page 13 to complete your quilt, using Templates G and H.

Fabric Requirements

☐ — 7½ yds.

▦ — 12⅛ yds.

▩ — 2⅜ yds.

Backing—
    If using horizontal seams—9 yds.
    If using vertical seams—7⅝ yds.

Batting—97″ x 113″

Variation 1

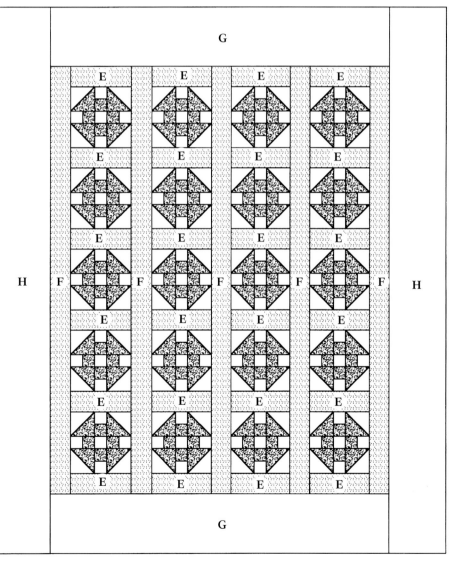

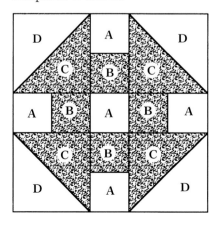

Variation 2—92" x 108"

Measurements given with seam allowances.

- A — Template given; cut 100
- B — Template given; cut 80
- C — 5$\frac{1}{4}$" x 5$\frac{1}{4}$"; cut 40; then cut in half diagonally
- D — 5$\frac{1}{4}$" x 5$\frac{1}{4}$"; cut 40; then cut in half diagonally
- E — 8$\frac{5}{8}$" x 8$\frac{5}{8}$"; cut 2; then cut in half diagonally
- F — 11$\frac{7}{8}$" x 11$\frac{7}{8}$"; cut 7; then cut in half diagonally
- G — 11$\frac{1}{2}$" x 11$\frac{1}{2}$"; cut 12
- H — 15$\frac{1}{2}$" x 63$\frac{1}{4}$"; cut 2
- I — 15$\frac{1}{2}$" x 108$\frac{3}{4}$"; cut 2

Fabric Requirements

 — 2$\frac{3}{8}$ yds.

 — 4$\frac{3}{4}$ yds.

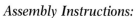 — 6$\frac{7}{8}$ yds.

Backing—
    If using horizontal seams—9 yds.
    If using vertical seams—7$\frac{5}{8}$ yds.

Batting—97" x 113"

Assembly Instructions:

1. To create one Monkey Wrench Block:

    A. Sew long sides of Template C and Template D together. Repeat 3 more times. (4 blocks total.)

    B. Sew a Template A to a Template B. Repeat. (2 strips total.)

    C. Sew a C/D Unit to opposite sides of a vertical A/B Unit. Repeat. (2 strips total.)

    D. Sew a Template A to a Template B. Sew a Template A to the A/B Unit. Sew a Template B to the A/B/A Unit. Sew a Template A to the A/B/A/B Unit.

    E. Sew three strips together as shown on diagram below to create block.

    F. Repeat steps 1A through 1E 19 more times. (20 blocks total.)

2. See How to Assemble Your Quilt, Diagram 2, page 12.

3. Follow Border Application Diagram on page 13 to complete your quilt, using Templates H and I.

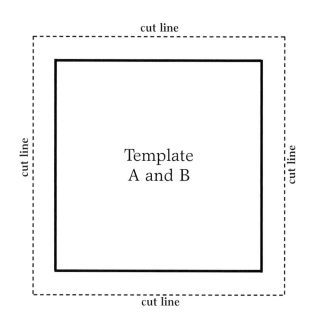

Template
A and B

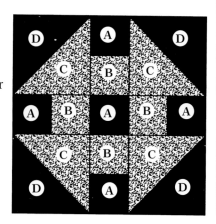

Variation 2

186

Carolina Lily

Approximate size—93" x 109"

Measurements given with seam allowances.

A — Template given; cut 240
B — Template given; cut 60
C — Template given; cut 40
D — Template given; cut 20
E — Template given; cut 40
F — Template given; cut 40
G — Template given; cut 40
H — Template given; cut 40
I — Template given; cut 20
J — Template given; cut 20
K — Template given; cut 40
L — Template given; cut 40
M — Template given; cut 20
N — Template given; cut 60
O — $8^5/8$" x $8^5/8$"; cut 2;
   then cut in half
   diagonally
P — $11^7/8$" x $11^7/8$"; cut 7;
   then cut in half
   diagonally
Q — $11^1/2$" x $11^1/2$"; cut 12
R — 4" x 63"; cut 2
S — 4" x $85^1/4$"; cut 2
T — $12^1/2$" x $69^3/4$"; cut 2
U — $12^1/2$" x $109^1/4$"; cut 2

Fabric Requirements

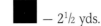 — $2^1/2$ yds.

□ — $14^3/4$ yds.

 — $3^1/4$ yds.

Backing—
   If using horizontal seams—$9^1/8$ yds.
   If using vertical seams—$7^3/4$ yds.

Batting—98" x 114"

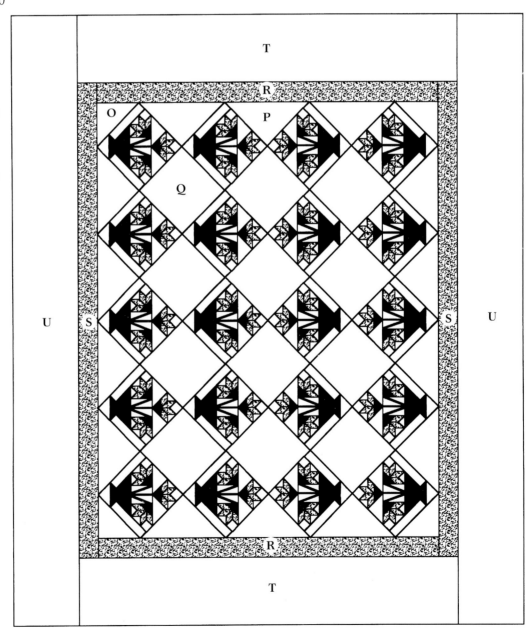

Assembly Instructions:

1. To create one Carolina Lily Block:

   A. Sew together 4 Template A's.

   B. Insert 2 Template C's and 1 Template D into top of A/A/A/A Unit.

   C. Sew Template B to the bottom of Unit to form a square.

   D. Sew a Template H to A/B side of square. Sew another Template H to B/A side of square. (Unit 1.)

   E. Sew together 4 Template A's. Repeat.

   F. Insert a Template E into one corner of A/A/A/A Unit. Insert a Template E into the opposite corner of the second A/A/A/A Unit.

   G. Insert a Template F into the top center of each Unit.

   H. Insert a Template G into the remaining corner of each Unit.

   I. Sew a Template B to the bottom of both Units.

   J. Sew Template I between the two Units to create horizontal strip. (Unit 2.)

   H. Sew bottom of Unit 1 to top of Unit 2. (Unit 3.)

   I. Sew Template J to bottom of Unit 3. (Unit 4.)

   J. Sew Template L to Template K. Repeat.

   K. Sew L/K to lower left side of Unit 4. Sew second L/K to lower right side of Unit 4. (Unit 5.)

   L. Sew Template M to bottom of Unit 5.

   M. Fold under edges of Templates N and slipstitch into position as shown on diagram. Adjust lengths as needed.

   N. Repeat steps 1A through 1M 19 more times. (20 blocks total.)

2. See How to Assemble Your Quilt, Diagram 2, page 12.

3. Follow Border Application Diagram on page 13 to complete your quilt, using Templates R through U.

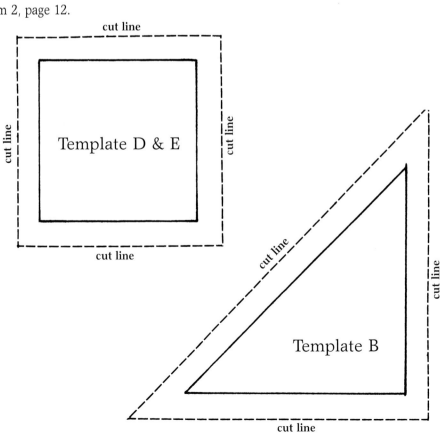

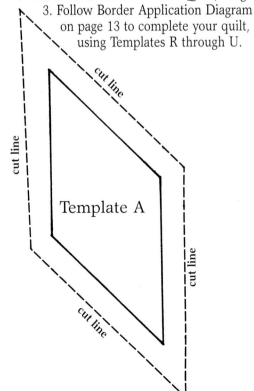

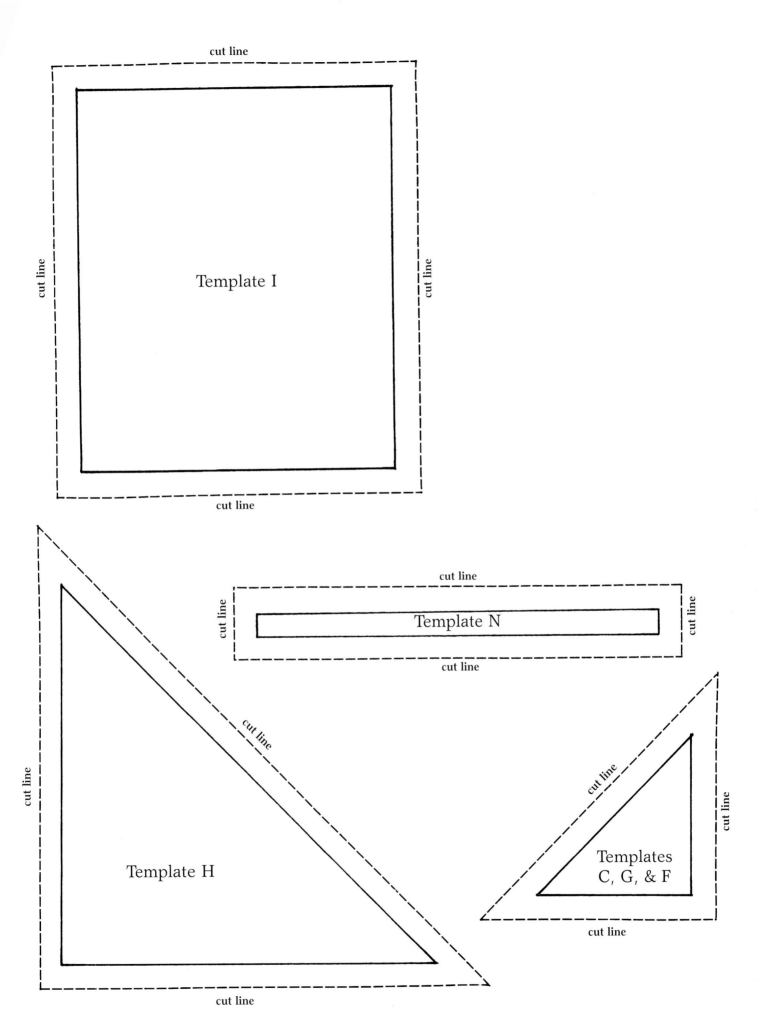

Template I

Template N

Template H

Templates
C, G, & F

cut line

189

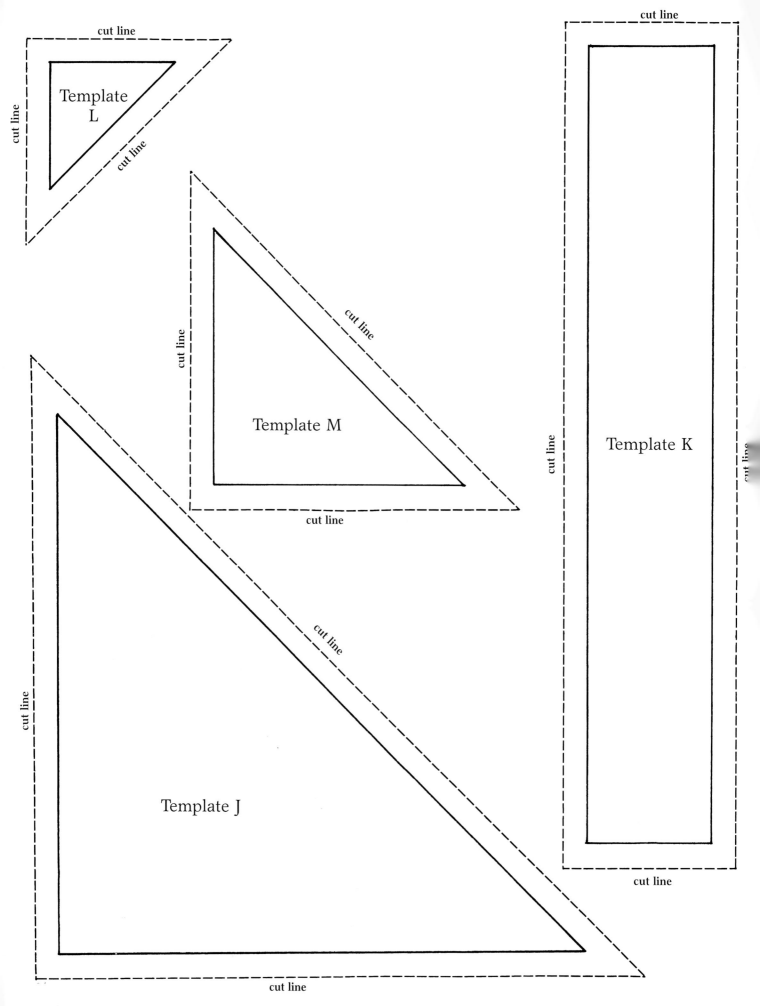

cut line

Template
L

cut line

cut line

cut line

cut line

cut line

Template K

cut line

Template M

cut line

cut line

Template J

cut line

cut line

cut line

190

Crown of Thorns

Approximate size—93½" x 109½"

Measurements given with seam allowances.

A — 2¾" x 2¾"; cut 100
B — 2¾" x 2¾"; cut 80
C — 3⅛" x 3⅛"; cut 160; then cut in half diagonally
D — 3⅛" x 3⅛"; cut 160; then cut in half diagonally
E — 8⅞" x 8⅞"; cut 2; then cut in half diagonally
F — 12⅛" x 12⅛"; cut 7; then cut in half diagonally
G — 11¾" x 11¾"; cut 12
H — 3½" x 64⅛"; cut 2
I — 3½" x 86"; cut 2
J — 12½" x 70⅛"; cut 2
K — 12½" x 110"; cut 2

Fabric Requirements

 — 8⅜ yds.

 — 5⅝ yds.

 — 5⅛ yds.

Backing—If using horizontal seams—9⅛ yds.
If using vertical seams—7¾ yds.

Batting—98½" x 114½"

Assembly Instructions:

1. To create one Crown of Thorns Block:

A. Sew long side of Template D to long side of Template C. Repeat 15 more times. (16 blocks total.)

B. Sew together Row 1, working from left to right.

C. Sew together Row 2, working from left to right.

D. Repeat with 3 remaining rows.

E. Sew Strip 1 to Strip 2.

F. Sew Strip 3 to other side of Strip 2.

G. Repeat with remaining strips.

H. Repeat Steps 1A through Step 1G 19 more times. (20 blocks total.)

2. See How to Assemble Your Quilt, Diagram 2, page 12.

3. Follow Border Application Diagram on page 13 to complete your quilt, using Templates H through K.

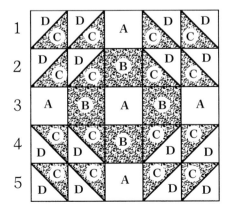

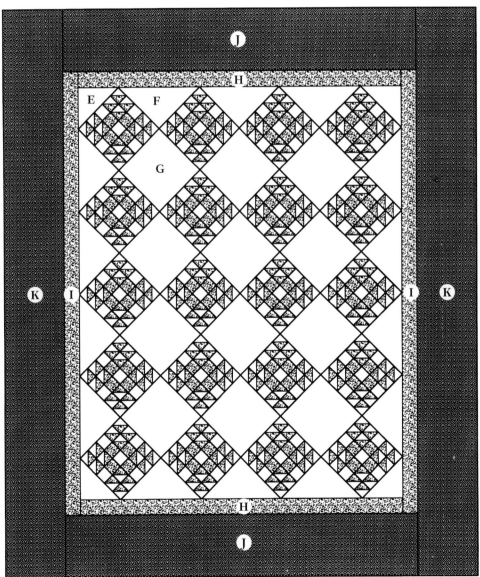

191

Bear Paw

Approximate size—93¹/₂" x 109"

Measurements given with seam allowances.

  A — 2" x 2"; cut 20
  B — 5" x 2"; cut 80
  C — 3¹/₂" x 3¹/₂"; cut 80
  D — 2³/₈" x 2³/₈"; cut 160; then cut in half diagonally
  E — 2³/₈" x 2³/₈"; cut 160; then cut in half diagonally
  F — 2" x 2"; cut 80
  G — 8³/₈" x 8³/₈"; cut 2; then cut in half diagonally
  H — 11³/₈" x 11³/₈"; cut 7; then cut in half diagonally
  I — 10¹/₂" x 10¹/₂"; cut 12
  J — 4¹/₂" x 59⁷/₈"; cut 2
  K — 4¹/₂" x 83"; cut 2
  L — 13¹/₂" x 67⁷/₈"; cut 2
  M — 13¹/₂" x 108³/₄"; cut 2

Fabric Requirements

☐ — 13⁷/₈ yds.

▨ — 6³/₈ yds.

Backing—
  If using horizontal seams—9 yds.
  If using vertical seams—7³/₄ yds.

Batting—98¹/₂" x 113"

Assembly Instructions:

1. To create one Bear Paw Block:

A. Sew long sides of Template D and Template E together. Repeat 15 more times. (16 blocks total.)

B. Sew a D/E Unit to another D/E Unit. Repeat 7 more times. (8 strips total.)

C. Sew a Template C to a D/E Unit. Repeat 3 more times. (4 blocks total.)

D. Sew a Template F to end of a D/E square. Repeat 3 more times. (4 strips total.)

E. Sew D/E/F Strip to C/D/E Strip to create block. Repeat 3 more times (4 blocks total) to create Unit 1.

F. Sew a Unit 1 to the long side of a Template B. Sew another Unit 1 to the other long side of the same Template B. Repeat. (2 strips total.)

G. Sew Template A to the short end of a Template B. Sew the short end of another Template B to the opposite side of the same Template A.

H. Sew three strips together as shown on diagram.

I. Repeat steps 1A through 1H 19 more times. (20 blocks total.)

2. See How to Assemble Your Quilt, Diagram 2, page 12.

3. Follow Border Application Diagram on page 13 to complete your quilt, using Templates J through M.

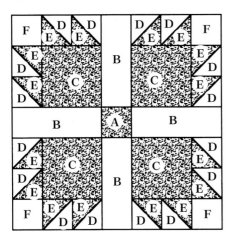

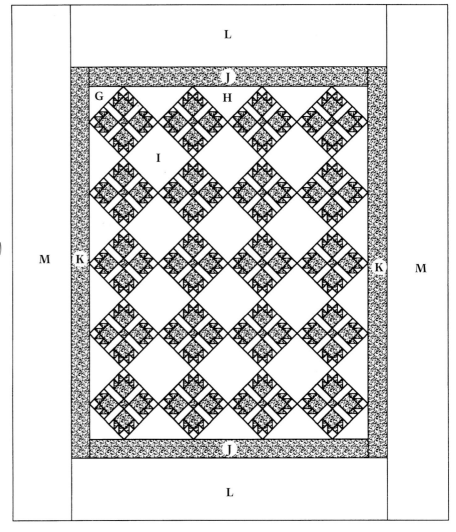

192

Pinwheel

Variation 1—92" x 108"
Measurements given with seam allowances.

A — Template given; cut 80
B — 4¾" x 4¾"; cut 40; then cut in half diagonally
C — 8⅝" x 8⅝"; cut 2; then cut in half diagonally
D — 11⅞" x 11⅞"; cut 7; then cut in half diagonally
E — 11½" x 11½"; cut 12
F — 3½" x 62¾"; cut 2
G — 3½" x 102¼"; cut 2
H — 12½" x 68¾"; cut 2
I — 12½" x 108¼"; cut 2

Fabric Requirements

☐ — 13⅞ yds.

▦ — 13⅞ yds.

▨ — 6⅜ yds.

Backing—
    If using horizontal seams—9 yds.
    If using vertical seams—7⅝ yds.

Batting—97" x 113"

Assembly Instructions:

1. To create one Pinwheel Block:
    A. Sew Template B to Template A. Repeat 3 times. (4 triangles total.)
    B. Sew Unit B/A to Unit B/A. Repeat. (Unit 1).
    C. Sew Unit 1 to Unit 1 to create block below.
    D. Repeat steps 1A through 1C 19 more times. (20 blocks total.)
2. See How to Assemble Your Quilt, Diagram 2, page 12.
3. Follow Border Application Diagram on page 13 to complete your quilt using Templates F through I.

Variation 1

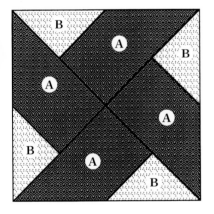

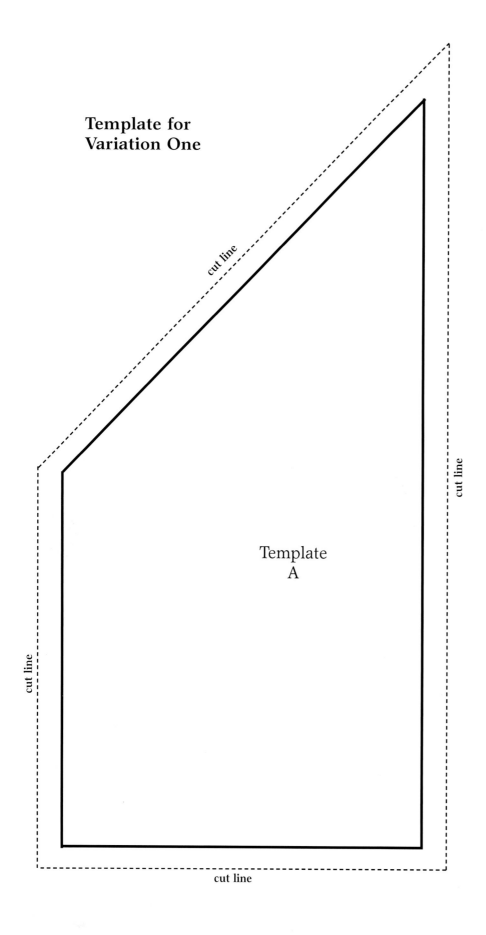

**Template for
Variation One**

cut line

cut line

cut line

Template
A

cut line

194

Variation 2—92" x 108"

Measurements given with seam allowances.

- A — 4³/₄" x 4³/₄"; cut 40; then cut in half diagonally
- B — 3⁵/₈" x 3⁵/₈"; cut 80; then cut in half diagonally
- C — 3¹/₄" x 6"; cut 80
- D — 8⁵/₈" x 8⁵/₈"; cut 2; then cut in half diagonally
- E — 11⁷/₈" x 11⁷/₈"; cut 7; then cut in half diagonally
- F — 11¹/₂" x 11¹/₂"; cut 12
- G — 3¹/₂" x 62³/₄"; cut 2
- H — 3¹/₂" x 102¹/₄"; cut 2
- I — 12¹/₂" x 68¹/₄"; cut 2
- J — 12¹/₂" x 108¹/₄"; cut 2

Assembly Instructions:

1. To create one Pinwheel Block:

A. Sew Template B to Template A. Sew another Template B to the other side of Template A. Repeat 3 times. (4 strips total.)

B. Sew Template C to A/B Unit. Repeat 3 times. (4 blocks total.)

C. Sew 4 blocks together as shown to create large block.

D. Repeat steps 1A through 1C 19 more times. (20 blocks total.)

2. See How to Assemble Your Quilt, Diagram 2, page 12.

3. Follow Border Application Diagram on page 13 to complete your quilt, using Templates G through J.

Fabric Requirements

— 4³/₄ yds.

— 3¹/₂ yds.

— 7¹/₄ yds.

— 1 yd.

Backing—
If using horizontal seams—9 yds.
If using vertical seams—7⁵/₈ yds.

Batting—97" x 113"

Variation 2

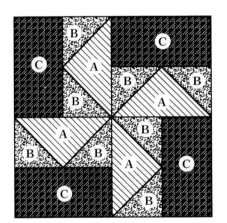

Variation 3—92" x 108"

Measurements given with seam allowances.

A — 4³/₄" x 4³/₄"; cut 40; then cut in half diagonally
B — 3⁵/₈" x 3⁵/₈"; cut 80; then cut in half diagonally
C — 4³/₄" x 4³/₄"; cut 40; then cut in half diagonally
D — 3⁵/₈" x 3⁵/₈"; cut 80; then cut in half diagonally
E — 8⁵/₈" x 8⁵/₈"; cut 2; then cut in half diagonally
F — 11⁷/₈" x 11⁷/₈"; cut 7; then cut in half diagonally
G — 11¹/₂" x 11¹/₂"; cut 12
H — 3¹/₂" x 62³/₄"; cut 2
I — 3¹/₂" x 102¹/₄"; cut 2
J — 12¹/₂" x 68³/₄"; cut 2
K — 12¹/₂" x 108¹/₄"; cut 2

Fabric Requirements

 — 9³/₄ yds.

 — 3 yds.

 — 5³/₈ yds.

Backing—
 If using horizontal seams—9 yds.
 If using vertical seams—7⁵/₈ yds.

Batting—97" x 113"

Assembly Instructions:

1. To create one Pinwheel Block:

A. Sew Template B to Template A. Sew another Template B to the other side of Template A. Repeat 3 times. (4 strips total.)

B. Sew Template D to Template C. Sew another Template D to the other side of Template C. Repeat 3 times. (4 strips total.)

C. Sew A/B Unit to C/D Unit. Repeat 3 times. (4 blocks total).

D. Sew 4 blocks together as shown to create large block.

E. Repeat steps 1A through 1D 19 more times. (20 blocks total.)

2. See How to Assemble Your Quilt, Diagram 2, page 12.

3. Follow Border Application Diagram on page 13 to complete your quilt, using Templates H through K.

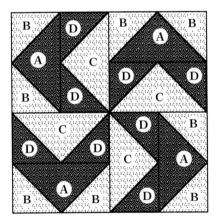

Variation 3

196

Garden Maze

Approximate size—96" x 111"

Measurements given with seam allowances.

A — Template given; cut 30
B — Template given; cut 120
C — Template given; cut 120
D — 2" x 9½"; cut 98
E — 3½" x 9½"; cut 49
F — 9½" x 9½"; cut 20
G — 3½" x 66½"; cut 2
H — 3½" x 87½"; cut 2
I — 12½" x 72½"; cut 2
J — 12½" x 111½"; cut 2

Assembly Instructions:

1. To create one Garden Maze Block:

A. Sew Template C to Template B. Sew another Template C to opposite side of Template B. Repeat.

B. Sew Template A to one end of Template B. Sew another Template B to opposite side of Template A.

C. Sew together 3 pieces, as shown on diagram, to create block.

D. Repeat steps 1A through 1C 29 more times. (30 blocks total.)

2. To create one Garden Maze Strip:

A. Sew long side of a Template D to long side of a Template E. Sew another Template D to opposite side of Template E.

B. Repeat 48 more times. (49 strips total.)

3. Sew an A/B/C Block to each short end of a D/E Strip. Add another D/E Strip. Repeat until you have 5 Blocks and 4 Strips sewn together into a horizontal strip as shown on diagram. Repeat 5 times. (6 strips total.)

4. Sew a D/E Strip to each side of F Block. Add another F Block. Repeat until you have 5 Strips and 4 Blocks sewn together in a horizontal strip as shown on diagram. Repeat 4 times. (5 strips total.)

5. Sew strips together from top to bottom as shown on diagram.

6. See How to Assemble Your Quilt, Diagram 1, on page 12.

7. Follow Border Application Diagram on page 13 to complete your quilt, using Templates G through J.

Fabric Requirements

☐ — 8¼ yds.

▦ — 8⅝ yds.

Backing—
If using horizontal seams—9¼ yds.
If using vertical seams—8 yds.

Batting—101" x 116"

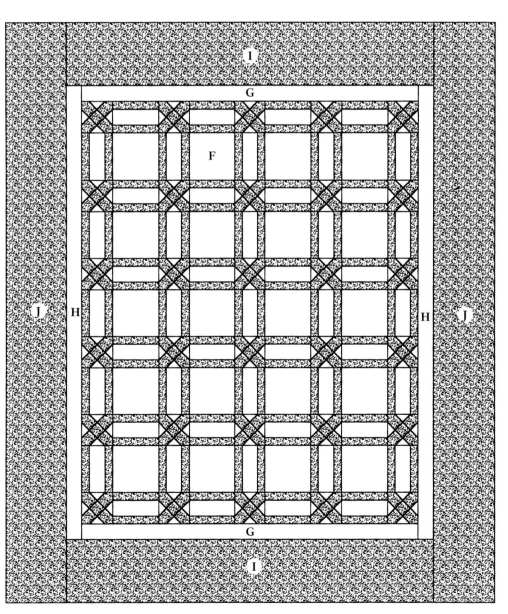

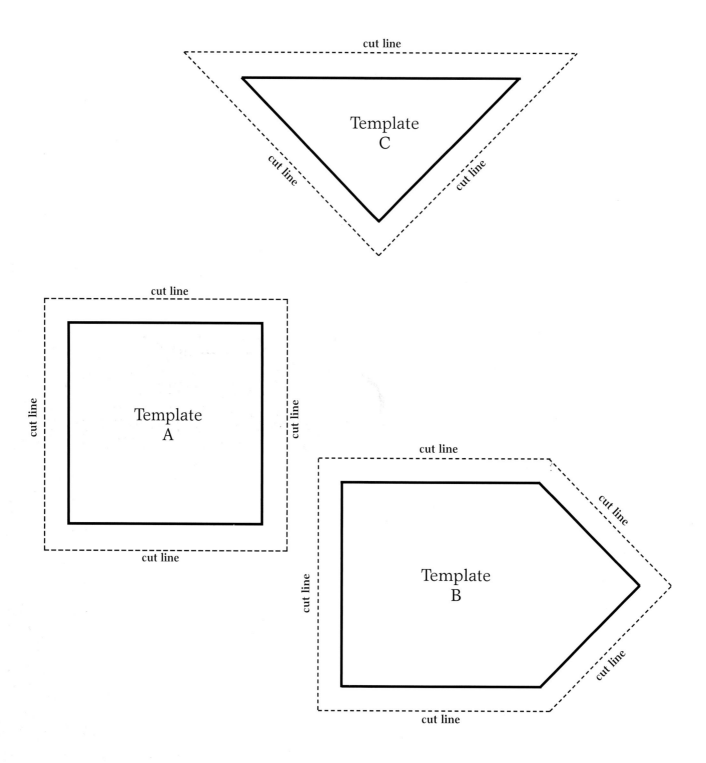

cut line

Template
C

cut line

cut line

cut line

Template
A

cut line

cut line

cut line

cut line

cut line

Template
B

cut line

cut line

cut line

Railroad Crossing

Approximate size—90" x 109½"

Measurements given with seam allowances.

A — 9½" x 9½"; cut 18
B — 1½" x 5"; cut 48
C — 1½" x 5"; cut 96
D — 1½" x 5"; cut 96
E — 1½" x 5"; cut 96
F — 1½" x 5"; cut 96
G — 7¼" x 7¼"; cut 2; then cut in half diagonally
H — 5⅜" x 5⅜"; cut 7; then cut in half diagonally
I — 9⅞" x 9⅞"; cut 5; then cut in half diagonally
J — 5½" x 5½"; cut 17
K — 4" x 57¾"; cut 2
L — 4" x 83⅞"; cut 2
M — 13½" x 64¾"; cut 2
N — 13½" x 109⅞"; cut 2

Fabric Requirements

 — 1¼ yds.

 — 1⅞ yds.

 — 1¼ yds.

 — 1¼ yds.

 — 3½ yds.

 — 9½ yds.

Backing—
　If using horizontal seams—
　　9⅛ yds.
　If using vertical seams—7½ yds.

Batting—95" x 114½"

Assembly Instructions:

1. To create one Railroad Crossing Strip:
　A. Sew Template F to Template E.
　B. Sew Template D to F/E Unit.
　C. Continue adding pieces so that final strip is F/E/D/C/B/C/D/E/F.
　D. Repeat 47 times. (48 strips total.)
2. See How to Assemble Your Quilt, Diagram 1, page 12.
3. Follow Border Application Diagram on page 13 to complete your quilt, using Templates K through N.

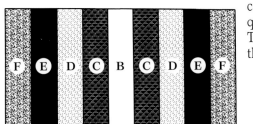

Double Wedding Ring

Approximate size—92" x 109"

Measurements given with seam allowances.

A — 2" x 2"; cut 80
B — Template given; cut 160
C — Template given; cut 160
D — Template given; cut 160
E — Template given; cut 160
F — Template given; cut 160
G — 2" x 2"; cut 80
H — Template given; cut 80
I — Template given; cut 32
J — Template given; cut 14
K — Template given; cut 4
L — 2½" x 68½"; cut 2
M — 2½" x 89½"; cut 2
N — 10½" x 72½"; cut 2
O — 10½" x 109½"; cut 2

Fabric Requirements

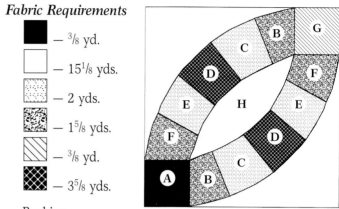

■ — ⅜ yd.
□ — 15⅛ yds.
▓ — 2 yds.
▓ — 1⅝ yds.
▨ — ⅜ yd.
▦ — 3⅝ yds.

Backing—
   If using horizontal seams—9⅛ yds.
   If using vertical seams—7⅝ yds.

Batting—97" x 114"

Assembly Instructions:

1. To create one Double Wedding Ring:
  A. Sew Template C to Template B.
  B. Sew Template D to B/C Unit.
  C. Sew Template E to B/C/D Unit.
  D. Sew Template F to B/C/D/E Unit (Strip 1).
  E. Sew Template H to inside of Strip 1 (Strip 2).
  F. Sew Template B to Template A.
  G. Sew Template C to A/B Unit.
  H. Sew Template D to A/B/C Unit.
  I. Sew Template E to A/B/C/D Unit.
  J. Sew Template F to A/B/C/D/E Unit.
  K. Sew Template G to A/B/C/D/E/F Unit (Strip 3).
  L. Sew Strip 3 to Strip 2 to create oval.
  M. Repeat 79 times (80 ovals total).

2. Sew oval to one side of Template I. Sew a second oval to the top of Template I. Repeat 31 times (32 partial blocks total).

3. Sew 4 blocks together to make strip. Repeat 4 times (5 strips total).

4. Sew 3 partial blocks together to make strip. Repeat 3 times (4 strips total).

5. Sew strip of 4 blocks to strip of 3 blocks. Add a strip of 4 blocks to bottom of strip of 3 blocks. Continue alternating 3 and 4 block strips until all strips are used.

6. Sew a Template K in each corner of the quilt.

7. Sew 4 Template J's along each long side of quilt, and 3 Template J's along the top and along the bottom.

8. Follow Border Application Diagram on page 13 to complete your quilt, using Templates L through O.

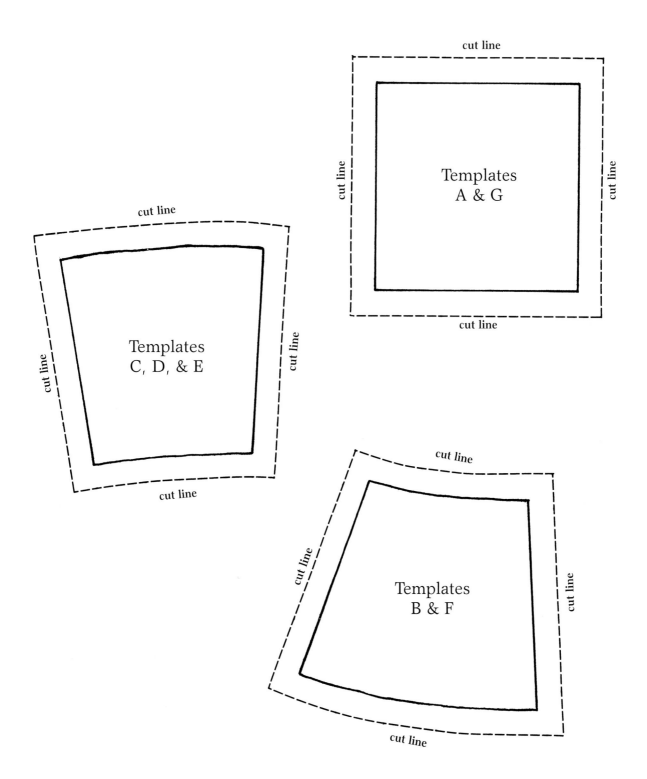

Templates
A & G

cut line
cut line
cut line
cut line

Templates
C, D, & E

cut line
cut line
cut line
cut line

Templates
B & F

cut line
cut line
cut line
cut line

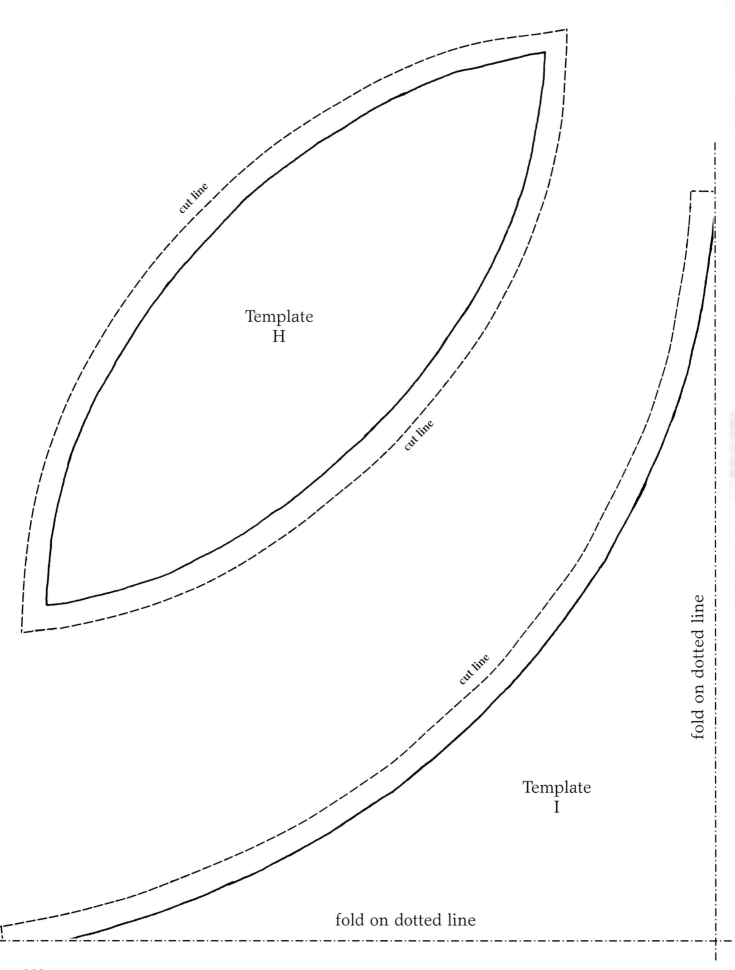

cut line

Template
H

cut line

cut line

Template
I

fold on dotted line

fold on dotted line

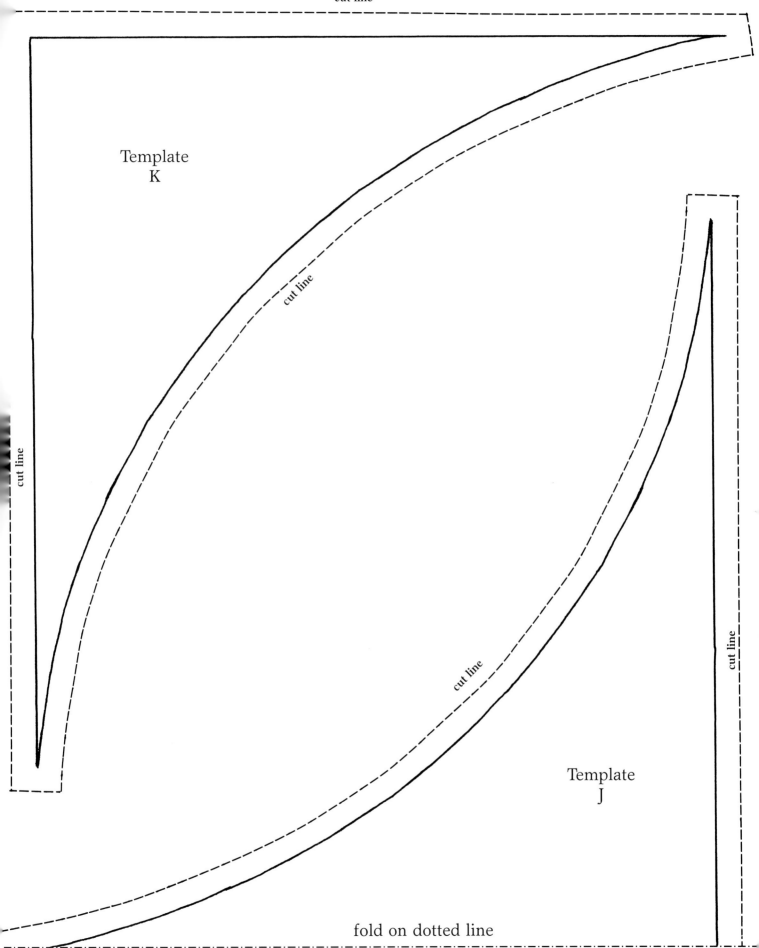

cut line

Template
K

cut line

cut line

cut line

Template
J

cut line

fold on dotted line

Diagonal Triangles

Approximate size—90" x 108"

Measurements given with seam allowances.

A — 3⅞" x 3⅞"; cut 52; then cut in half diagonally
B — 3⅞" x 3⅞"; cut 260; then cut in half diagonally
C — 3⅞" x 3⅞"; cut 52; then cut in half diagonally
D — 3⅞" x 3⅞"; cut 52; then cut in half diagonally
E — 3⅞" x 3⅞"; cut 52; then cut in half diagonally
F — 3⅞" x 3⅞"; cut 52; then cut in half diagonally
G — 3½" x 60½"; cut 2
H — 3½" x 84½"; cut 2
I — 12½" x 66½"; cut 2
J — 12½" x 108½"; cut 2

Fabric Requirements

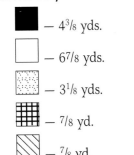

— 4⅜ yds.

— 6⅞ yds.

— 3⅛ yds.

— ⅞ yd.

— ⅞ yd.

— ⅞ yd.

Backing—
  If using horizontal
    seams—9 yds.

  If using vertical seams—
    7½ yds.

Batting—95" x 113"

Assembly Instructions:

1. Sew long side of a Template A to long side of a Template B. Repeat 103 times. (104 blocks total.)

2. Sew long side of a Template C to long side of a Template B. Repeat 103 times. (104 blocks total.)

3. Sew long side of a Template D to long side of a Template B. Repeat 103 times. (104 blocks total.)

4. Sew long side of a Template E to long side of a Template B. Repeat 103 times. (104 blocks total.)

5. Sew long side of a Template F to long side of a Template B. Repeat 103 times. (104 blocks total.)

6. See How to Assemble Your Quilt, Diagram 1, page 12.

7. Follow Border Application Diagram on page 13 to complete your quilt, using Templates G through J.

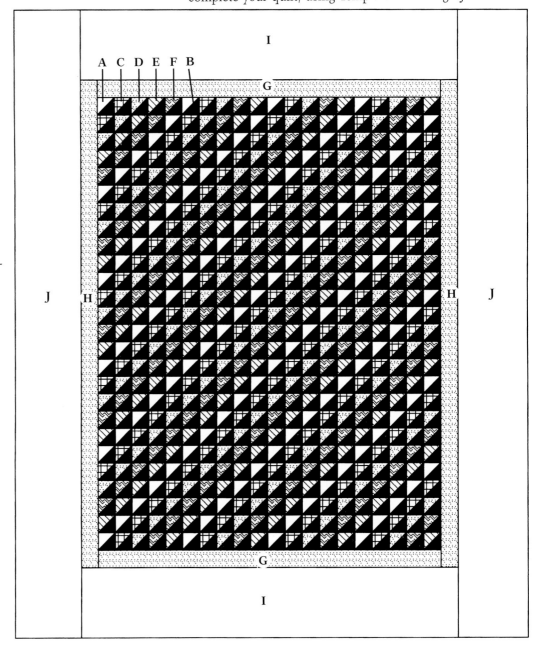

Drunkard's Path

Approximate size—90" x 112"

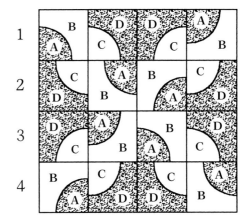

Measurements given with seam allowances.

A — Template given; cut 96
B — Template given; cut 96
C — Template given; cut 96
D — Template given; cut 96
E — $3^1/2$" x $66^1/2$"; cut 2
F — $3^1/2$" x $94^1/2$"; cut 2
G — $9^1/2$" x $72^1/2$"; cut 2
H — $9^1/2$" x $112^1/2$"; cut 2

Assembly Instructions:

1. To create one Drunkard's Path Block:

    A. Sew curved side of Template A to curved side of Template B. Repeat 7 more times. (8 blocks total.)

    B. Sew curved side of Template C to curved side of Template D. Repeat 7 more times. (8 blocks total.)

    C. Sew together Row 1, working from left to right.

    D. Repeat process with Rows 2, 3, and 4.

    E. Sew Row 1 to Row 2.

    F. Sew Row 3 to Row 2.

    G. Sew Row 4 to Row 3 to create block.

    H. Repeat steps 1A through 1G 11 more times. (12 blocks total.)

2. See How to Assemble Your Quilt, Diagram 1, page 12.

3. Follow BOrder Application Diagram on page 13 to complete your quilt, using Templates E through H.

Fabric Requirements

 — $6^5/8$ yds.

 — $7^1/8$ yds.

Backing—If using horizontal
    seams—$9^3/8$ yds.
If using vertical
    seams—$7^1/2$ yds.

Batting—95" x 119"

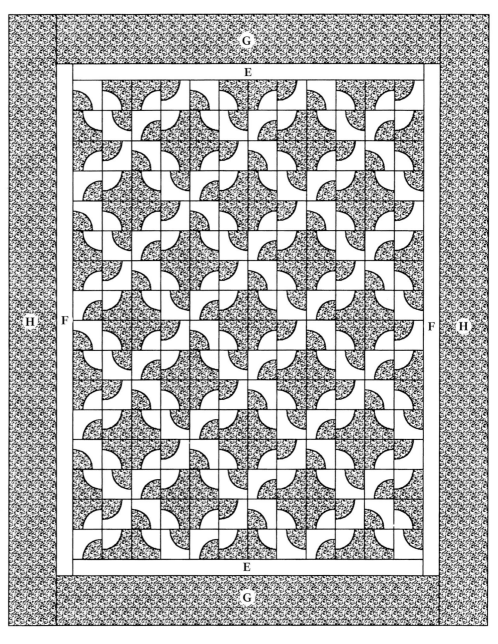

205

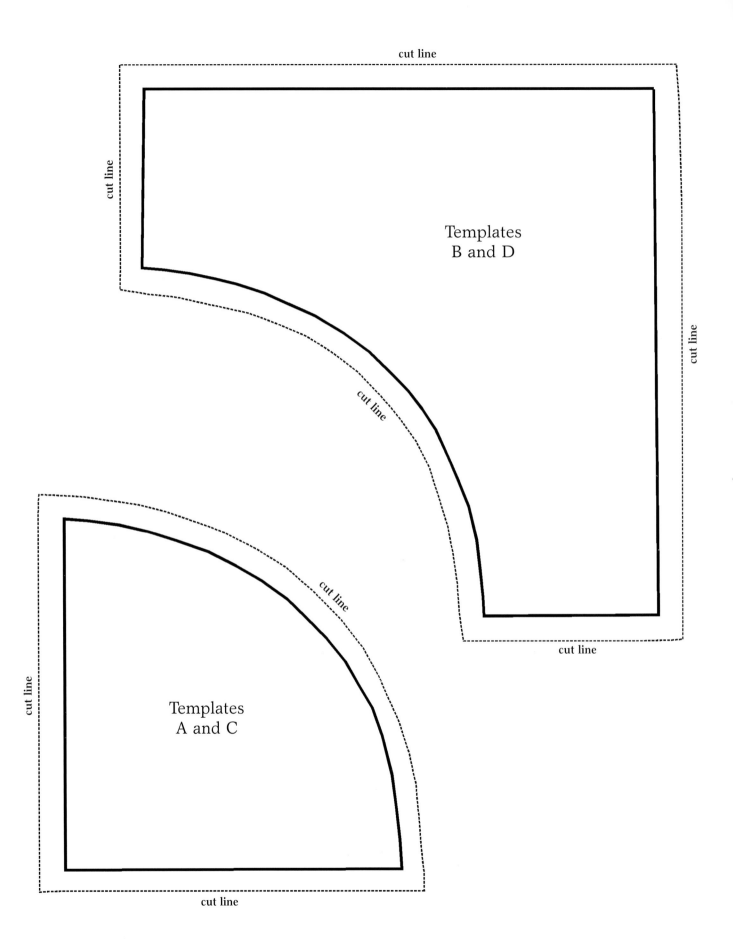

cut line

cut line

cut line

Templates
B and D

cut line

cut line

cut line

Templates
A and C

cut line

cut line

Tree of Life

Approximate size—90¹/₂″ x 110″

Measurements given with seam allowances.

- A — 4⁷/₈″ x 4⁷/₈″; cut 6; then cut in half diagonally
- B — 4⁷/₈″ x 4⁷/₈″; cut 6; then cut in half diagonally
- C — 2⁷/₈″ x 2⁷/₈″; cut 12; then cut in half diagonally
- D — Template given; cut 24
- E — 4¹/₂″ x 4¹/₂″; cut 12
- F — 2¹/₂″ x 2¹/₂″; cut 24
- G — 2⁷/₈″ x 2⁷/₈″; cut 150; then cut in half diagonally
- H — 2⁷/₈″ x 2⁷/₈″; cut 114; then cut in half diagonally
- I — 6⁷/₈″ x 6⁷/₈″; cut 12; then cut in half diagonally
- J — 14¹/₂″ x 14¹/₂″; cut 6
- K — 14⁷/₈″ x 14⁷/₈″; cut 5; then cut in half diagonally
- L — 10³/₄″ x 10³/₄″; cut 2; then cut in half diagonally
- M — 4″ x 59⁷/₈″; cut 2
- N — 4″ x 86³/₄″; cut 2
- O — 12¹/₂″ x 66⁷/₈″; cut 2
- P — 12¹/₂″ x 110³/₄″; cut 2

Fabric Requirements

☐ — 10¹/₂ yds.

▨ — 3¹/₂ yds.

▦ — 5¹/₂ yds.

Backing—If using horizontal seams—9¹/₈ yds.
  If using vertical seams—7¹/₂ yds.

Batting—95¹/₂″ x 115″

Assembly Instructions:

1. To create one Tree of Life Block:

A. Sew long side of Template A to long side of Template B.

B. Sew Template C to Template D. Repeat.

C. Sew A/B Block to C/D Block.

D. Sew Template E to another C/D Block.

E. Sew strip A/B/C/D to strip C/D/E.

F. Sew long side of Template H to long side of Template G. Repeat 18 more times. (19 blocks total.)

G. Sew together Row 1, working from left to right, ignoring Template I.

H. Sew together Row 2, working from left to right, ignoring Template I.

I. Sew together Row 3, working from left to right, ignoring Template I.

J. Sew Row 1 to Row 2. (Unit 1)

K. Sew Row 3 to Row 2. (Unit 2)

L. Sew Template I to Unit 2.

M. Sew three G/H Blocks together. (Unit 3)

N. Sew two G/H Blocks together. (Unit 4)

O. Sew Template G to Unit 4. (Unit 5)

P. Sew Template G to a G/H Block. (Unit 6)

Q. Sew Unit 3 to Unit 5. Sew Unit 6 to Unit 5. (Unit 7) Sew Template G to bottom of Unit 7. (Unit 8)

R. Sew Unit 8 to block A/B/C/D/E.

S. Repeat steps 1a through 1R 11 more times. (12 blocks total.)

2. See How to Assemble Your Quilt, Diagram 2, page 12.

3. Follow Border Application Diagram on page 13 to complete your quilt, using Templates M through P.

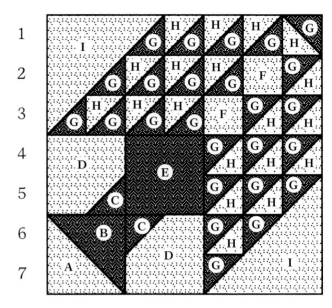

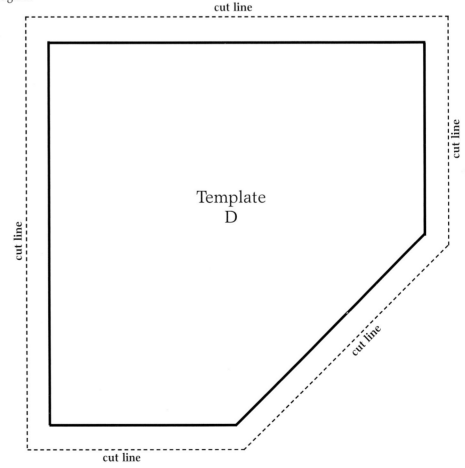

208

Bachelor's Puzzle

Approximate size—91$\frac{1}{2}$" x 112$\frac{1}{2}$"

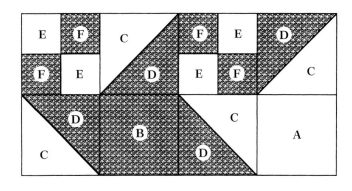

Measurements given with seam allowances.

A — 4" x 4"; cut 54
B — 4" x 4"; cut 54
C — 4$\frac{3}{8}$" x 4$\frac{3}{8}$"; cut 119; then cut in half diagonally
D — 4$\frac{3}{8}$" x 4$\frac{3}{8}$"; cut 119; then cut in half diagonally
E — 2$\frac{1}{4}$" x 2$\frac{1}{4}$"; cut 260
F — 2$\frac{1}{4}$" x 2$\frac{1}{4}$"; cut 260
G — 3" x 67"; cut 2
H — 3" x 93"; cut 2
I — 10$\frac{1}{2}$" x 72; cut 2
J — 10$\frac{1}{2}$" x 113; cut 2

Fabric Requirements

 — 7$\frac{1}{4}$ yds.

 — 9$\frac{3}{4}$ yds.

Backing—If using horizontal
        seams—9$\frac{3}{8}$ yds.
    If using vertical
        seams—7$\frac{5}{8}$ yds.

Batting—96$\frac{1}{2}$" x 117$\frac{1}{2}$"

Assembly Instructions:

1. To create one Bachelor's Puzzle Block:

A. Sew a Template F to a Template E. Repeat 259 times. (260 strips total.)

B. Sew an E/F Strip to an F/E Strip, to form block. Repeat 129 times. (130 blocks total.)

C. Sew long side of a Template C to the long side of a Template D. Repeat 236 times. (237 blocks total.)

2. See How to Assemble Your Quilt, Diagram 1, page 12.

3. Follow Border Application Diagram on page 13 to complete your quilt, using Templates G through J.

Rolling Stone

Approximate size—93″ x 108″

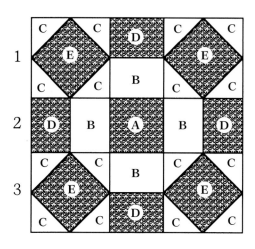

Measurements given with seam allowances.

A — $3^{1}/4''$ x $3^{1}/4''$; cut 20
B — $2^{1}/2''$ x $3^{1}/4''$; cut 80
C — $2^{7}/8''$ x $2^{7}/8''$; cut 160; then cut in half diagonally
D — $2^{1}/2''$ x $3^{1}/4''$; cut 80
E — Template given; cut 80
F — $11^{1}/4''$ x $11^{1}/4''$; cut 12
G — $11^{5}/8''$; cut 7; then cut in half diagonally
H — $8^{1}/2''$ x $8^{1}/2''$; cut 2; then cut in half diagonally
I — 4″ x $61^{3}/8''$; cut 2
J — 4″ x $83^{1}/2''$; cut 2
K — 13″ x $68^{3}/8''$; cut 2
L — 13″ x $108^{1}/2''$; cut 2

Fabric Requirements

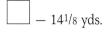 — $14^{1}/8$ yds.

 — $4^{3}/8$ yds.

Backing—
    If using horizontal
        seams—9 yds.
    If using vertical
        seams—$7^{3}/4$ yds.

Batting—98″ x 113″

Assembly Instructions:

1. To create one Rolling Stone Block:

    A. Sew a Template C to each side of Template E. Repeat 79 more times. (80 blocks total.)

    B. Sew a Template D to a Template B. Repeat 79 more times. (80 blocks total.)

    C. Sew together Row 1, working from left to right.

    D. Sew together Row 2, working from left to right.

    E. Sew together Row 3, working from left to right.

    F. Sew Row 1 to Row 2. Sew Row 3 to Row 2 to create block.

    G. Repeat steps 1A through 1F 19 more times. (20 blocks total.)

2. See How to Assembly Your Quilt, Diagram 2, page 12.

3. Follow Border Application Diagram on page 13 to complete your quilt, using Templates I through L.

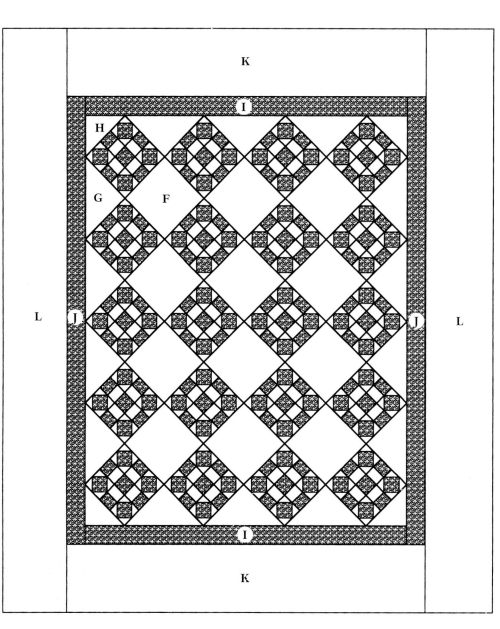

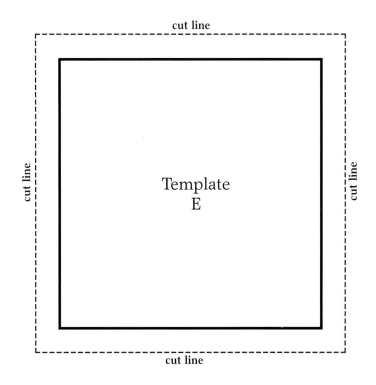

cut line

cut line

Template
E

cut line

cut line

Quilting Templates

Following are several traditional quilting templates given in full size. Many of the templates extend over several pages. To use, pull out template section. Match corresponding letters along dotted lines and tape pages together to form the complete template.

Circular Feather—i

To create finished template, match corresponding letters along dotted lines, and tape.

One quarter of the Circular Feather is given. To make a complete circle, trace the section given, make a one-quarter turn, and trace again. Repeat until circle is complete.

Completed pattern motif will look like this:

Trim along dotted lines.

Circular Feather—ii

Trim along dotted lines.

Trim along dotted lines.

Circular Feather—iii

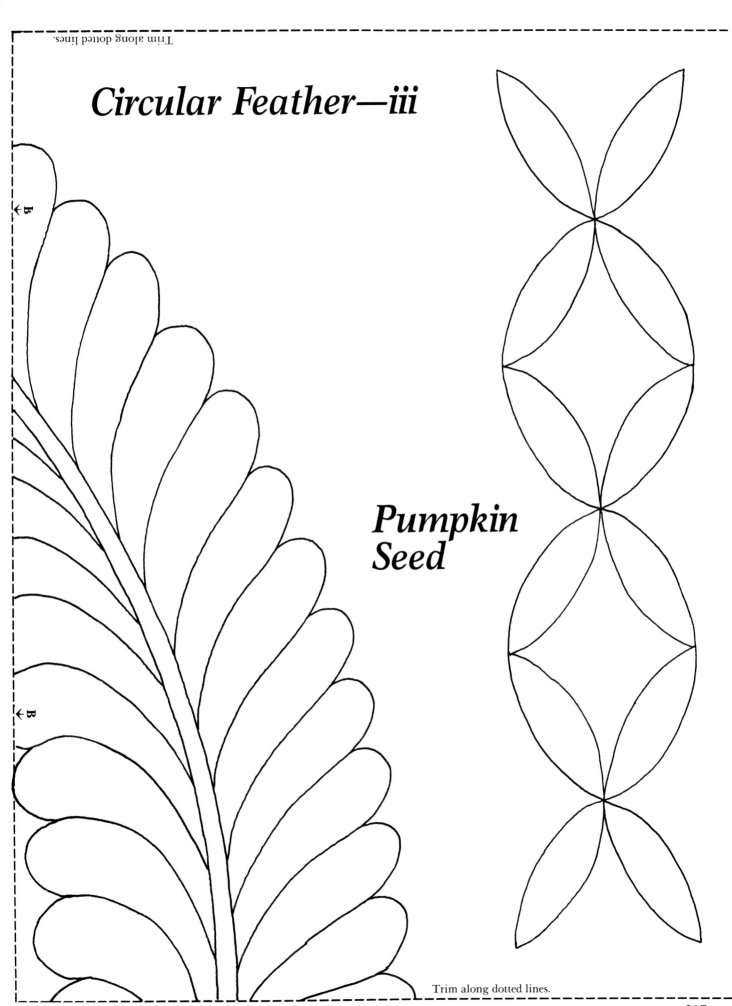

B

B

Pumpkin Seed

Triangular Rose—i

To create finished template, match corresponding letters along dotted lines, and tape.

Completed pattern motif will look like this:

Triangular Rose—ii

A

A

B

B

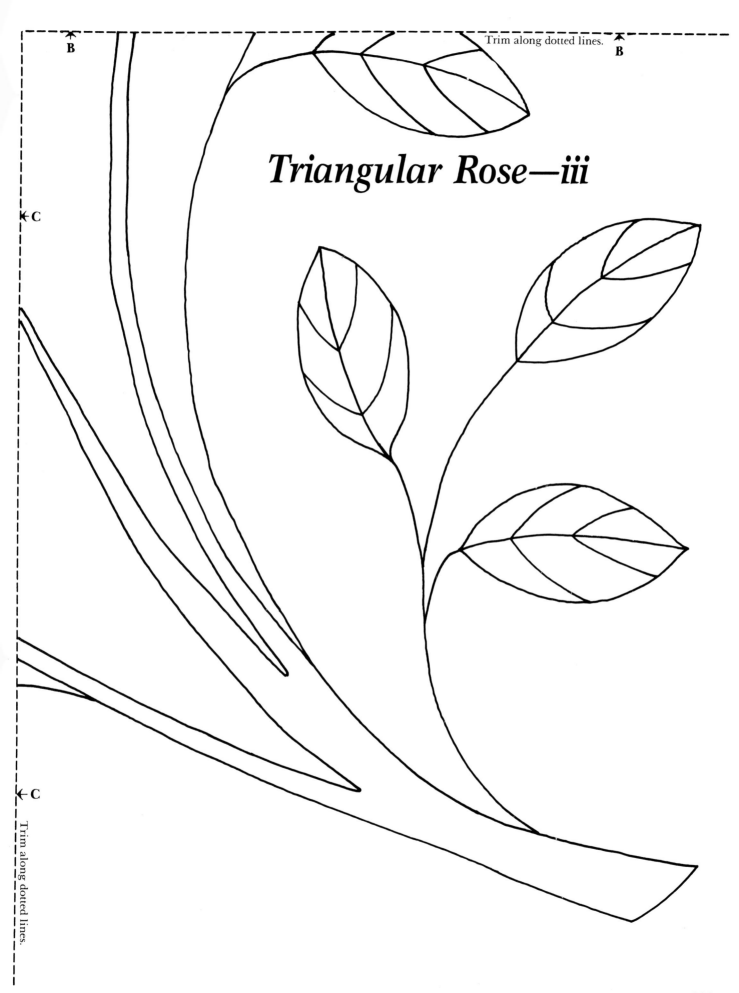

C

Triangular Rose—iii

C

D

D

Triangular Rose—iv

← E

C →

C →

← E

225

Triangular Rose—v

Trim along dotted lines.

*Ivy
Leaf*

E →

E →

Feather Border—i

Trim along dotted lines

← A

Completed pattern motif will look like this:

To create finished template, match corresponding letters along dotted lines, and tape.

Feather Border—ii

A

B

B

Trim along dotted lines.

C

C

Feather Border—iii

B

B

D

D

Trim along dotted lines.

Feather Border—iv

E ←

E ←

C ↓

C ↓

Trim along dotted lines.

Feather Border—v

Trim along dotted lines.

E

E

D

D

107

Grapes with Leaves

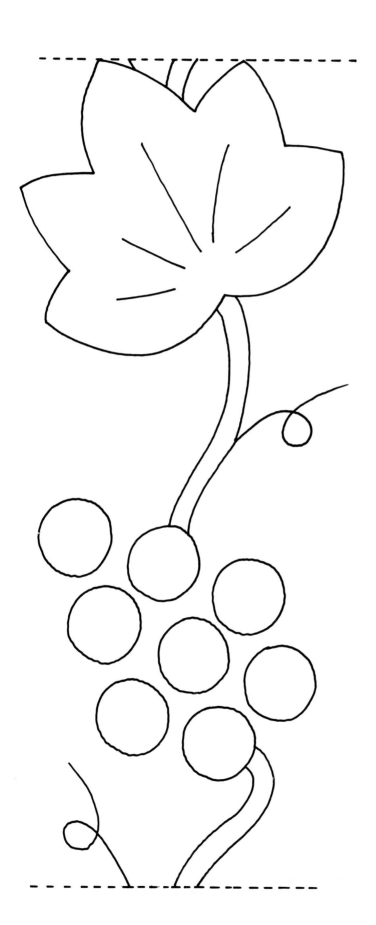

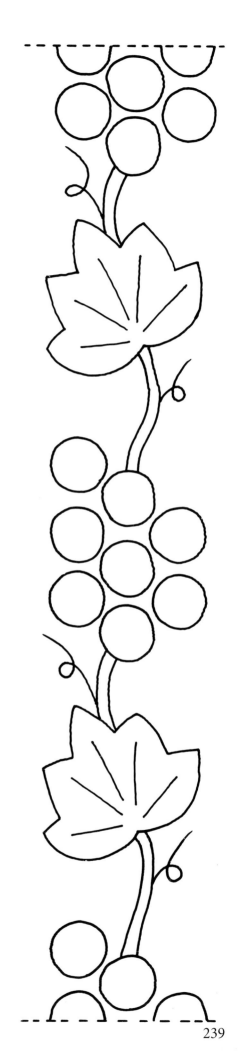

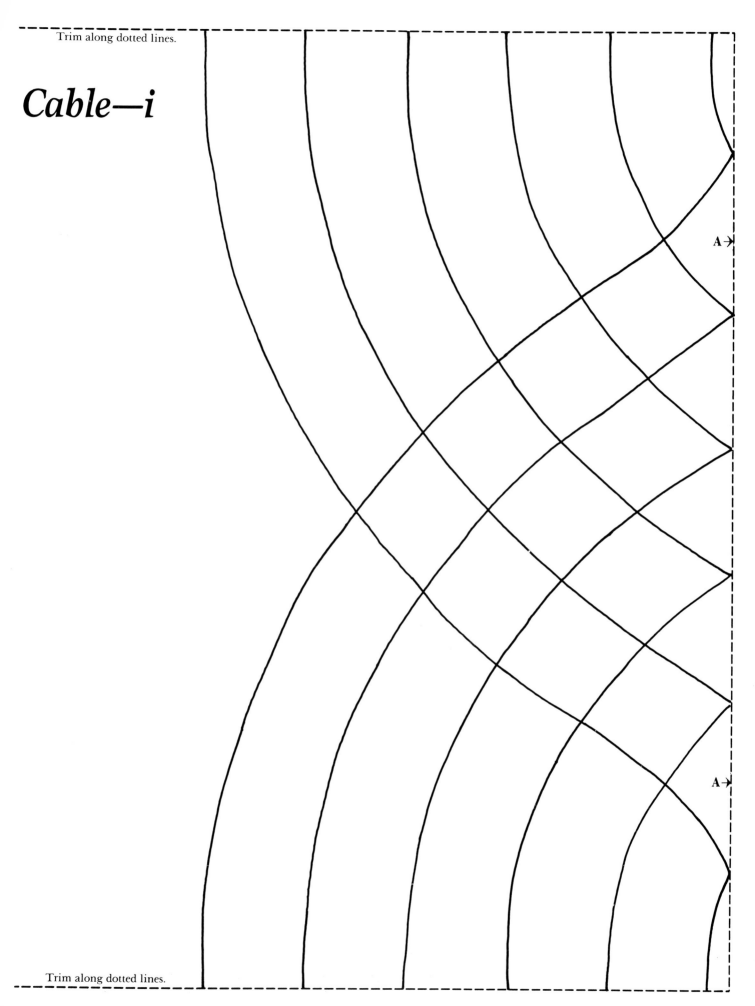

Trim along dotted lines.

Cable—i

A→

A→

Trim along dotted lines.

241

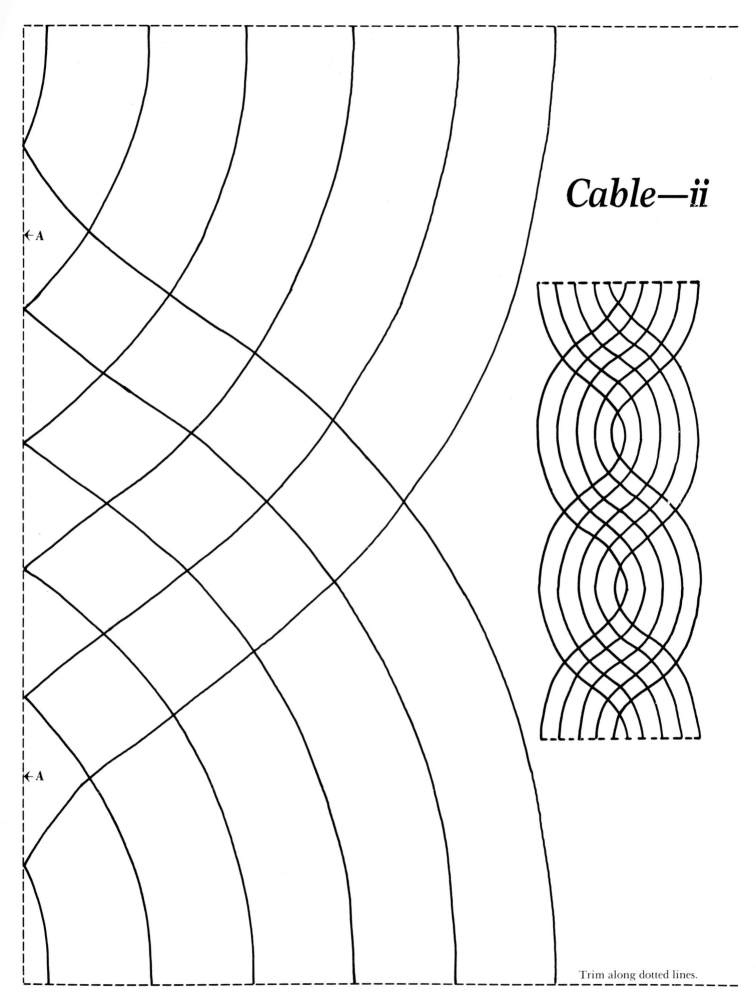

Cable—ii

←A

←A

Trim along dotted lines.

Cable—iii

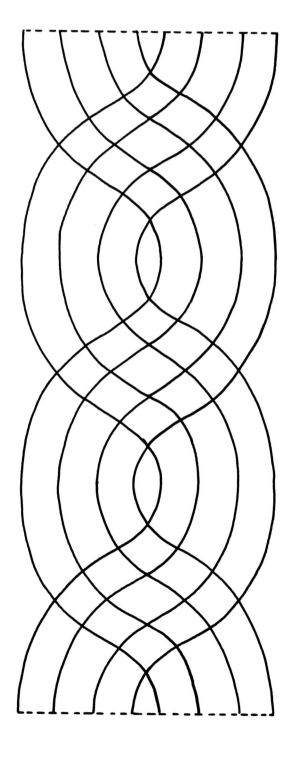

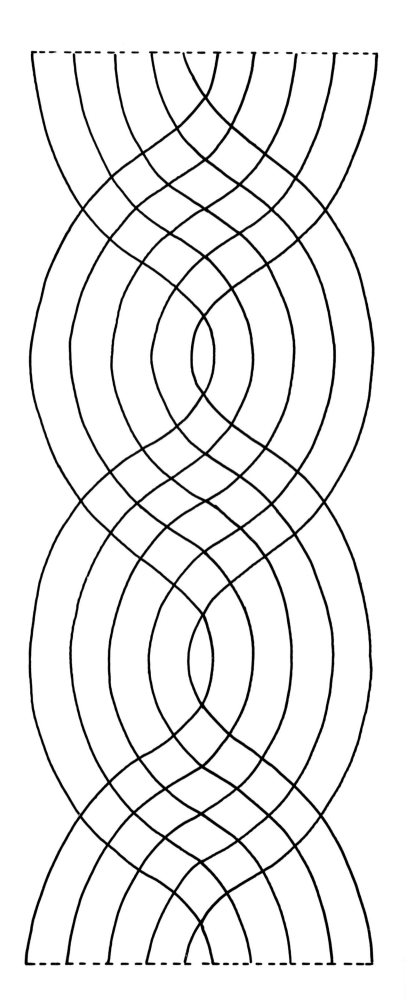

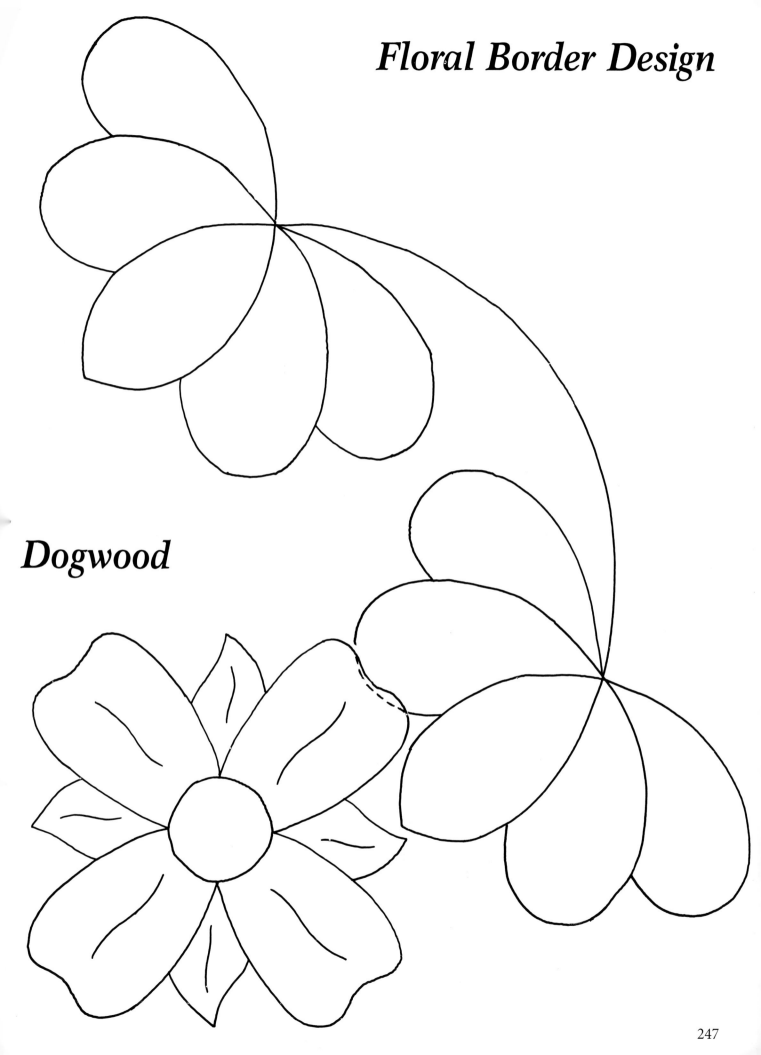

Floral Border Design

Dogwood

Readings and Sources

Cross-Reference

Pellman, Rachel T. *Amish Quilt Patterns*. Good Books, Intercourse, Pennsylvania, 1998.

About Antique Amish Quilts

Bishop, Robert and Elizabeth Safanda. *A Gallery of Amish Quilts*. E.P. Dutton and Company, Inc., New York, New York, 1976.

Granick, Eve Wheatcroft. *The Amish Quilt*. Good Books, Intercourse, Pennsylvania, 1989.

Haders, Phyllis. *Sunshine and Shadow: The Amish and Their Quilts*. Universe Books, New York, New York, 1976.

Horton, Roberta. *Amish Adventure*. C & T Publishing, Lafayette, California, 1983.

Lawson, Suzy. *Amish Inspirations*. Amity Publications, Cottage Grove, Oregon, 1982.

Pellman, Rachel and Kenneth. *Amish Crib Quilts*. Good Books, Intercourse, Pennsylvania, 1985.

_____. *Amish Doll Quilts, Dolls, and Other Playthings*. Good Books, Intercourse, Pennsylvania, 1986.

_____. *A Treasury of Amish Quilts*. Good Books, Intercourse, Pennsylvania, 1992.

Pottinger, David. *Quilts from the Indiana Amish*. E.P. Dutton, Inc., New York, New York, 1983.

About Other Quilts

Beyer, Jinny. *Patchwork Patterns*. EPM Publications, McLean, Virginia, 1979.

Haders, Phyllis. *The Warner Collector's Guide to American Quilts*. The Main Street Press, New York, New York, 1981.

Holstein, Jonathan. *The Pieced Quilt: An American Design Tradition*. New York Graphic Society, Boston, Massachusetts, 1973.

Houck, Carter and Myron Miller. *American Quilts and How to Make Them*. Charles Scribner's Sons, New York, New York, 1975.

Leone, Diana. *The Sampler Quilt*. Leone Publications, Santa Clara, California, 1980.

Orlovsky, Patsy, and Myron Orlovsky. *Quilts in America*. McGraw Hill Book Company, New York, New York, 1974.

About the Amish

Bender, H.S. *The Anabaptist Vision*. Herald Press, Scottdale, Pennsylvania, 1967.

Braght, Thieleman J. van. Comp. *The Bloody Theatre; or, Martyrs Mirror*. Scottdale, Pennsylvania, 1951.

Budget, The. Sugarcreek, Ohio. A weekly newspaper serving the Amish and Mennonite communities.

Devoted Christian's Prayer Book. Pathway Publishing House, Aylmer, Ontario, 1967.

Family Life. Amish periodical published monthly. Pathway Publishing House, Aylmer, Ontario.

Gingerich, Orland. *The Amish of Canada*. Conrad Press, Waterloo, Ontario, 1972.

Good, Merle. *An Amish Portrait*. Good Books, Intercourse, Pennsylvania, 1993.

Good, Merle and Phyllis Pellman Good, *20 Most Asked Questions about the Amish and Mennonites*. Good Books, Lancaster, Pennsylvania, 1995.

Good, Phyllis Pellman. *The Best of Amish Cooking*. Good Books, Intercourse, Pennsylvania. 1984.

Good, Phyllis Pellman and Rachel Thomas Pellman. *From Amish and Mennonite Kitchens*. Good Books, Intercourse, Pennsylvania, 1984.

Hostetler, John A. *Amish Society*. Johns Hopkins University Press, Baltimore, Maryland, 1980.

Kaiser, Grace H. *Dr. Frau: A Woman Doctor Among the Amish*. Good Books, Intercourse, Pennsylvania, 1997.

Keim, Albert N. *Compulsory Education and the Amish*. Beacon Press, Boston, Massachusetts, 1975.

Klassen, Walter. *Anabaptism: Neither Catholic nor Protestant*. Conrad Press, Waterloo, Ontario, 1975.

Kraybill, Donald B. *The Puzzles of Amish Life*. Good Books, Intercourse, Pennsyvania, 1995.

Nolt, Steven M. *A History of the Amish*. Good Books, Intercourse, Pennsylvania, 1992.

Stoltzfus, Louise. *Amish Women*. Good Books, Intercourse, Pennsylvania, 1994.

Index

About the Authors

Rachel and Kenneth Pellman are also the co-authors of *Amish Crib Quilts*; *Amish Doll Quilts, Dolls, and Other Playthings*; and *A Treasury of Amish Quilts*.

They work together in a business related to designing fabric projects. They live near Lancaster, Pennsylvania, with their two sons.